Sino-Japanese Relations After t

Since the end of the Cold War China and Japan have faced each other as powers of relatively equal strength for the first time in their long history. As the two great powers of East Asia the way they both compete and cooperate with each other and the way they conduct their relations in the new era will play a big part in the evolution of the region as a whole.

This textbook will explore in detail the ways in which politics has shaped the thinking about history and identity in both China and Japan and explain the role political leadership in each country has played in shaping their respective nationalisms. Michael Yahuda traces the evolution of the relationship over the two decades against the framework of a rising China gaining ground on a stagnant Japan, and analyzes the politics of the economic interdependence between the two countries and their cooperation and competition in Southeast Asia and in its regional institutions.

Concluding with an examination of the complexities of their strategic relations and an evaluation of the potentialities for conflict and coexistence between the two countries, this is an essential text for students and scholars of Sino-Japanese and East Asian International Relations.

Michael Yahuda is Professor Emeritus of International Relations at the London School of Economics, UK, and visiting scholar at the Sigur Center for Asian Studies, The Elliot School, George Washington University, USA.

"Michael Yahuda's extraordinary contributions to understanding Asia's foreign relations reach a new milestone in this clear and comprehensive treatment of the region's most important relationship. Detached and discerning analysis, adroit use of International Relations theories, and careful weighing of alternatives show a difficult path ahead, short of armed conflict."

– Robert Sutter, George Washington University, USA

"Michael Yahuda's *Sino-Japanese Relations After the Cold War: Two tigers sharing a mountain* fills a persistent need for a solid textbook on Asia's most important bilateral relationship. It is comprehensive in its scope, lucid in its conclusions, well balanced in its treatment of both history and new strategic realities, and always eminently readable."

– Richard Bush, The Brookings Institution, USA

"During the first two decades following the normalization of Sino-Japanese relations in the early 1970s, Japan and China managed to maintain amicable ties in spite of a relative lack of economic engagement and human exchanges. Since the early 1990s, however, the growing interdependence of the two countries has also been marked by underlying tensions and serious disputes as a long-term power shift from Japan to China occurs. Yahuda, a leading authority in the field, offers us a cogent and dispassionate analysis of the ways in which these two tigers can learn to share the same mountain."

– Ryosei Kokubun, President, National Defense Academy of Japan

"Focusing on China-Japan relations in the post-Cold War period, Michael Yahuda explains, with great skill, the historical, political, economic and strategic complexities of this most important East Asian bilateral relationship. In particular, he demonstrates how economic interdependence and a growing tripartite institutionalisation in Northeast Asia have thus far mitigated against conflict. Highly accessible, Yahuda's insightful and balanced view offers us a refreshing antidote to the more alarmist interpretations of Sino-Japanese relations."

– Caroline Rose, University of Leeds, Executive Director, White Rose East Asia Centre, UK

Sino-Japanese Relations After the Cold War

Two tigers sharing a mountain

Michael Yahuda

LONDON AND NEW YORK

First published 2014
by Routledge
2 Park Square, Milton Park, Abingdon, Oxon OX14 4RN

and by Routledge
711 Third Avenue, New York, NY 10017

Routledge is an imprint of the Taylor & Francis Group, an informa business

© 2014 Michael Yahuda

The right of Michael Yahuda to be identified as author of this work has been asserted by him in accordance with the Copyright, Designs and Patent Act 1988.

All rights reserved. No part of this book may be reprinted or reproduced or utilised in any form or by any electronic, mechanical, or other means, now known or hereafter invented, including photocopying and recording, or in any information storage or retrieval system, without permission in writing from the publishers.

Trademark notice: Product or corporate names may be trademarks or registered trademarks, and are used only for identification and explanation without intent to infringe.

British Library Cataloguing in Publication Data
A catalogue record for this book is available from the British Library

Library of Congress Cataloging in Publication Data
Yahuda, Michael B.
Sino-Japanese relations after the Cold War : two tigers sharing a mountain /
Michael Yahuda.
pages cm.
Includes bibliographical references and index.
ISBN 978-0-415-84307-2 (hardback) -- ISBN 978-0-415-84308-9 (paperback) -- ISBN 978-0-203-74029-3 (ebook) 1. China--Foreign relations--Japan. 2. Japan--Foreign relations--China. 3. China--Foreign economic relations--Japan. 4. Japan--Foreign economic relations--China. 5. China--Foreign relations--1976- 6. Japan--Foreign relations--1989- I. Title.
DS740.5.J3Y25 2013
327.51052--dc23
2013005010

ISBN: 978-0-415-84307-2 (hbk)
ISBN: 978-0-415-84308-9 (pbk)
ISBN: 978-0-203-74029-3 (ebk)

Typeset in Sabon
by Taylor and Francis Books

Printed and bound in Great Britain by
TJ International Ltd, Padstow, Cornwall

To my Grandchildren

Rachael
Aisha
Omi
Emily
Hannah
Jacob
Nina
Zack
Eli

Contents

Preface

Research for this book first began in 2005, when I was fortunate to be awarded a year's fellowship at the Woodrow Wilson International Center for Scholars in Washington DC. At that time it seemed as if Sino-Japanese relations were heading in a downwards spiral irretrievably towards military conflict and that my task was to explain this sorry state of affairs and how such conflict could be averted, perhaps through the good offices of the United States. However, with the "breaking of the ice" between them in August 2006, which also coincided with North Korea's first nuclear test, it became apparent that a more complex dynamic of relations was at play between China and Japan – the two great powers of East Asia.

I then put my project on hold as I turned to other research activities including, amongst others, revising a textbook on the international politics of the Asia-Pacific. But I continued to follow developments in Sino-Japanese relations and it gradually became apparent to me that despite the enormity of their differences, heightened by their proximity, the potentiality for conflict between them was less than I had supposed. Although military clashes between the two great powers of East Asia are entirely possible, especially in the East China Sea, with the potential for escalation, neither seeks open warfare and it seems that longer-term peaceful coexistence between China and Japan is the more likely outcome. I then returned once again to the task of writing this book.

In addition to drawing on the usual sources for researching a book of this kind, such as formal documents, statements by leaders and governments, interviews by leaders and other people of influence, scholarly journals, books, newspapers and so on, I have been privileged down the years beginning in the late 1970s and continuing every two years on average to have access to government officials and notable scholars in both countries. Discussions and interviews with them have deepened my understanding and enriched my knowledge in ways that extend far beyond the written word. Out of respect for their desire not to be formally named and in order to encourage them to continue to talk with me in confidence I have kept their names confidential.

During these years I have benefited immensely from the many seminars and talks that have been open to me, first at my original home institution the London School of Economics and Political Science and since 2003 at the Sigur Center for Asian Studies of the Elliott School of International Affairs, George Washington University. I shall remain grateful to the Wilson Center, which first encouraged me to research this subject, and to Bob Hathaway, Director of its Asia Program, for his continued support and advice. I learned a great deal from the many meetings and talks to which I was invited by the Brookings Institution and in that regard I am especially grateful to Richard Bush, Jeffrey

Bader and the visiting scholars there who are too numerous to mention. I wish to register my thanks to Dr. Satu Limaye, Director of The East–West Center in Washington, for having invited me to participate in seminars of great interest. I have also benefited greatly from attending meetings at the Center for Strategic and International Studies and at the International Institute for Strategic Studies, both in Washington DC.

It is a pleasure to record my special thanks to two colleagues at the Sigur Center: to Professor Mike Mochizuki, whose profound views on Japan's foreign relations have influenced me more than he will know; and above all to my dear friend Professor Shambaugh with whom I have been close since we first met at the University of Michigan, Ann Arbor in 1985.

I am deeply grateful to Dr. Liselotte Odgaard who read and commented on the whole first draft and to the suggestions and criticisms of the four anonymous reviewers selected by the publishers. Of course I alone am responsible for any remaining errors and shortcomings of the book.

Above all I cherish the unstinting support of my wife, Ellen. She has been an indispensable note taker of my interviews in Asia over the course of many years, a wonderful and patient traveling companion on those many research visits. In addition she has borne with resilience and good cheer my inevitable long absences in researching and writing this book.

Introduction

China and Japan are the two great powers of East Asia, who are both rivals and partners. They emerged from the Cold War as rough equals for the first time in their long history, but then a dynamic and rising China seemingly has been in the process of passing a declining Japan. It has already replaced Japan as the second largest economy in the world and it is on path to surpass the American economy within a decade or so. China is often regarded as already a superpower and there is a considerable literature on China's potential conflict with the United States based on International Relations theories of the transition of power in international political systems. In fact China's leaders regard the United States as the key opponent to China's rise to the great power stature they crave. Both Beijing and Washington appear to assume that Japan will be of little consequence in the rivalry between the two titans, the United States and China. I shall argue that Japan's significance as a possible constraint on China's rise and search for greatness cannot so readily be overlooked or dismissed. Consequently China and Japan will have to find ways to coexist in the East Asian region. Hence I suggest that contrary to the old Chinese saying, "Two tigers can't occupy the same mountain," China and Japan, as the two tigers of Northeast Asia, will have to learn how to share the same mountain.

Although a remorselessly rising China is challenging Japan's territorial integrity by its use of force in pursuit of its claims in the East China Sea and it is threatening to reduce Japan's standing to a secondary position, the prospects for major military conflict are limited. It will be argued in this book that China will be constrained both by the effects of the possible breakdown of the economic interdependence with Japan and by Japan's alliance with the United States. A breakdown in China's economic relations with Japan would have damaging effects for the Chinese economy and could threaten the basis for the rule of China's Communist Party (CCP), which relies heavily on the continued rapid growth of the economy and on the social stability which that provides. Japan's alliance with the United States is the geostrategic lynchpin for America's position in the Western Pacific and beyond. Even if it were to be weakened, Chinese strategists fear that Japan could very rapidly transform itself into a formidable military power replete with nuclear weapons.

Japan's economy may not have grown much in the two decades since the end of the Cold War and the comparison with the way the Chinese economy has grown by leaps and bounds may make its economic outlook appear dismal. But the Japanese economy still retains impressive strengths. It is a highly developed economy with advanced technology and a capacity for technological innovation that places it at the top of the production chains, which are crucial to the growth of the Chinese economy. Combined with its financial strength and relative sophistication and its accumulated foreign direct investment (FDI) in East and Southeast Asia, Japan is a major economic player in the region.[1] The Chinese and Japanese economies are highly interdependent. Indeed that interdependence has been institutionalized, as together with South Korea the respective leaders have met regularly on an annual basis since 2003 to confirm and advance the agreements reached by lower officials to facilitate deepening economic exchanges between the three countries. This tripartite arrangement, which excludes the United States, has been formalized with the establishment of a secretariat in Seoul.[2]

From a strategic perspective, Japan may seem constrained by its "Peace Constitution" to be limited to but a narrow form of self-defense, which does not allow it to deploy offensive weaponry, but nevertheless it disposes of a high-tech advanced navy, deemed by many to be the most powerful in East Asia. Moreover Japan has changed its military posture by adopting a more "dynamic" orientation in defense of its southerly islands and even increasing its defense expenditure for the first time in nine years – albeit by only 0.6 percent. But nevertheless it was an important signal. More importantly, Japanese security is guaranteed by its alliance with the United States and by the American nuclear umbrella. Thus when the US Secretary of State, Condoleezza Rice, hastened to Japan (and South Korea) in the aftermath of North Korea's first nuclear test in August 2006 to reassure Tokyo that the American nuclear deterrent still applied, she also implicitly assured Beijing that Tokyo would not go nuclear. What has given rise to heightened tensions between China and Japan since 2008 over seemingly barren islands in the East China Sea is China's emergence as a maritime power. In order to gain access to the Western Pacific China's naval vessels have to traverse straits between Japanese islands (in both the main islands as well as in the Okinawa chain). Although these are designated as international straits, the Chinese are concerned that they could be closed to its shipping in the event of military conflict. If China fears being hemmed in the coastal waters of the East China Sea, Japan fears a potential blockade of its vital trade routes that might follow increased Chinese control of adjacent waters. From a Chinese perspective, these considerations deepen Japan's interest in the continued separation of Taiwan from China, which goes against China's core interest of unifying the country.

The way leaders addressed questions of history at home greatly affected the relationship between the two powers. During Mao's lifetime the principal claim to the historical legitimacy of the Chinese Communist Party (CCP) was the victory over the Kuomintang (KMT) in the civil war (1946–49), which was linked to the carrying out of class struggle that was central to Mao's rule at home and which formed a significant part of his vision of the outside world. From Mao's perspective the terrible Japanese invasion (1931–45) was mitigated by the fact that it so weakened the KMT as to facilitate his ultimate victory. However, after Mao's death, under the leadership of Deng Xiaoping, China foreswore class struggle and sought the unity of the Chinese people in order to focus on economic development. Far from being the class enemy the KMT on Taiwan was now to be wooed as a fellow compatriot in playing its part in the grand project of rejuvenating China. This led to a new emphasis on Chinese nationalism, especially as communism had lost its allure after the demise of the Soviet Union and after the opening of the country to the international capitalist market. This had the effect of changing the historical basis for the legitimacy of CCP rule from victory over the KMT in the civil war to victory over the Japanese aggressors. The change from the Mao to the Deng era first took effect in the 1980s even though Japan was seen as a key player in modernizing the

Chinese economy. This brought Japan into the domestic political argument in China between the more market-oriented reformers and the more conservative CCP traditionalists. Japan thus became an important factor in the Chinese discourse about identity. In the 1990s and the first decade of the twenty-first century enmity towards Japan assumed central importance in the new nationalism encouraged by the CCP, which became a pillar in the CCP claims to legitimacy. At the same time the new and sharper nationalism was not congruent with China's economic dependence on foreign economic relations in which Japan was a major player. Thus there was political tension between the two pillars on which CCP legitimacy rested.

Japanese views about its identity and its place in the world in the post-Cold War period were also greatly affected by the relationship with China. China was central to the debates in Japan going back to the nineteenth century as to how to balance Japan's Asian and Western identities.[3] With the end of the Pacific War and the American occupation (1945–52) the Japanese were not called to account for their brutal aggression, to the extent of the Germans. Although he did lose his divine status, the Emperor was kept in office without any inquiry into his role as the leader of the nation during the war (1931–45). As the Cold War began in earnest, the United States began in 1947 to regard Japan as a pillar of the West in East Asia. As a means of encouraging its economic recovery the Occupation administration allowed former administrators of the Japanese empire (including those who had been indicted as war criminals) to play major roles in the reconstruction. The most prominent of these, Nobusuke Kishi, actually served as prime minister (1957–60). Not surprisingly, these men, many of whom came to dominate the Liberal Democratic Party (LDP) which ruled Japan almost uninterruptedly for more than five decades, resisted attempts to face up to Japan's history of aggression and tended to portray the war in positive terms as a war of resistance to the West. Nevertheless the debate about Japan's identity was somewhat subdued during the Cold War.[4]

However, it resurfaced as Japan sought to redefine itself in the light of the changes wrought by the demise of the Soviet Union and the end of the so-called San Francisco system, which had set the parameters for domestic politics and for Japan's place in the world. These changes virtually spelled the end of the Socialist Party as a significant political force, shifting the mainstream of Japanese politics to a more conservative direction. Notwithstanding attempts by some Japanese leaders and governments to offer apologies of a kind for the wars of aggression, others of ministerial rank including even some prime ministers from time to time watered down the apologies – sometimes to the extent of denying that apologies were called for. Such statements outraged opinion in South Korea and China, which had borne the brunt of Japanese aggression.

Interpretations of history became highly politicized and they became a major factor in Sino-Japanese relations (and also in Korean–Japanese relations, but these fall outside the main subject of this book). Beginning in the 1980s, but intensifying in the 1990s and into the twenty-first century, China's leaders continued to demand fuller apologies from their Japanese equivalents, who in turn regarded the Chinese demands as cynical political maneuvers to put Japan at a disadvantage. The often violent anti-Japanese demonstrations in China had a profoundly negative effect in Japan as registered by opinion polls, which showed deepening distaste for China. The growth of Chinese economic and military power became a factor in Japanese debates about the extent to which Japan should modify its commitment to the pursuit of peace amid a minimal defense doctrine. China thwarted Japanese aspirations to use its unique constitutionally based status as a peace-loving country to become a permanent member of the UN Security Council. As Chinese military pressure on Japan has deepened the Japanese have begun to pursue a more active military strategy, leading to debates as to whether Japan should assume for the first time the commitment to participate in collective defense, meaning that it should cease to be simply the recipient of American military assistance in the event of an attack on Japan and be ready to contribute to the defense of its ally too.

The end of the Cold War also changed the character of Japan's alliance with the United States. The demise of the Soviet Union removed their common enemy so Japan came under American pressure to play a more active security role not only in the East Asian region, but also internationally. Japan was often found wanting, largely because of the continuing attachment to the Peace Constitution, which ironically had been imposed by the American Occupation in 1946–47. Nevertheless Washington and Tokyo were able to reach agreements that allowed for expanding the roles of Japan's Self Defense Forces (SDF), even though in practice these did not involve taking part in actual conflict. However, it was growing Chinese power that began to raise more fundamental questions about the efficacy of the alliance in practice. For example, to what extent would the United States assist Japan in the event of military incidents with China in the East China Sea, when the United States is still seeking to cooperate with China in many areas of vital American interests?

Notwithstanding the prospects of skirmishes between them in the East China Sea there is no sign of imminent warfare between China and Japan. Japan possesses great naval power and although the country is dedicated to a narrow version of self-defense, it is a formidable opponent. China cannot take lightly a Japan whose alliance with the United States is still at the heart of the structure of America's military presence and strategy in the Asia-Pacific. Chinese strategists, who might otherwise welcome a loosening of the alliance and a reduction in American deployments in the region, also worry about a Japanese response that could yet prompt Japan to become a "normal" country again replete with offensive weaponry including nuclear power. A significant weakening of the American strategic overlay would be a "game changer," but as argued earlier, major constraints against open warfare between these two proud countries would still remain. Moreover, there is the danger that they would exhaust themselves to the advantage of neighboring India and Russia, not to mention the United States.

However, Northeast Asia is subject to dynamic change and the relationship between China and Japan, the second and third largest economies in the world and the two greatest powers of East Asia, is the key to whether or not the region will continue to develop peacefully as the second decade of the twenty-first century unfolds. The United States, as the ally of the former and the putative global partner of the latter, plays a critical role in shaping the dynamics of the relationship. As a result there is unease in both countries about how the US balances its cultivation of the two powers. So far the US has played a major role in limiting the incipient conflict between the two. But much as Japan and others in East Asia rely upon the US as a hedge against China's rapidly growing military power, doubts have arisen about the American capacity and willingness to continue to guarantee their security. Despite the decision by the Obama administration in 2011 to "pivot to Asia" or to "re-balance" its forces towards the Pacific, many of its Asian allies and partners worry about the prospects of Washington being able to do so in practice. In particular they are concerned about the effects of America's deep-set political gridlock and about both the short- and long-term consequences of America's slow economic recovery from the financial crisis of 2008. Since the turn of the twenty-first century the established order in East Asia is increasingly being challenged by the rise of China. China has replaced the US as the major trading partner of all of America's East Asian allies and its military is seeking to circumscribe the strategic space in the region American forces have enjoyed for the past six decades. China's rise as a military power in the region has begun to challenge the established order in East Asia and the American role as the provider of public goods and the guarantor of regional security has come under pressure. Moreover, the first to experience the consequences of China's newfound maritime power are its maritime neighbors, including Japan.

As the defender of the status quo, Japan lacks the strategic space to consider a variety of options in accommodating China's rise. In effect Japan can either accept Chinese dominance or resist it. It can resist it through the alliance with the United States or, in the event of the alliance being found wanting, Japan retains the option of becoming militarily self-reliant. This has created a new dynamic, which the governments of both China and Japan are seeking to contain. Perhaps it is their close proximity that makes it difficult for these two very different countries to forge lasting amicable relations. Meanwhile the other great and medium powers including India, Russia, Australia, Indonesia and Vietnam are repositioning themselves, with China and Japan competing for linkages with them. It is within that broad context that China and Japan began to face each other anew with an incentive to redefine their priorities and to rethink their basic political identities. At stake in their relationship is how the order in East Asia may unfold amid the possibility of armed conflict. Underlying their disputes over the ownership of rocky islands in the sea between them and the related seabed with its oil and gas resources, as well as over history and other specific issues is the fear that China or Japan may undermine the aspirations of the other. If Japan fears that China's rise may end in the marginalization of Japan and perhaps even its subordination to understandings between China and America, China fears that Japan, together with the United States or perhaps alone, as a revitalized military power, may prevent it from uniting with Taiwan and generally obstruct China's rise to the great power status to which it aspires. China has successfully stabilized the security of its continental border regions and established workable relations with both Russia and India so that they are unlikely to combine with the United States against it.[5] In the Chinese view, that leaves Japan as the only neighboring power that has the capacity to limit its rise and its emergence as a major maritime force.[6]

A security dilemma exists between them in which the acquisition of new weapons systems, seen as defensive by the one is regarded as offensive by the other. Thus Japan's procurement of missile defense systems is regarded by the Chinese as designed to undermine their deterrence capabilities and therefore as offensive. Japan in turn sees the rapid growth of Chinese military spending, the modernization of the armed forces and especially China's acquisition of a significant ocean-going maritime capability as potentially threatening and destabilizing. Each side distrusts the other's aims with regard to the future of the Korean peninsula and they openly contest the other's attempts to extend influence in Southeast Asia. More broadly, they hedge against each other in the great power diplomacy of the region. Arguably it is only the United States that ensures the strategic stability of the region and which provides the public goods that have ensured the free flow of goods and markets, which have underpinned the economic success of East Asia as a whole and of these two great powers. Yet the United States is seen by both

China and Japan as potentially destabilizing, but for opposite reasons: China fears American containment; but Japan fears American abandonment.

In the process of redefining and reinvigorating the alliance with Japan in the second half of the 1990s, the United States not only set new demands for Japanese participation in regional and more general security, but intentionally or not, it also raised new security issues for Sino-Japanese relations that in themselves affected their respective domestic debates about identity. As far as Japan was concerned the alliance with the US raised afresh the long-standing concern that the US might embroil Japan unwillingly in external conflicts particularly with China, or alternatively that the US might neglect Japan in the new strategic environment, especially in pursuit of engagement with China. If Japan feared both entanglement and abandonment by the US, China also had concerns of its own about the US alliance with Japan. Did this serve Chinese interests by obviating the need for Japan to become an independent military power capable of projecting force? Or, on the contrary, did the alliance in the post-Cold War era constitute a new means of containing China and preventing it from rising to the great power status to which most Chinese have felt their country is entitled for at least one hundred years?

It will be seen that Sino-Japanese relations are highly complex, spanning several dimensions that are inter-related. These include interlocking issues of identity, history, economic interdependence, strategy and the international context – among the most notable. No one theory could hope to do justice in seeking to explain the dynamics of this complex relationship. Accordingly, the following chapters will draw on the three main theories of International Relations: Constructivism, which puts the onus on how views of reality are "socially constructed";[7] Liberal Internationalism, which argues that "complex interdependence" entails deepening cooperation as opposed to conflict;[8] and Realism, which focuses on state power in an anarchical international system.[9] The chapters here broadly follow Sino-Japanese relations in sequence in accordance with these theories.

The book will begin with a chapter which will explore in greater detail the ways in which politics has shaped the thinking about history and identity in both China and Japan and which will explain the role political leadership in each country has played in shaping their respective nationalisms. It will argue that these matters have been contested among the elites in both China and Japan and that the manifestations of nationalism in each country have led to repercussions in the other.

The next two chapters will trace the evolution of the relationship over the two decades since the end of the Cold War against the framework of a rising China gaining ground on a more stagnant Japan. The fourth and fifth chapters will analyze respectively the politics of the economic interdependence between the two countries and their cooperation and competition in Southeast Asia and in its regional institutions. The sixth chapter will examine the complexities of their strategic relations and the book will conclude with an evaluation of the potentialities for conflict and coexistence between these two very different neighboring countries. It will suggest that these two great East Asian powers will have to develop strategies and mechanisms for their mutual coexistence as two tigers sharing the same mountain.

Notes

1 Claude Meyer, *China or Japan: Which will Lead Asia?* (New York: Columbia University Press, 2011).

2 Kent Calder and Min Ye, *The Making of Northeast Asia* (Palo Alto, CA: Stanford University Press, 2010).
3 Michael J. Green, "Japan in Asia," in David Shambaugh and Michael Yahuda (eds.), *International Relations of Asia* (Lanham, MD: Rowman and Littlefield Publishers, 2008), pp.170–91.
4 See, John W. Dower, *Ways of Forgetting, Ways of Remembering: Japan in the Modern World* (New York: The New Press, 2012).
5 Robert Kagan, *The World America Made* (New York: Alfred A. Knopf, 2012), p.127.
6 For example, Ye Zicheng, one of China's most highly regarded thinkers of foreign affairs, argues that Japan in the twenty-first century may be "in decline but [it is] still capable of being a world power." See his *Inside China's Grand Strategy*, edited and translated by Steven I. Levine and Guoli Liu (Lexington: The University Press of Kentucky, 2011), p.145 and the discussion which follows on how the two should cultivate cooperative relations.
7 The key tenets of this theory, on which there is a vast literature, may be found in Alexander Wendt, *Social Theory of International Politics* (Cambridge: Cambridge University Press, 1999).
8 The classic text for this theory, which may be traced to the eighteenth century and on which there is also a considerable literature, is Robert O. Keohane and Joseph S. Nye, *Power and Interdependence* (Boston, MA: Little, Brown, 1977).
9 Writings on this theory may be traced to ancient Greece, ancient India and ancient China. The literature on this theory is more than vast, but a more contemporary classic is Hans Morgenthau, *Politics Among Nations* (New York: Knopf, 1948).

Chapter 1

Politics of history and identity

From the Mao era to the early reform period of the 1980s

Most writers on contemporary Sino-Japanese relations pay much attention to the historical legacy of Japan's brutal aggression in Asia in the first half of the twentieth century and to the failure of the Japanese adequately to come to terms with the history of those atrocities. It is further asserted that until Japan does address that history adequately it will remain a running sore in Japan's relations with China and the two Koreas. I will argue that such a view is too simplistic. A careful account of when and how animosity towards Japan in China came to be based on these historical charges will show that these took place because of changes in the domestic politics of identity within China, rather than because of a continuing sense of grievance stemming from when Japanese atrocities actually took place. To be sure there are many Chinese families who share memories of the wartime depredations of the Japanese, but it was the Chinese leadership which determined whether or not to make these historical grievances into public issues in the conduct of relations with Japan. The role of the leaders in authoritarian China has clearly been crucial in determining the extent to which public demonstrations can take place against an important foreign country. Whatever the character of individual and collective memories and the emotionalism to which they give rise, governments take other factors into account in their interactions with each other. The Chinese government, for example, at different times has chosen to downplay the question of history in its dealings with Japan. In the Mao period comparatively little attention was given to past Japanese aggression, but beginning in the 1980s and culminating in the 1990s and the first fifteen years of the twenty-first century, hostility towards Japan because of the history question reached unprecedented heights. Between 2006 and 2009, as we shall see in chapter 3, China's leaders took a more pragmatic course of cultivating relations with Japan and they stifled possible anti-Japanese demonstrations and the media reported more objectively about Japan. However, in 2010 and again in 2012 the Chinese authorities encouraged anti-Japanese demonstrations once again, this time in response to what were regarded as Japanese attempts to enhance their claims to the Senkaku/Diaoyu islands in the East China Sea also claimed by China.

By the latter stage a gap had begun to grow between the popular nationalistic attitudes of the younger generation and the more pragmatic views of the leaders.[1] The evolution of these viewpoints, as I shall show, was greatly influenced by changes in the international system (notably the end of the Cold War and its aftermath) and by changes in the way Chinese and Japanese debated their respective identities, as well as by political changes in their respective countries.

During Mao's totalitarian rule there was no social space for such grievances to be aired unless specifically called for by the leadership. Although there is now more social space for the airing of grievances and the government is interested in paying heed to public opinion, that space is still heavily circumscribed, especially in the foreign policy arena, and the authorities have means at their disposal to curtail, or even prevent, demonstrations not to their liking.[2]

Approaches towards Japan during Mao's rule

As noted in the Introduction, Mao did not greatly emphasize his country's grievances against Japan. In part that was due to his domestic agenda and in part to the international context. Upon the establishment of the People's Republic of China (PRC) in 1949, Mao Zedong famously declared that the Chinese people have stood up and that never again would they be humiliated. He also placed the "New China" within the Communist bloc and pledged to develop a socialist system within the country. He neatly integrated nationalism or patriotism with socialism or communism. One of the main themes of his program was the emphasis on class struggle. Chinese history was rewritten to reflect the significance of class struggle as the main driving force of the country's development.[3] Modern history was written with the aim of showing that it was only with the rise of the Communist Party that it became possible for the Chinese people to overcome their feudal past, imperialist oppression and the "bureaucratic-capitalism" of the KMT.[4] Only by building socialism, according to Mao, would the Chinese people be able to embark on the nationalist road to wealth and power that would make the country great again. In contrast to his successors, Mao tended to put the blame for China's earlier abject condition during the "century of shame and humiliation" on domestic failures which made the country vulnerable to foreign aggressors rather than on the foreigners.

Mao sought to build the Chinese nation anew. Although he claimed that the Communist Party of China had played the main role in the defeat of Japan in 1945, he put the main stress of his historical claim to legitimacy on the defeat of the KMT in the civil war that followed, which culminated in the foundation of the new state, the People's Republic of China, in October 1949. The KMT had been supported and armed by the US (albeit not wholeheartedly). Hence Mao claimed to have repulsed the forces of feudalism and imperialism as well as to having defeated the KMT in the civil war as his primary achievement. This claim drew strength and immediacy from the continued presence of the defeated KMT on the island of Taiwan, especially once it enjoyed the protection of the American Seventh Fleet from June 1950 after the North Korean invasion of the South.

Japan did not get off altogether lightly in domestic Chinese propaganda. For example, popular histories such as school textbooks, films and children's comics all portrayed scenes from the war, with graphic depictions of the cruelties of Japanese soldiers. But the key point is that in most of these presentations the main emphasis was directed towards the alleged shortcomings and even betrayals by KMT stereotypes. The war with Japan was not depicted as a war between the two nations, but rather between the Chinese people and "the small handful of Japanese militarists" assisted by counter-revolutionary Chinese traitors.[5] In other words, the "lesson" was to be prepared for betrayal by class enemies, especially in wartime, who would tend to side with the external enemy.

Throughout the Mao era (1949–76) class struggle at home was linked with the issue of the "liberation of Taiwan." The presence of class enemies who might support Chiang Kai-shek was a constant theme of Mao's rule. More broadly, class struggle within China was integrated with resistance to imperialism outside China. Children's comics, films, TV programs and even Jiang Qing's revolutionary Peking operas that dealt with the War of Resistance Against Japan consistently stressed the dangers of domestic class enemies who would betray the heroic resisters to the Japanese. In a rural context they would be depicted as landlords and in the cities as capitalists (usually singled out by the wearing of scholarly gowns and fedora hats), but they were all associated with the KMT.[6]

The link between the betrayal of the revolution at home and a sell-out to imperialism abroad was evident in Mao's treatment of the Soviet Union after Khrushchev became leader. Mao's argument was that the betrayal of the Bolshevik revolution came about after Khrushchev succeeded Stalin, when he began what Mao regarded as a series of revisionist policies in opposition to the main tenets of Marxism–Leninism. Mao instigated the Cultural Revolution by arguing that there were similar revisionists who sought to betray the revolution in China, leaders who were close to him just as Khrushchev "nestled" beside Stalin only to go against him after his death.[7]

Although the defense treaty with the Soviet Union of February 14, 1950 was targeted at "Japan, or any country allied with it," Mao encouraged his countrymen to distinguish between the governing elite and the people. This was a distinction he applied retroactively, arguing that it was the government at the time and not the Japanese people as a whole, who was responsible for the war. Mao tended to lend his support to the leftist forces within Japan who supported the peace constitution and opposed the defense treaty with the United States. His aim was to try and encourage the Japanese to renounce their security ties to the United States. He welcomed the development of economic ties proposed by Prime Minister Yoshida at the end of the American occupation in 1952, as this constituted an open break with the American imposed trade embargo with China. In talks with the Indian Prime Minister Nehru in 1954, Mao referred to Japan as being "bullied" and its people as being "oppressed" (by the US). A year later he said that it would be "good" if Japan were to become "strong and prosperous."[8] Later in 1955 Mao told a delegation of members of the Japanese Diet that they shared a common interest in pushing away "the hand [of the US] weighing over our heads." Then, in sharp contrast to what Chinese leaders were to say after his death, Mao went on to say: "In the past, ordinary Chinese did not like the Japanese; now we like you very much ... The debts of the past are not an obstacle, nor are the present difference in social systems. Let bygones be bygones." Mao added:

> As you have formally apologized for the debts you incurred in the past, it is not reasonable to ask you for payments of those debts. You cannot be asked to apologize everyday, can you? It is not good for a nation to constantly feel guilty, and we can understand this point.

He then returned to his main argument about their common need to "make the United States withdraw its hands."[9]

Given the significance of KMT-ruled Taiwan in Mao's entire political strategy this favorable view of Japan was challenged by the continued links between some leading conservatives of Japan's ruling LDP and senior members of the KMT including Chiang Kai-shek. This was especially troubling for Beijing when first, Prime Minister Kishi visited Taiwan in 1957, to be followed by Prime Minister Sato in 1967. Both were seen in Beijing as right-wingers who sought to establish in effect "two Chinas," undermining the sovereign claims of the PRC. They were criticized for allegedly seeking to revive Japan as a military power and to oppose the PRC in conjunction with the United States with whom Japan's security treaty had been renewed in 1960. The agreement with the US on the reversion of Okinawa to Japan in 1971 was seen as confirming these right-wing aims. It was then that Chinese propaganda began to warn about the revival of Japanese militarism and indeed Cultural Revolution leftists made great play with the issue. Not only was that at a time of the Cultural Revolution, but it was also when Chinese foreign policy was in flux just prior to the rapprochement with the United States. And it also reflected Chinese concern about Sato's attempt to link up South Korea and Taiwan with the Japan–US alliance.[10]

All of these concerns dropped away in 1971–72, when Kissinger and Nixon agreed in effect to help China in its confrontation with the Soviet Union and also to stop challenging China's claim to Taiwan. After recovering from the "shock" of being given only three minutes' advanced notice of the announcement of Kissinger's visit in 1971, the Japanese government was keen to establish diplomatic relations with the PRC, which the United States, on account of its formal recognition of Taiwan as the Republic of China, was still unable to do. But Mao continued to distinguish between the pro-KMT right-wingers and others in the governing LDP. Japan's Prime Minister Sato was rebuffed when he attempted to open negotiations for normalizing relations in 1972. The position of the Chinese government was thought to have played a part in the LDP decision to replace Sato with the more moderate Tanaka, who then proceeded to normalize relations.[11] On meeting Mao Tanaka immediately began to apologize for Japan's aggression in the past, when he was apparently stopped by Mao, who said that he was grateful to Japan, for without the war he would not have been able to seize power. Mao also refused to consider the issue of reparations.[12] But the Chinese side did insist that Japan accept the Potsdam Declaration on Taiwan. The precise text of the joint statement was that Japan "fully understands and respects" the reaffirmation by China that Taiwan is an "inalienable part" of its territory. Although the Japanese position fell short of formally recognizing the Chinese claim, it did in effect constitute a retreat from the assertion of Japan having a security interest in Taiwan, as was stipulated in the Nixon–Sato communiqué of November 1969. The agreement with Japan allowed it to maintain non-governmental economic and social links with Taiwan and its non-official institutional representation on the island was to serve as a model for all other countries. The Chinese side also accepted that the Japanese side need only "acknowledge" rather than "recognize" the Chinese claim that Taiwan was an inalienable part of the PRC. In any event, the main issue for Mao in 1972 was to try and recruit Japan into his united front against the Soviet Union.[13] Hence Japan was not required to renounce any key aspect of the San Francisco Peace Treaty of September 1951, which the Chinese government had denounced at the time.

Mao regarded Japan as another potential major ally against the Soviet Union and at one point he chided Dr. Kissinger for not paying enough attention to Japan.[14] Japan, which had been so used to deferring to the United States on questions of security strategy, seemed little bothered by the "anti-hegemony" (read anti-Soviet) clause that was included in the document of recognition. But under later Soviet pressure they did try to resist Chinese insistence upon such a clause in the build up to the signing of a peace and friendship agreement in 1978. The issue typified the difference between China's leaders, who did think deeply about security matters, and the Japanese, who by and large did not.[15]

The opening to China also provided Japan with an opportunity to redress the wholly Western orientation of its general policies and outlook. Ever since it began modernizing at the time of the Meiji restoration in 1868 Japan had been torn between considering itself as belonging to the West or to Asia. After its defeat in 1945, Japan's orientation was to the West. There was never a concerted attempt to reach out to the new Asian governments in a spirit of reconciliation by acknowledging its past aggression and its moral obligation to pay reparations. These, it was claimed, had been dealt with by law in the framework of the San Francisco Peace Treaty by which Japan extended relatively small amounts of official reparations due to its relatively poor conditions at the time. Moreover, because these were tied to Japanese companies, they contributed to Japan's post-war recovery as much as they helped the states in Southeast Asia.[16] The recognition of South Korea in 1965 and the payment of reparations resulted more from American pressure than from any Japanese initiative.[17] Nevertheless some Japanese had fondly imagined that Japan could act as the bridge between China and the United States – an attitude that intensified the sense of shock from Washington's sudden rapprochement with Beijing in 1971 of which they only had a few minutes' notice.

Notwithstanding the Japanese enthusiasm for their new opening to China in 1972, the Chinese did not succeed in drawing Japan formally into their anti-Soviet coalition until 1978 (two years after Mao's death and after four years of negotiations) when, under the newly established leadership of Deng Xiaoping, the two sides signed a treaty of peace and friendship.[18] The preamble included a phrase about their common opposition to "hegemonism" – Beijing's code word for the Soviet Union at that time. Under Soviet pressure the Japanese had succeeded in modifying the first Chinese drafts by specifying in particular that the treaty be not aimed at any third party, nevertheless the new treaty still served the Chinese purpose. As Deng explained:

> some people did not understand why China had formerly opposed the Japanese–U.S. Security Pact but now found it possible to understand the relations between Japan and the United States. Likewise, why China opposed the revival of Japanese militarism but now appreciates the fact that Japan has its own self-defense forces. Viewing this in terms of global strategy, this helps to postpone war, extending the period of peace.[19]

In other words, for the first thirty years of its existence the official Chinese view of Japan was determined by Mao's view of the centrality of class struggle and by broader strategic concerns. The one centered on a view of China's identity as a revolutionary power and the other on concerns about China's national security. Of course in Deng's perspective it was only the latter that mattered in 1978.

Japan's identity under the Yoshida Doctrine

The way in which Japan's identity was constructed after its defeat in 1945 did not lead to an outlook that encouraged it to reflect on its horrific conduct of the war in East Asia, let alone prepare it to atone for the cruelties its soldiers had visited upon the tens of millions of people they had conquered. Moreover unlike Germany, the other main aggressor in the Second World War, Japan did not become a party to economic and military multilateral alliances with neighboring states that would have required it to make itself acceptable as a legitimate partner to its neighbors. Rather than thinking of themselves as terrible victimizers of others, Japanese have tended to think of themselves as victims of the war. All the fighting by Japanese armies took place well away from the Japanese home islands and the horrors of war did not impress themselves on most Japanese until their mainland was devastated by American bombing in the first months of 1945, culminating in the Atomic bombing of Hiroshima and Nagasaki in August, which brought the war to an end. The Japan that the Americans first occupied after the surrender in August 1945 was a desolate and ruined land, with its people reduced to shocked penury.[20]

The early American attempts to transform Japan into a new kind of democracy that would never be able to wage war again was soon put aside in 1947 by the advent of the Cold War, when the United States determined to rebuild Japan as its main pillar of support in the Cold War in Asia. By this stage, however, Japanese had begun to play a greater role in shaping their own destiny, so that by the end of the American occupation in 1952 Japan, under the leadership of Prime Minister Shigeru Yoshida, had developed a unique approach to domestic and international affairs, subsequently called the "Yoshida Doctrine." This famously relied on the Peace Constitution of 1946 (which was promulgated before the advent of Cold War considerations) and the security treaty with the United States to enable Japan to focus exclusively upon economic development and to avoid any foreign military entanglements by relying exclusively on the United States to provide for its security.[21] The 1951 San Francisco Peace settlement in effect set the structure for both the domestic system of Japan and its security dependency on the United States, as confirmed by the US Senate's ratification of the treaty between the two countries in 1952. A democratic Japan was nonetheless constrained in both its domestic and foreign affairs by the political structures imposed by the victorious United States. However, under the leadership of Prime Minister Yoshida, the Japanese were able to turn these developments to their advantage by focusing on economic recovery and by resisting American pressure to become an active political and military partner in the Cold War in East Asia.

The political system that emerged in 1955 (later called the "San Francisco system") was one that was dominated by the conservative LDP, with the Japanese Socialist Party (JSP) and other smaller parties in permanent opposition. The opposition, however, had sufficient representation to deny the conservatives the two-thirds majority needed to change the constitution. LDP leaders used the parliamentary strength of the JSP (which opposed the US alliance) as a means of resisting American pressure to contribute more to regional security. The LDP ruled in conjunction with a strong government bureaucracy with close ties to the big companies in what was seen as a mutually supportive triangular relationship – the so-called "iron triangle." The system gave rise to what has been called "realist mercantilism." By the 1970s the extraordinarily rapid growth of the economy had transformed Japan into a highly developed country, whose Gross Domestic Product (GDP), ranked second in the world only to the United States which made it a key driver of the other East Asian economies.[22]

This arrangement gave rise to three broad attitudes that were embedded in Japanese political life: on the right were traditional nationalists, who resented Japan's loss of autonomy and sought to restore what they regarded as Japan's essence; on the left were the pacifists and the socialists, who envisioned Japan as a pacific neutral country and who opposed the security ties with the US; and in the middle (the political mainstream) were the adherents to the Yoshida legacy.[23]

Japanese on the whole did not dwell much on their war of aggression in Asia. Their American occupiers had not pressed Japanese to atone for their war guilt. The United States government had deliberately retained the emperor (albeit as a secular rather than a divine head of state) even though the Japanese war had been fought in his name and with his knowledge and occasional participation.[24] Additionally, with the impact of the Cold War from 1947 onwards, the Americans allowed former managers and administrators of imperial Japan in China to contribute to the recovery of Japan in the expectation of rebuilding the country. It was under such conditions, for example, that Nobusuke Kishi (a former senior official in Manchuria and member of the wartime cabinet) was released from prison in December 1948, where he was awaiting indictment as a "Class A" war criminal, and went on to become prime minister in 1957. Furthermore, unlike West Germany, there was no equivalent of a Nazi Party to be extirpated, nor was Japan required to reach a reconciliation with neighboring countries in order to establish a regional community and a collective security treaty. American attempts to establish an East Asian equivalent to NATO failed in the early 1950s and hence the United States had to rely on a series of bilateral security treaties in which the US alone undertook region-wide responsibilities, while its partners focused exclusively on their own narrower interests (the so-called "hub and spokes system"). In short neither domestic nor external pressures forced Japanese to confront their ugly past. Instead the Yoshida Doctrine allowed them to pursue a course of virtual pacifism while concentrating their energies on economic development.

Elite Japanese attitudes towards China were a complex mixture of guilt for the aggression of the 1930s and 1940s, of condescension due to China's relative backwardness, of admiration for its past culture to which Japan was indebted and of eagerness to have access to the Chinese economy. In fact despite the alliance with the United States, Japan established economic relations with China in the early 1950s in defiance of the American trade embargo. Even before recognizing China in 1972 Japan had established a complex pattern of economic relations with the PRC that included a quasi-formal agreement and a series of private arrangements. As far as politics was concerned, until the onset of the Cultural Revolution in 1966 the Japanese left was on the whole sympathetic towards Maoist China and leading members of the JSP frequently visited Beijing. Moreover some leaders of the second rank in Beijing (notably Liao Zhengzhi) had personal links with senior members of the LDP and these had helped to smooth over some of the problems that arose in the 1950s and 1960s.[25] At the same time some of the more conservative elements of the LDP had personal ties to the KMT leaders in Taiwan, but the way in which the Taiwan issue was settled in 1972, upon recognition of the PRC, did not arouse vehement opposition within Japan.

The pragmatic basis on which economic relations with China were conducted and the personal ties which Japanese of different shades of opinion had with China stood in stark contrast to their total absence in the case of Sino-American relations. Some Japanese persuaded themselves that they could act as a bridge between China and the US. That would have helped to resolve the long-standing tension in the Japanese self-image as somehow being both an Asian and a Western country.

Thus there was little about Japan in the Maoist period which could have led Mao to change his approach towards the country. Interestingly, it was Japanese historians in the 1970s who were the first to write about the war of the 1930s and 1940s in China, leading to fierce debates with the right wing, which regarded their version of events as "masochistic history." But in view of the anger the Chinese were to display about these matters in the 1980s and 1990s it is remarkable that no attention was paid to these debates in China at that time.[26]

However, there is no doubt that the Yoshida Doctrine proved remarkably successful for Japan during the Cold War era. By the end of the 1980s Japan was being seen as about to overtake the US as the world's leading economy and Japanese took pride in their economic model and the political system under-pinning it, which was seen as providing them with the key role in East Asia.[27] But the bursting of the Japanese economic bubble in 1991 and the effects of the end of the Cold War brought about the demise of the Japanese "economic model" and the political order that had been set by the "San Francisco system." Japan then began to search yet again for a new political identity to replace the one that had proved inadequate to meet the challenges of the unexpected end of the Cold War order.

Deng's new identity for China

China had already begun the process of profound changes necessary to meet the challenges of the end of the Cold War ten years ahead of its demise with the collapse of the Soviet Union in 1991. The death of Mao and the end of the Cultural Revolution in 1976 was marked by the disillusion of the Chinese people and their leaders with Maoist ideology and with his blood-thirsty policies of class struggle. If Mao had argued that only continuous revolution could enable China to recapture its past greatness, his successors held that China would be great again only by focusing on economic development without regard for revolutionary politics. Henceforth, China, as led by Deng Xiaoping from December 1978, would put the emphasis on patriotism alone as the means by which to appeal to the Chinese people. However, the transformation from a socialist to a market-led economic system was to lead to differences within the elite between the reformers and their more conservative colleagues, who wanted to retain a leading role for the state. Unwittingly, Japan came to be embroiled in China's new quest to promote patriotism amid the struggles for economic reform.

The abandonment of class struggle and the revolutionary ideology that accompanied it led to a new emphasis on patriotism and the unity of the Chinese people. This entailed reaching out to the ethnic Chinese overseas. Although they were not necessarily citizens of the PRC they were nonetheless regarded as fellow descendents from the mythical Yellow Emperor and hence part of the Chinese people. In fact the Chinese overseas (including the "compatriots" of Hong Kong, Macao and Taiwan, as well as those in Southeast Asia and beyond) were to play a major role as "foreign" investors in China throughout the modernizing period. The stress on the unity of the Chinese people also led to a new approach to Taiwan. Instead of regarding the KMT on Taiwan as the reactionary remnant of the party and of the class enemies who had been defeated in the civil war, from whom the people on Taiwan had to be "liberated," the KMT was now seen as a potential partner in a new united front of the Chinese people.[28] This meant that for the first time since 1949 the KMT and its supporters, principally on Taiwan, were to be officially included within the ranks of the "people." Mao had famously excluded them as among the 5 percent of the Chinese population who, as enemies, were denied membership of "the people" (*renmin*).

China's post-Mao leaders could no longer base their historical claim for legitimacy on the victory of the CCP over the KMT in the civil war. Instead, the legitimacy of the CCP was seen to have stemmed from the historic victory over Japan. By claiming that the CCP had played the leading role both in mobilizing the Chinese people and in fighting the

Japanese invaders, the CCP could more easily place itself as the leading defender of China and its people. As we shall see, this also led the CCP to present itself as the embodiment of China and as the core of the nation.

This transformation of the identity of China and the CCP had the unintended effect of worsening relations with Japan. The deterioration in relations with Japan was less in the realms of policy or economic relations than in the realms of perceptions and attitudes. Within China the treatment of the history of the War of Resistance to Japan underwent a change of emphasis. No longer was reference made to the alleged traitorous position of the KMT. Films and comic books no longer dwelt on how sinister KMT types were only thwarted at the last minute from betrayals by the heroic measures of workers and peasants. Instead the war was treated as one in which the people (including the KMT) were united in resistance to the cruel Japanese aggressors. Thus the pathway was now clear to raising the long suppressed memories of the war of resistance to Japan and to demand proper restitution.

Ironically, at the very time in which Japan was being excoriated as the past enemy, which had not come to terms with its evil doings, some of China's leaders were looking to Japan as an example of an East Asian country that had successfully taken the path to a modernity of the kind that China now sought. A group of Party leaders who had visited Japan in the autumn of 1978 were so impressed by its high levels of industrial and technological development and the degree of affluence that they returned determined to modernize China as quickly as possible.[29] The foreign affairs section of the authoritative Report of the General Secretary to the 12th Communist Party National Congress of September 1982, which addressed relations with specific countries, gave pride of place to Sino-Japanese relations stating the objective "to remove all obstacles to developing bilateral ties to ensure lasting friendship between the Chinese and Japanese peoples for generations to come."[30] Japan came to be treated in contradictory fashion: throughout the 1980s China's powerful and all-embracive propaganda organs presented Japan as an object of hatred, yet others in the Chinese elite saw Japan as a kind of economic model to be emulated.

The international strategic situation had also begun to change from a Chinese perspective in a way that no longer required the courting of Japan as a potential ally: in 1978–79 China's leaders feared a possible strategic encirclement by the Soviet Union and its supposed proxy Vietnam, a fear that was increased by the Soviet invasion of Afghanistan in late 1979. It was within that context that China had invaded Japan briefly in 1979 and the peace treaty with Japan reached in 1978 doubtless helped Deng Xiaoping prepare the ground for the attack on Vietnam. However, within a year or two it became apparent to Beijing that the Soviet Union was becoming bogged down in Afghanistan and that Vietnam was unable to wipe out Khmer resistance in Cambodia. By 1982 Chinese fears of the threat from the Soviet Union had abated sufficiently for an official reformulation of its foreign policy at the 12th Party Congress to that of an "independent foreign policy of peace." Instead of basing policy on opposition to the Soviet Union, China's leaders now proposed to play a more measured role between the two superpowers. Consequently, Deng no longer saw the Japan–US Alliance in the same positive light as before.

If the international situation had become more benign from a Chinese perspective, there were continuing political divisions at home. China's leaders had settled the question of how to look at the Mao era in the 1981 Resolution on Party History in which the War of Resistance to Japan was also revisited as a triumph of the CCP, without reference to alleged betrayals by KMT types. However, by this stage new problems had arisen. The country was recovering from the wounds and the social upheavals of the Cultural Revolution as it embarked on an entirely new course in carrying out a transition towards market based economic reforms, while trying to retain state controls and without undermining the power of the CCP. There was, however, tension among China's leaders throughout the 1980s between those who advocated both political and economic reforms and those who sought to limit the role of the market and to retain the main bastions of Party and state controls.[31] The differences between the two sides led to what has been described as "cycles of loosening and tightening" as the push for change threatened instability and therefore led to a tightening-up, which in turn led to the stifling of reform and hence led to a loosening of the reins, which then again led to a tightening and another cycle.[32] As a way of reconciling both tendencies, China was now said to be at "the early stage of socialism" and it was said to be practicing "socialism with Chinese characteristics." None of these vague terms was ever defined or explained with any precision. Not surprisingly, perhaps, Chinese people who had been disillusioned with ideology by the Cultural Revolution, were described now as living in a "spiritual vacuum," as the contrast between socialist doctrine and Party practice was diverging so markedly.[33]

One way of countering this was to carry out patriotic education campaigns. Indeed it was in the midst of such a campaign in the summer of 1982 that China's leaders first made an issue of the revision of a history textbook by the Ministry of Education in Japan. Interestingly, this occurred only once China's leaders had concluded that the Soviet Union did not pose an immediate threat and that therefore the strategic relations with Japan had correspondingly declined in importance. The Chinese objection to the supposed revision of the textbook was based entirely on a report in a Japanese newspaper, as China had not yet trained adequate researchers after the Cultural Revolution who could claim expertise in Japanese affairs. As it happened the newspaper turned out to be mistaken. Nevertheless the Chinese pressed the Japanese side, which at that point was caught up in a dispute between the Education and Foreign Affairs Ministries, with the former resisting the latter's insistence upon an apology. In the end the prime minister intervened in favor of the latter and issued an expression of regret, which was eventually accepted by the Chinese side.[34] Whatever the merits or demerits of the Chinese case, China's leaders had used the history question with regard to Japan for domestic purposes, they had succeeded in extracting an official Japanese apology and they were able to claim the moral high ground over Japan.

If that illustrated one dimension of the Chinese approach to Japan, the following incident demonstrated another: In October 1983 the conservatives (or leftists) launched an "anti-spiritual pollution campaign" against what they saw as excessive liberalism, which they associated with an increase in crime and growing Westernization as expressed even in clothes styles and love for "decadent music." The campaign was soon halted as it was seen to threaten economic reform and the opening to the outside. One of the reform leaders, Premier Zhao Ziyang, pointed out, "*Japanese* capitalists are postponing agreements with us ... because they are frightened by the ... movement to eliminate spiritual pollution."[35] (emphasis added) Here the implicit view of Japan was as a vital player in the economic modernization of China. This was given sartorial symbolism by Hu Yaobang during his official visit to Japan later that month, when he wore a Western suit throughout instead of the customary Mao suit favored by the conservatives.

Meanwhile a host of problems in carrying out the reforms combined with levels of inflation not seen since the establishment of the PRC resulted in significant social unrest especially in China's cities. By 1985 students became restive because of poor living conditions and anger at the privileges of the children of leaders, among other reasons. Throughout the summer of 1985 a huge propaganda campaign was launched among students excoriating Japan for its wartime atrocities, pointing out that the death toll for the 1937 Nanjing massacre exceeded that of both the atomic bombs dropped on Japan. The first major student demonstration against Japan took place on September 18, the anniversary of Japan's invasion of Manchuria. This was ostensibly occasioned by the first ever visit by a Japanese prime minister to the Yasukuni Shrine honoring the souls of dead soldiers, which included since 1978 those of the top fourteen A class war criminals condemned to death at the Tokyo War trials, who had been responsible for Japan's invasion of China in the 1930s. Students protested Japan's "new economic invasion" and some went on to criticize the Chinese authorities for not taking a stronger stand against Japan. In November further student demonstrations took place.[36]

The other more positive image of Japan was also extolled in the period of student protests. Under the auspices of the Commission for Sino-Japanese Friendship in the Twenty First Century, as patronized by the leaders Hu Yaobang and Nakasone Yasuhiro (the same prime minister who had given offense by his visit to the Yasukuni Shrine) Japan was held up in the general media and in specialist journals as a model of modernization.[37] In explaining the role of Deng Xiaoping in accelerating the growth and opening of the Chinese economy in the 1980s, his biographer, Ezra Vogel, noted the significance of Japanese advice, management training and the transfer of advanced technology and management techniques from Japan.[38] As Allen Whiting pointed out, in the years 1984–86 aspects of Japanese education, inventiveness and Japanese society as well as its economic development were singled out for praise.[39] The duality of attitudes towards Japan reflected a tension that was evident in views of Japan held by China's leaders. The duality can also be seen as implying differing views about China's identity and its future course. The reformist view called for integrating China into the international economy via Japan, even at the cost of weakening its socialist identity, whereas the conservative view was more concerned about China's socialist identity and regarded what the reformers sought as an encouragement of "bourgeois liberalization."

An additional issue was the perceived military potential of Japan. Especially from the mid-1980s Japan was regarded as a highly developed economic superpower, which was in the process of outstripping American economic influence, especially in the East Asian region. Given the pronounced realism of China's second echelon of leaders headed by Deng Xiaoping, there was concern lest Japan's economic power should be translated into military strength, especially if rightist forces should gain in influence. Given their Leninism they had little understanding of democracy and the rule of law and it was unlikely that they saw these pillars of the post-war Japanese political system as effective bulwarks against militarization. At the same time China's leaders saw the two countries as economically complementary and they expected Japan to invest greatly and to transfer high levels of technology as well. In addition to which China's post-Mao leaders saw their country as the principal victim of Japan's past aggression, and in the 1980s many Japanese agreed. This sense of guilt made most Japanese leaders susceptible to the demands of Chinese leaders for remorse and restitution. Chinese leaders felt a sense of entitlement as epitomized by Deng Xiaoping's remark to a visiting Japanese politician in

June 1986 that Japan should help China more than the US or the Europeans as it "has the biggest debt to China. In 1972 China did not ask for reparations. Frankly speaking, we harbor dissatisfaction over this point."[40]

Chinese sensitivity over the question of Japan and how to treat it was reflected in political struggles among the leadership. As the struggle over the reforms intensified in the mid-1980s, Hu Yaobang, the leading reformist and advocate of developing a special relationship with Japan, was forced to resign. As Christopher Hughes has shown, a difference was evident in the public speeches of Hu Yaobang and the then Vice Premier Li Peng about the patriotism required of the young, with Hu giving a speech in November 1986 defining "sober-minded patriots" as people who go beyond thinking of their country's welfare to reach out to people in Japan and other countries. Li, however, declared the following month the young could contribute to development only if they formed an organized and disciplined force under the leadership of the Party.[41] The linkage between the question of Japan and domestic elite politics was made explicit by Japanese diplomats who reported that top Chinese officials had asked for their "help" with internal divisions by not "making demands."[42]

Japanese perspectives

For Japan the 1980s were a vindication of its long-standing policy of economic realism derived from the Yoshida Doctrine, by which Japan built its economy through international trade and a degree of mercantilism, while continuing to rely upon the United States security guarantee. By this stage Japan was defraying much of the cost for maintaining US bases in Japan and it substantially increased its contributions to international organizations including the World Bank, the IMF, the United Nations and the Asian Development Bank. Japan became the world's largest creditor and also the world's largest aid donor. Japanese Official Development Assistance (ODA) was targeted for strategic commercial purposes mainly at Asian countries. What Kenneth Pyle has called "economic realism" allowed for the pursuit of regional hegemony by economic means. Japan was often described as an "economic giant and a political or military pygmy," yet the country's relative autonomy in its production of leading edge high-technology gave it the capacity to switch very rapidly to becoming a major military power should circumstances warrant that. Indeed its potential to do so could be used for diplomatic and strategic purposes. Influential Japanese extolled Japan as a modern merchant state. Indeed a majority of Japanese took pride in Japan's newfound status and regarded their country as superior to the West.[43]

However, this adaptive (or reactive) Japanese state that relied on the US for its defense and as a market for 40 percent of its exports was perceived by many Japanese as lacking a coherent Japanese identity. Views were deeply divided between a substantial proportion of the population who saw themselves as either progressives or right-wingers, some of whom were in the LDP. The progressives had accepted the pacifist agenda of the first two years of the US occupation and they adhered to a socialist agenda. They coalesced under the banner of the Japanese Socialist Party. The right-wingers saw Japan's dependency on the United States as demeaning. But the conservatives, who wielded power in association with the bureaucracy and big business, tended to adhere to the Yoshida Doctrine. The deep political divide was bridged by the politically cynical practice by which the JSP received a proportion of the spoils of government in return for tacit burden sharing of the Yoshida guidelines, which accepted the peace constitution and the limitations set on the

Japanese military. Thus much of the sparring between them was inconsequential. In fact the conservative government found the opposition of the JSP useful in order to resist demands from the US that Japan accept more of the military strategic burdens, by claiming that there was insufficient support among the people.[44] Furthermore, having seen the repercussions in China occasioned by his visit to the Yasukuni Shrine, Nakasone refrained from doing so again in order to save the Chinese reformist Hu Yaobang from further criticism for his pro-Chinese views.[45]

The more conservative wing of the LDP had long shared the view of the more extreme right-wingers that the strategic subordination to the United States was wounding to Japan's national pride. But they did not share the rightist nationalist argument that Japan should return to the ideals of imperial Japan. When the LDP's Yasuhiro Nakasone, who had long advocated greater autonomy in defense, became prime minister (1982–87) he attempted to change the established policy, not only by seeking to remove the constraint that limited the defense budget to 1 percent of GDP, but also to make the economy less mercantilist, so as to enable Japan to play a leadership role in the global economy. He also sought to reform the rigid educational system to help internationalize Japan. But his efforts failed largely because of obstruction by Japan's domestic system, which allowed great scope for bureaucratic and vested interests to block change.[46]

The main area where the ideological clash between the progressives and the rightist elements in the LDP took place was over the interpretation of the history of Japan's invasion of Korea and China in the first half of the twentieth century. In the late 1940s progressive historians wrote extensively in refutation of the wartime imperial history justifying its war. However, with the onset of the Cold War thousands of leftists were purged from important institutions and by the mid-1950s the Ministry of Education demanded that textbooks avoid harsh criticism of Japan's role in the Pacific War. The aim was to instill national pride in being Japanese. Beginning in a small way in the late 1960s and then growing in volume in the 1970s and becoming a virtual cottage industry, progressive historians and rightists clashed over what had happened in the war.[47] At issue was the larger question of Japan's identity and its relations with its neighbors, notably China and Korea.

When the Chinese and the Koreans, beginning in 1982, started to protest alleged textbook revisions, rightists and a good number of conservatives regarded the Chinese criticisms and the demands for apologies as interference in Japan's domestic affairs. But the government and the majority of the LDP took the view that Japan had to show sensitivity to Chinese sensibilities in particular. As has been suggested they were affected by a measure of guilt, but there was also a view that Japan had to be sensitive to Chinese views so as to avoid exacerbating tensions in the giant country at a difficult time in its transition. It was argued that an unstable China would be damaging for Japan and Japan had an important role to play in helping China to develop economically. That perhaps reflected Japanese confidence in its leading role in East Asia in accordance with the "flying geese" model.

Such attitudes gave birth to what was later seen as the period of "friendship diplomacy" that lasted until the relations began to sour in the early 1990s. The Japanese government gave way on questions of history, as seen in the 1982 episode. Similarly, Nakasone cancelled all plans he may have had to visit the Yasukuni Shrine following the intensity of the Chinese reaction to his first visit. Nakasone also fired his education minister after the Chinese objected to the minister's complaint that Japanese textbooks were showing the country's history in too negative a light. A high ranking diplomat who reacted adversely to angry remarks by Deng Xiaoping by saying that the Chinese paramount leader had become "hard headed" with age was also dismissed in response to Chinese outrage and in the end the prime minster extended a personal apology. More broadly, as Mike Mochizuki put it, "there was an implicit understanding that in exchange for forgoing its demand for reparations China would receive economic assistance from Japan."[48] Tokyo provided three loan packages of Yen 300 billion, 470 billion and 810 billion to cover the years 1979–93. These huge sums from (which were also of benefit to) Japanese firms, played a significant role in constructing the initial infrastructure on which China's rapid industrialization was built.

As far as China and Japan were concerned, the relationship entered a more troubled phase in the 1980s. Since the strategic anti-Soviet glue that bound China and Japan together had lost its force, other more troublesome dimensions of the relationship began to surface. These included new stirrings of nationalism on both sides, the significance of the differences between their two political systems and the way the relationship became an issue in the elite politics of the two sides. Thus even before the end of the Cold War many of the issues of identity that were to bedevil their relationship in the 1990s and early part of the twenty-first century were already apparent.

Notes

1 This is the main argument of Zhao Suisheng, *A Nation-State by Construction: Dynamics of Modern Chinese Nationalism* (Palo Alto, CA: Stanford University Press, 2004).
2 See for example, James Fallow, "Arab Spring, Chinese Winter," *The Atlantic Magazine*, September 2011. www.theatlantic.com/magazine/archive/2011/09/arab-spring-chinese-winter/8601. Accessed March 27, 2012.
3 Hu Sheng, *From the Opium War to the May 4th Movement* (Peking: Foreign Languages Press, reissued in 1991) and his *Imperialism and Chinese Politics* (Peking: Foreign Languages Press, 1955). See also Shouyi Bai, *An Outline of Chinese History* (Peking: Foreign Languages Press, 1982).
4 See for example, Mao Tse-tung, "The Chinese Revolution and the Chinese Communist Party," in his *Selected Works*, Vol. II (Peking: Foreign Languages Press, 1965), pp.305–34 and his "On New Democracy," ibid., pp.339–84.
5 See also, Rana Mitter, "Behind the Scenes at the Museum: Nationalism, History and Memory in the Beijing War of Resistance Museum, 1987–97," *The China Quarterly* No. 161, March 2000, pp.279–93.
6 Yinan He, *Search for Reconciliation* (Cambridge: Cambridge University Press, 2009), p.135. See also her "National Mythmaking and the Problems of History in Sino-Japanese Relations" (Paper delivered at the Conference on Memory of War, 24–25 January 2003, MIT).
7 Roderick MacFarquhar and Michael Schonhals, *Mao's Last Revolution* (Cambridge, MA: Harvard University Press, 2006), "Introduction," pp.1–13.
8 *Mao Zedong on Diplomacy* (Beijing: Foreign Languages Press, Second Printing, 2007), p.126 and p.160.
9 Ibid., pp.169–74.
10 Wolf Mendl, *Issues in Japan's China Policy* (London: Macmillan, 1978), p.19 and p.25.
11 Ibid., pp.57–68.
12 Ross Terrill, *The New Chinese Empire, And What It Means for the United States* (New York: Basic Books, 2003), pp.283–84. See also, Mao's "Conversation on Meeting with Mr. and Mrs. Wilcox, Communist Party of New Zealand Secretary, February 9, 1964," in *Mao Zedong Sixiang Wansui* (A Red Guard Publication, September 1967), p. 327.
13 Yinan He, "National Mythmaking," p.19, cites an internal policy document by Mao to this effect.

14 Michael Yahuda, *The International Politics of the Asia-Pacific, 1945–1995* (London and New York: Routledge, 1996), p.134.
15 Hidenori Ijiri, "Sino-Japanese Controversy since the 1972 Diplomatic Normalization," *The China Quarterly* No. 124, December 1990, pp.639–61. He regarded this as one of the structural weaknesses of Japanese diplomacy in dealing with China.
16 Shoko Tanaka, *Post-War Japanese Resource Policies and Strategies: The Case of Southeast Asia* (Ithaca, NY: Cornell University Press, 1986) and J.L. Vellut, "Japanese Reparations to the Philippines," *Asian Survey* Vol. 3, No. 10, July 1963, pp.496–506.
17 Wolf Mendl, *Japan's Asia Policy* (London and New York: Routledge, 1995), p.64.
18 For text and analysis see R.K. Jain, *China and Japan 1949–1980* (Oxford: Martin Robinson, revised 2nd edition, 1981), Chapter 7, "Peace and Friendship Treaty," pp.107–21.
19 Cited by Liao Chengzhi in his report to the Standing Committee of the National People's Congress on Deng Xiaoping's visit to Japan (November 4, 1978).
20 John W. Dower, *Embracing Defeat: Japan in the Wake of World War II* (New York: W.W. Norton, 1999).
21 For an extensive account and analysis see, Kenneth B. Pyle, *Japan Rising: The Resurgence of Japanese Power and Purpose* (New York: Public Affairs, Perseus Books, 2007), Chapter 8, "The Yoshida Doctrine as Grand Strategy."
22 Ibid., p.265.
23 Richard J. Samuels, *Securing Japan: Tokyo's Grand Strategy and the Future of East Asia* (Ithaca, NY: Cornell University Press, 2007), Chapter 5, "The Discourse," pp.109–32.
24 John W. Dower, *Empire and Aftermath: Yoshida Shigeru and the Japanese Experience, 1878–1954* (Cambridge Council on East Asian Studies, 1979).
25 Mendl, *Japan's Asia Policy*, Chapter 1, "Japan's Policy 1945–71."
26 Ibid., pp.64–68.
27 For elaboration of these developments see, Ezra Vogel, *Japan as Number One* (Cambridge, MA: Harvard University Press, 1979), Chalmers Johnson, *MITI and the Japanese Miracle* (Palo Alto, CA: Stanford University Press, 1982) and Paul Kennedy, *The Rise and Fall of Great Powers* (New York: Random House, 1988). See also examples of Japanese hubris cited by Chalmers Johnson, *Japan, Who Governs? The Rise of the Developmental State* (New York: W.W. Norton, 1995), p.88.
28 See, "National People's Congress Standing Committee Message to Taiwan Compatriots," *Xinhua*, December 31, 1978; and the further elaboration by Marshal Ye Jianying's nine point proposal of September 30, 1981 (*Xinhua*).
29 Richard Baum, quoting a memoir by the Party's leading theoretician, Deng Liqun, who later was regarded as a conservative: *Burying Mao: Chinese Politics in the Age of Deng Xiaoping* (Princeton, NJ: Princeton University Press, 1994), pp.57–58.
30 http://bjreview.com.cn/90th/2011–content_357550_9.htm.
31 Harry Harding, *China's Second Revolution: Reform After Mao* (Washington, DC: The Brookings Institution, 1987), Chapter 4, pp.70–97.
32 Baum, *Burying Mao*. This cycle is one of the themes of the book. See, e.g., Chapter 3, "The First Fang/Shou Cycle," pp.66–93.
33 See the discussion by Suisheng Zhao, in his *A Nation-State by Construction: Dynamics of Modern Chinese Nationalism* (Palo Alto, CA: Stanford University Press, 2004), Chapter 6, "The Rise of State-Led Pragmatic Nationalism: An Instrumental Response to the Decline of Communism in China," pp.209–47.
34 For an extensive treatment see, Caroline Rose, *Interpreting History in Sino-Japanese Relations* (London and New York: Routledge, 1998).
35 For details see, Baum, *Burying Mao*, pp.155–63.
36 For details see, Allen S. Whiting, *China Eyes Japan* (Berkeley: University of California Press, 1989), pp.51–79.
37 Nakasone in fact soon apologized for the visit and made a point of never going there again.
38 Ezra F. Vogel, *Deng Xiaoping and the Transformation of China* (Cambridge, MA: Harvard University Press, 2011), pp.462–64.
39 Whiting, *China Eyes Japan*, pp.80–92.
40 Ibid., p.158.

41 Christopher R. Hughes, "Japan in the politics of Chinese leadership legitimacy: recent developments in historical perspective," *Japan Forum* Vol. 20, No. 2, 2008, pp.251–52.
42 Whiting, *China Eyes Japan*, p.57.
43 Pyle, *Japan Rising*. The quote is on p.258 and the paragraph draws on his pp.258–62.
44 See ibid., pp.262–70.
45 Akihiko Tanaka, "The Yasukuni Issue and Japanese International Relations," in Tsuyoshi Hasegawa and Kazuhiko Togo (eds.), *East Asia's Haunted Present: Historical Memories and the Resurgence of Nationalism* (Westport, CT: Greenwood Publishing Group, 2008), pp.127–28.
46 J.A.A. Stockwin, *Governing Japan* (Oxford: Blackwell, 3rd edition, 1999), pp.62–67.
47 For accounts of the disputes about history see, Takashi Yoshida, *The Making of the "Rape of Nanking": History and Memory in Japan, China and the United States* (Oxford: Oxford University Press, 2006); Joshua A. Fogel (ed.), *The Nanjing Massacre in History and Historiography* (Berkeley: University of California Press, 2000).
48 Mike M. Mochizuki, "Dealing with a Rising China," in Thomas U. Berger, Mike M. Mochizuki and Jitsuo Tsuchiyama (eds.), *Japan in International Politics: The Foreign Policy of an Adaptive State* (Boulder, CO: Lynne Rienner, 2007), p.235.

Chapter 2

The post-Cold War transformation

The 1990s

The end of the Cold War in East Asia led to profound transformations in Asia generally and in Sino-Japanese relations in particular. This was not immediately apparent as there were no great upheavals as in Europe, where communist regimes collapsed, new states came into existence, the EU was enlarged and the Western alliance system was expanded with its *raison d'être* changed. In Asia, the communist parties of China, North Korea and Vietnam stayed in power, the American series of bilateral alliances (the so-called "hub and spokes system") remained intact and the Korea and Taiwan conflicts remained as relics from the Cold War. However, the disintegration of the Soviet Union suddenly brought to an end the primary global axis of conflict that had marked the Cold War between the United States and the Soviet Union in Asia, as elsewhere. It changed the nature of security in the region and it opened the way for the development of pan Pacific and East Asian regional institutions. The disintegration of the Soviet Union freed both China and Japan of the only immediate source of aggression against them. It also had the effect of making them rethink their bilateral relations as they had become simultaneously independent great powers for the first time in their long history. In the absence of the perception of a common Soviet threat, the United States, as the sole superpower, and its regional allies found it necessary to re-calibrate their alliances to meet new circumstances in order to ensure that their interests in common were not overshadowed by newly emerging differences. Finally, both the Chinese and the Japanese found that the disintegration of the Soviet Union and the end of bipolarity had profound implications for their domestic politics, their senses of identity, as well as for the character of their security and foreign policies, which suddenly faced new challenges and opportunities.

Patriotic China

In China, where the leadership was still torn by the divisions of the 1980s exacerbated by the ramifications of the Tiananmen disaster, the sudden disintegration of the Soviet Union deepened the discord among the top leaders. Conservative or leftist forces had gained political traction in Beijing, as Deng Xiaoping was held in certain respects to be responsible for Tiananmen. Deng was not only the prime instigator of the reforms and the loosening up that accompanied them, but he was the one who had appointed Hu Yaobang and Zhao Ziyang to the top positions, whose liberal reforms were directly blamed for the challenge to the authority of the Party represented by the demonstrations in Tiananmen and in many cities throughout China.

The collapse of the Soviet Union raised the question for the CCP of how to account for that "disaster" so as to avoid a similar fate. The conservatives or the "left" in China blamed the collapse on the prevalence of "bourgeois liberalism" aided and abetted by the long-term effects of what was perceived as a Western policy of "peaceful evolution" – a policy designed to subvert communist systems from within by encouraging the spread of "bourgeois liberalism." Accordingly, they favored tighter central controls by subordinating the market to state direction of the economy and by restricting the openness to the international (capitalist) economy. They were also critical of the decentralization of economic decision-making to the provinces, for giving them too much autonomy and denuding the center of many of the powers necessary to direct the economy. Additionally, they sought the rehabilitation of communist ideology and even of class struggle.

The reformers, however, argued that the principal reason for the collapse of the Soviet Union was its failure to meet the economic needs of its citizens rather than the ideological influence of the West. Led by Deng Xiaoping, they called for a new push for further reforms and the opening of the economy still wider, claiming that the advantage of socialism lay in enhancing production. It was in that spirit that Deng Xiaoping successfully overcame his "leftist" opposition in the course of his famous "Southern Tour" of January and February 1992. The importance of socialist and communist ideology was played down as Deng and his associates emphasized patriotism and economic development as the key ideals that have appealed to Chinese people since they were first enunciated at the end of the nineteenth century by Sun Yat Sen, the common father figure of the CCP and the KMT. By pushing the country once again into a pattern of high economic growth, reform and openness, Deng changed the course of China.[1]

It is important to recognize that although Deng prevailed in 1992 the political differences between leftists and reformers continued in one form or another through the 1990s and well into the twenty-first century. The former emphasized the need to address growing inequalities, problems of social welfare and to protect the country from the ill effects of globalization and possible Westernization, and the latter emphasized the need to press on with economic growth through expanding the role of the market and linkages to the international economy, increasing the rule of law, recognizing the private right to own property and so on. Intellectual currents, associated respectively with the so-called "New Left" and the so-called "Liberals," represented these two approaches.[2] However, both "schools" were united in their insistence that the key priority was to retain the rule of the CCP. Moreover they both regarded the United States and its democratic allies including Japan as ideologically committed to the undermining of CCP rule through their promotion of democracy. They took to heart the professions of successive American presidents of their desire to see China democratize in due course and they further took note of the many American governmental statements that this was among the goals to be served by the policy of engagement.

As a result this perceived adverse external pressure was never absent from the debates about reform. If much of the ideology and practice of socialism had been discredited and replaced by "patriotism" as the means by which the leadership could appeal to the Chinese people, the question arose as to what would be the patriotic "ideal" which could bind China together under the leadership of the CCP.

If it were not to be based on a socialistic rejection of Western capitalism, it would be one based on the nationalism emanating from Sun Yat Sen of a hundred years earlier, which called for the building of a strong united and prosperous China that would never again be humiliated.[3] The new historical claim to legitimacy of the CCP was presented as stemming from having defeated Japan, united the country and provided the conditions for stability and economic growth. A new kind of spiritual dimension was added to the role and function of the CCP as the upholder of China's dignity, culture and continuity with its past glory. The Chinese Communist Party was portrayed as the embodiment of "Chineseness."[4]

It was to serve these ends that a huge campaign of "patriotic education" was launched in 1993. Following on from the damage to the credibility of the CCP after the Tiananmen disaster, the new leader Jiang Zemin sought to burnish the leading role of the CCP by presenting it as the only force to have saved China from the hundred years of humiliation at the hands of foreigners, and the only one capable of regenerating the country so that it could be restored to the greatness that was its due. Focusing especially on primary and secondary schools, a countrywide program of films and television documentaries was issued that focused on the war with Japan and on promoting national pride. The Party's Central Committee issued an outline of a patriotic education curriculum to cover all students from kindergartens all the way through to universities. This curriculum replaced in effect the programs on communist ideology that had been compulsory since the 1950s. The new curriculum emphasized the Party's view of China's national conditions in the current historical period, taking into account the situation in the economic, political, military, social and cultural fields as well as the country's demography and physical resources. The purpose was to enhance among the young a sense of their historical mission and responsibility. As the campaign developed, the curriculum was extended to include a latter-day Confucianism that focused on themes of loyalty and obedience. Important patriotic people from China's past were glorified so as to present the CCP as continuing in their patriotic tradition. China was defined as a multi ethnic country in which all the ethnic groups living within China's current borders were regarded as being part of the Chinese people since ancient times. Finally, the CCP was not only glorified, but it was portrayed as the ultimate defender of Chinese interests.[5] As we shall see, this new nationalistic definition of China and of the historic role of the CCP were to have a marked impact on the deterioration of relations with Japan in the 1990s.

Uncertain Japan

In Japan, the end of the Cold War brought about the end of the "San Francisco system," to which it had given rise. In domestic politics this hastened the decline of the JSP and in effect shifted the center or mainstream of Japanese politics further in a conservative direction. At the same time the end of the Cold War also brought to an end the one party rule of the LDP, which thereafter required other parties to join it in coalition governments and at one point temporarily even lost its position as a governing party. A new electoral system was introduced in 1994 ending the multiple seat constituencies in favor of single seat constituencies. Henceforth the only successful candidate was the one with the most votes. This marked the transition from a centrifugal to a centripetal system, which had the effect of moving the main political parties towards the center. It also spelt the end of the JSP as a major party because it could no longer win seats based on minority leftist votes in multiple seat districts.[6] But it did not have the effect of transforming Japanese politics into a coherent two party system.

Debates about Japan's identity, which had been subdued during the Cold War and especially during Japan's triumphal decade of the 1980s, now resurfaced. Particularly significant were the different visions put forward by two prominent LDP members, Ichiro Ozawa and Takemura Masayoshi. Ozawa's 1993 book, *Blue Print for a New Japan* called for the emergence of a "normal" Japan that would have its economy deregulated and that would be prepared to take risks in foreign affairs, participate in collective security and enhance national power and prestige. Takemura replied a year later with the book, *Japan: A Small But Shining Country*, in which he argued against deregulating the economy and raising the country's international profile in favor of a more quietist country. There were also calls in the early 1990s for Japan to return to its Asian character in the light of the more favorable economic trends in East Asia (if not in Japan at that time).[7] However, as the 1990s wore on these views were overtaken by the very real pressure from the missile and possible nuclear threat from North Korea and from the economic and military rise of China.

In external affairs the first Gulf War of 1990/91 forced the Japanese to recognize that the character of their alliance with the United States had changed irrevocably. Japan was criticized for providing only monetary assistance to a war in which its own vital oil supplies were at risk, while others risked the lives of their own soldiers. Thereafter the Americans demanded more from Japan, effectively bringing to an end the Cold War arrangement of leaving security arrangements to the US, while Japan focused on economics and paid the lion's share of the costs of basing American forces on its territory. The Japanese Diet promptly broke what had hitherto been considered a taboo and changed its laws to allow its Self Defense Forces (SDF) to leave Japanese shores to participate in UN peacekeeping. The first Japanese peacekeepers were dispatched to Cambodia in 1992, albeit under conditions that forbade them to engage in combat.[8]

In 1994 as the United States prepared for a possible war with North Korea Japan was once again found wanting as its government indicated to its American ally that it would find great difficulties in meeting American demands for various logistic assistance and for curtailing the $600 million remittances sent by resident Koreans to North Korea.[9] Notwithstanding its lackluster performance during those two major crises and indeed before the last one had quietened down, Japan in May 1994 formally let it be known that it was seeking permanent membership of the UN Security Council.[10] The junction of the two events may be seen as illustrative of the lack of bureaucratic coordination in a troubled political system. There had been long-standing caution about the wisdom of this, as it was thought by many that Japan was not yet ready to assume all the obligations that might be incurred, but the pressure from the Ministry of Foreign Affairs (MOFA, within whose provenance UN affairs was bureaucratically located) prevailed in part because there was international recognition that the UN system needed reform to meet the new post-Cold War conditions. The clear implication for Japan, however, was that it sought the prestige of great power status.

One indication of unease among other sections of the Japanese government was the successful resistance to the proposal by some in the LDP that Japan should embrace the obligation of collective security as allowed by the UN Charter and contribute to armed conflicts involving its American ally. Indeed, as already noted, the Japanese had proved to be unable, as well as reluctant, to participate militarily in the 1990/91 Gulf War or in the American preparation for a possible war with North Korea in 1994, even though North Korea had just tested a Nodong missile, whose range could reach Japan.

From a Japanese perspective the uncertain situation was made much worse by the bursting of its asset bubble in 1991 and the collapse of its much vaunted economic model. Only a few months earlier it was commonly argued that the Japanese model was superior to American style capitalism. The American Senator Paul Tsongas put it graphically at the time, "the Cold War is over ... and Japan won."[11] The 1990s became a decade of economic stagnation. Much needed reforms were delayed or not carried out. The much praised bureaucracy and the interlocking character of business and the banks were now perceived to be the problem rather than the solution, especially as the prestige of the major ministries of the government was undermined by corruption scandals. Japan could no longer present itself as an economic model for Asia and the world beyond.

The sense that an era had come to an end and that a new uncertain one had begun was reinforced in Japan by the earlier death of the Showa Emperor in January of 1989. His death provided the occasion for opening up once again the debate about Japan's responsibility for the war. Several cities opened Peace museums, which were critical of Japan's role in the war, while at the same time recording memories of local wartime losses. The Hiroshima and Nagasaki Museums added new materials critical of Japan's war. Conservative nationalist groups went on a counter-offensive. Some had already criticized middle-school textbooks as "self-flagellating" and now, unlike in the previous two decades, they not only sought to end criticism of Japan's wars in the 1930s and 1940s, but they also sought to change public opinion in favor of future rearmament.[12] Moreover, the end of the Cold War marginalized the pacifist groups who had advocated for "unarmed neutrality" in the era of bipolarity. It had become outdated by the new insecurities in the region. For one thing, North Korea had begun to threaten regional stability; for another, Japanese police in 1992 concluded that the North Korean intelligence service had abducted people registered as missing from the Japanese coastline. In addition, the emergence of China as a military power was giving rise to concern especially after its nuclear tests in 1994. Opinion polls began to show acceptance of the legitimacy of the SDF and a readiness to consider revision of the constitution, if not Article 9 – the famous peace article.[13]

The end of the Cold War changed the international environment differently for China and Japan. For the first time since the establishment of the People's Republic in 1949 and indeed for the first time in the modern era China was free from possible attack by a superior military power. China gained greater strategic latitude as it was able to reduce its extensive military deployments from the North, where they had formed defensive lines against a possible Soviet attack and to focus more on increasing its influence in its neighbors in East Asia and in the newly formed states in Central Asia. Unlike the Western countries, the neighboring Asian countries did not impose sanctions on China after Tiananmen and even the one Asian country that did, Japan, did so minimally and it ended those very quickly. Meanwhile Indonesia and Singapore established diplomatic relations with China in 1990. The better pattern of relations with neighbors paved the way for China's re-entry into international society after the relative ostracism it had suffered in response to Tiananmen. Meanwhile China's experience of rapid economic growth, economic reform and deepening engagement with the international economy coincided with the unleashing of the forces of globalization now that the economic divisions occasioned by the Cold War were over. China became a major beneficiary of the new tide of globalization.

Yet as we have seen, Japan faced a deteriorating international environment for which it was unprepared. It continued to depend on the alliance with the United States for its security, but it was unable to meet US demands that it should contribute militarily to security in the region and the wider world. The Cold War understanding, which enabled Japan to concentrate on its economy while the United States took care of its security, no longer worked in the same way. The relative weakening of the ties with the United States coincided with the decline of Japan's appeal as an economic model in East Asia. Far from being the economic leader in the region, Japan was soon perceived to be in decline as its rates of foreign investment (FDI) in Southeast Asia were reduced. The relatively closed character of its domestic economy that had served Japan so well up until 1990 had now become an obstacle to its capacity to benefit from the high tide of globalization that was sweeping the world. The fact that Japan remained America's most important Asian ally with the world's second largest economy, with the largest investments in Southeast Asia, did little to mitigate a sense of adversity.[14]

Within Japan this gave rise to a sentiment that the country could no longer continue simply to adjust and adapt to changing circumstances as it carried out mercantilist practices under the security umbrella of the United States. If Japan were to be able to uphold its position in international society it would have to take more proactive steps to defend its position.[15] There was an urge to be more assertive and autonomous in international affairs, but there was still the residual desire to be seen as uniquely a peace-loving country. One way in which the difference between the two was sometimes depicted was the question whether Japan should seek to be the Britain or the Switzerland of Asia.

Richard Samuels has addressed the issue by identifying four broad viewpoints along two axes centering on the questions of the use of force and the relationship with the United States. Two viewpoints accept that it may be necessary to use military force: first the "neoautonomists," whom he sees as heirs to traditional nativists and who seek autonomy from the United States. Second are the "normal nation-alists," whom he sees as heirs to "Big Japanists" who seek prestige through strength. The main difference between them is that the former want to distance Japan from the US and the latter want to embrace it. The other two groupings object to the use of military force, but are also divided on the question of relations with the US. The first, the "Pacifists," heirs to the unarmed neutralists of the Cold War period, seek autonomy through prosperity, and want distance from the US; and the second, the "middle power internationalists," heirs to "Small Japanists," seek prestige through prosperity, and want to embrace the US.[16]

In practice, however, the differences were less clear-cut and their impact on domestic Japanese public opinion reflected that. The Pacifists, who had been marginalized by the end of the Cold War, nevertheless continued to influence public opinion, as shown by the persistent public aversion to the prospect that Japanese armed forces engaged in Peace Keeping Operations (PKO) should be put in harm's way and suffer casualties. It mattered not whether they operated under UN or American auspices. Similarly, the leading politician Ozawa, who is regarded by Samuels as a "normal nation-alist who favors hugging the US" (which may have been true of the early 1990s), made it clear from the late 1990s onwards that he favored the deployment of the SDF only under the UN mandate. Moreover all the groups supported Japan's initial bid to become a permanent member of the UN Security Council in 1994, even though they may have differed about their motivation and their appreciation of the implications.[17] Perhaps the key point to be made is that the end of the Cold War undermined the consensus upholding the Yoshida Doctrine, without replacing it with a coherent alternative. Hence the basic premise of the Doctrine of operating within the constraints of Peace Article 9 of the Constitution and the strategic dependence on the United States remained in practice.

Sino-Japanese relations deteriorate

In a very real sense Japan was in a process of transition, as was China. But the difference was that Japan was doing so in the context of relative decline, whereas China was on the rise. The relative change in the experience of China and Japan after the end of the Cold War had a major impact on their relations with each other. From a Chinese perspective Japan ceased to be seen as a possible economic model. For example, in considering how to reform their state-owned enterprises (adapted from the now obsolete Soviet model) China's leaders tended to look to South Korea's *chaebols* rather than to Japan's major companies.[18] No matter that Japan had been instrumental in returning China to international respectability after Tiananmen, notably by arranging for the emperor to visit China in 1992 and by taking the lead in lifting sanctions, Japan tended to be seen in a bad light through the lens of China's new patriotism. Japan was seen as the aggressor who had not properly atoned for its misdeeds. From a Japanese perspective, China was no longer seen as a more backward country, which Japan was obligated to help develop economically and to which Japan should display sensitivity because of Japan's history of aggression. Instead China was perceived to be a more troublesome neighbor, whose leaders were prepared to use force ruthlessly against peaceful demonstrators at home, to test nuclear weapons without regard to neighboring countries in 1994 and even to engage in coercive diplomacy in 1995/96 against Taiwan by firing missiles, some of which came close to Japanese waters.

The Chinese in turn were outraged by the Japanese reaction to their policies. In particular they objected to Japanese protests on August 17, 1995 against China's nuclear tests. These did not contravene any treaty, as the Comprehensive Test Ban Treaty (CTBT) was not adopted by the UN General Assembly until a year later in September 1996 (which in any case meant that it was not legally binding as it would have been had it been a resolution of the UN Security Council). The Chinese had not tested nuclear weapons for a while and they sought to modernize their nuclear deterrent. The timing of the Japanese protest (only two days after the fiftieth anniversary of the end of the war) and the decision to suspend a symbolic amount of the Ministry of Foreign Affairs' Grants in Aid deepened China's ire. Although the amount was insignificant the Chinese government was indignant that it could be withheld at all and by Japan of all countries. Japan was portrayed to the Chinese people not only as the past aggressor who had yet to atone adequately, but also as a power that was now interfering in China's internal affairs by trying to use economic sanctions to oppose nuclear tests that the government regarded as central to its national security. At the same time Japan was still tightly bound to an America that stood accused of obstructing China's key national interests. From a Japanese perspective, China was contravening the spirit of the coming CTBT that was due to be approved by the UN, especially as all the declared nuclear powers (with the exception of France) had already stopped testing.

The change was reflected in the increasingly unfavorable views that the two sets of populations had of each other. In the 1980s the two sides held relatively positive views of each other. In Japan, where the Prime Minister's Office has conducted annual polls on the question since 1978, 70–75 percent of people felt affinity for China in the 1980s (the decade of "friendship diplomacy"). This dipped to around 50 percent in the wake of Tiananmen in 1989, where it remained for most of the 1990s. Indeed as relations deteriorated in response to the issue of the nuclear test of 1994 and the 1995/96 Taiwan crisis, those feeling affinity for China dropped to below 50 percent and for the first time those who claimed no feelings of affinity surpassed those who did. That figure did not begin to change until the political relationship began to change after Prime Minister Abe's visit to Beijing in October 2006.[19] Although systematic polling of Chinese views did not begin until the late 1990s, the available evidence suggests that Chinese perceptions of Japan followed a similar pattern. In the 1980s, despite evidence of some rancor, Chinese managers and officials considered that Japan was playing a valuable role in China's economic development.[20] By the 1990s attitudes had changed, as evident by the more abrasive attitude to the West in general and Japan in particular displayed in Chinese publications and as confirmed by my interviews with Chinese scholars.[21] A major survey by *China Youth Daily* published in December 1996 showed that only 14.5 percent had a favorable impression of Japan in contrast to 41.5 percent who had a poor impression of the country.[22]

The worsening of relations in the 1990s did not arise from the conscious adoption of hostile policies by either state against the other. Rather they arose as unintended consequences of changes in their broader responses to the new post-Cold War international environment and to their respective new socio-political changes at home. Internationally, China was seen to be rising and playing greater and more active economic and political roles in East Asia, even though it still ranked as a developing country, while Japan was seen to be relatively declining, even though it still ranked as a highly developed country with by far the larger economy. Chinese strategists also viewed Japan negatively as being capable of constraining China's rise.[23] In domestic affairs, China was becoming more nationalistic in response to government campaigns to foster a new sense of national identity centered on Communist Party rule. That had the unintended effect of casting Japan as the ultimate symbol of foreign aggression, which had humiliated the country for a hundred years until the establishment of the People's Republic in 1949. Japan, for its part, was seeking to come to terms with the consequences of the bursting of the economic bubble, which undermined popular faith in government and business institutions that had hitherto been regarded as the mainstay of the now disparaged "economic miracle." It was generally appreciated that the country needed to carry out fundamental reforms, but as Gerald Curtis observed, there has been considerable social change and adaptation by Japanese companies to address the challenges of the 1990s and changes to the political parties, but not a change in the political system fundamental enough to allow for effective cabinet government under prime-ministerial leadership.[24]

In both countries public opinion began to play an increasingly important and independent role in the deterioration of the Sino-Japanese relationship. In China the accelerated economic changes led to rapid social change, which loosened the party-state's social controls. Responding to the authorities' encouragement of patriotic sentiments the younger generation in particular became more overtly nationalistic. Perhaps the first indication of this, which attracted attention in both China and abroad, was the publication of the book *The China That Can Say No* by a number of younger intellectuals. In blunt and emotional language it excoriated mainly the United States, but also Japan, for hypocrisy in using idealist concepts such as human rights to criticize China, which were depicted as no more than smoke screens behind which the two pursued their national interests to keep China down. This main message had support within officialdom even though the book contained not-so-veiled criticism of the government.[25] Using electronic means of communication, text messages and so on, younger people were able to communicate across the country rapidly. As Peter Gries has pointed out, younger people in their twenties self-consciously adopted a nationalistic stance in the latter half of the 1990s and saw that as part of their identity as a distinctive generation, separate from those aged in their forties and fifties. Virulently anti-Japanese views became the common staple of messages on the Internet, some of which incited violence against Japanese and their alleged sympathizers. His book recounts in detail numerous public incidents in which student emotional nationalism burst out to the discomfort of mainly the Japanese, but also of the Chinese government, which stood accused of not being sufficiently robust in standing up against these alleged "anti-China policies."[26] By the late 1990s, Party leaders and those in charge of the country's foreign affairs became conscious of the gap between the emotional nationalism of the young and the more pragmatic nationalism of policy-makers. At one point the former foreign minister and leading figure in foreign affairs, Vice Premier Qian Qichen, told a student audience that the principal contradiction in China's foreign affairs was the difference between the patriotism of the young and that of the officials.[27]

The emergence of strident student nationalism in China coincided with the adoption of a more pragmatic foreign policy by China's leaders. They were stung by the adverse reaction in the region to their coercive diplomacy against Taiwan in 1995–96 and to their creeping assertiveness in pursuit of territorial claims in the South China Sea, as manifested by the occupation of Mischief Reef in 1995 which was also claimed by the Philippines. Beijing found it propitious for the first time to negotiate collectively with the ASEAN (Association of Southeast Asian Nations) countries over conduct in the South China Sea, thereby mollifying their concerns over what they saw as China's maritime assertiveness and ensuring that they would not openly align with the US against China in response to its military actions against Taiwan.[28] This marked the beginning of active Chinese multilateral diplomacy in Southeast Asia. Up until that point Chinese diplomacy in the region was marked by a certain reactive and cautious quality.[29] China's leaders had found that the diplomatic costs of using their country's superior weight to deal with its neighbors separately outweighed the short-term disadvantages of dealing with them on a multilateral basis. This meant abandoning the PRC's traditional diplomacy of emphasizing bilateral dealings, which reflected the long time imperial practice of treating the representatives of other countries on a one-to-one basis as bearers of tribute.

The Taiwan crisis came to an end in 1996 when the US sent two carrier-led battle groups to the vicinity. Having come close to the brink of conflict, Beijing and Washington took the opportunity to ameliorate relations. The new approach by Beijing reflected its broader policy agenda of embracing multilateralism to enhance its acceptance in the region and to deflect concern about the so-called "China threat theory." Both may be seen as continuing the emphasis on the centrality of enhancing domestic economic development and integrating the Chinese economy more closely with the outside world.[30] This more accommodating diplomacy was not only out of step with the new nationalism of the young, but it also failed to command universal support among the leaders in Beijing. The old divisions of the 1980s between the leftist/conservatives and the reformers had not been swept away by the success of Deng Xiaoping's economic policies of the 1990s. For example, in the summer of 1996 *The Economic Daily*, a newspaper under the aegis of the

State Council headed by Premier Li Peng (a leading leftist) published a series of fifteen articles critical of the impact of foreign capital on the Chinese economy that led to an authoritative rebuttal by the CCP's *People's Daily* on July 16.[31] The difference also reflected a dispute about power and the future direction of China as Jiang Zemin sought to consolidate his position as the unrivalled successor to Deng Xiaoping, who in 1995 had become irretrievably incapacitated by advanced age before his death two years later. Jiang had first leaned to the "left" before seeking once again to promote the cause of reform. His opening to the US, as consolidated by his successful visit to the US in 1997, and President Clinton's return visit the following year were an important part of the new orientation.

Japan, however, felt that it was in danger of being abandoned by its ally as Clinton became the first US president to visit China without stopping over in Japan. It was called "Japan by-passing." Many Japanese were also disturbed by Clinton's signing of a joint statement with Jiang condemning the Indian nuclear tests, which took place during his visit. They complained that this diminished Japan's status as it was not a party to the statement, suggesting that China and the US would attempt to work together in what was later to be called a G-2, to the exclusion of Japan – America's principal ally in the region. Even more importantly, the Japanese were not best pleased by Clinton's joining the Chinese in criticizing Japan for its conduct during the Asian Financial Crisis of 1997. The Japanese were also hurt by his unilateral declaration in China that the US would henceforth not support Taiwanese membership of international organizations for which sovereignty was a condition of membership. The Japanese government had not been consulted on a policy change in an area that touched on its vital security interests. Moreover the United States had failed to support Japan in its proposing to the Chinese that summit meetings be held with other major powers to consider common security issues.[32] These all combined to make Japanese fear that they were being sidelined at the expense of their troublesome neighbor. As we shall see, later that year when Jiang paid a visit to Japan, the Japanese government displayed its autonomy and its tacit rebuttal of the G-2 tendency by refusing to follow Clinton's new position on Taiwan.

The bombing of the Chinese embassy in Belgrade in May 1999, which was seen by all Chinese as deliberate, brought to the surface underlying fears of perceived American efforts to constrain the rise of China and of alleged attempts to Westernize the country. It also provided an opportunity for the leftists and hardliners in the leadership to derail Jiang's policies. Fiery speeches by Premier Li Peng and Defense Minister Chi Haotian calling on people to rally against the external "enemy" accompanied huge violent student-led demonstrations throughout China. Jiang played the key role in setting aside the animosity towards the United States and the opposition to globalization by deciding to accept with minor modifications the terms on offer for joining the World Trade Organization (WTO).[33]

The divide deepens

Japan, however, did not benefit from Jiang's new course. The new diplomacy towards neighbors, the engagement with the US and the consolidation of the integration with the international economy was not accompanied by a new approach towards Japan. First, the differences in the way the respective identities of China and Japan had developed since the end of the Cold War and the debates about those identities did not allow either side to regard the other with much sympathy and understanding. The underlying distrust between the two sides became manifest. Second, the two sets of leaders were unwilling to take the steps necessary to bridge the divide between the two countries. Third, as will be explored in chapter 6, the two were adversely affected by a security dilemma by which defensive measures by the one were perceived as offensive by the other.

As we have seen, the core of China's post-Cold War identity that emerged under the leadership of Jiang Zemin emphasized a new kind of patriotism/nationalism in which Japan's role as the cruel oppressor who had yet to atone for its aggression was an important element. Little reference was made to Japanese ODA, which had played a vital role in the early stages of the construction of major infrastructure projects such as road, rail, ports and power stations that helped kick start rapid economic growth. In 1995 Jiang orchestrated huge events to mark the fiftieth anniversary of the CCP's alleged triumph over Japan without reference to Japan's consistent turn towards peace and non-militarist policies since its defeat over fifty years earlier. Instead every instance of denial of wartime responsibility by Japanese politicians (who were dismissed from office for their pains) was played up by China's official media as evidence of a possible re-emergence of Japanese militarism similar to that of the 1930s. Japanese debates about "normalcy" were wrenched out of context to be portrayed as arguments for the resumption of a military role, replete with capabilities to project force (including perhaps nuclear weapons) to complement Japan's economic and technological prowess. At no point did the official media take into account that Japan's defense budget was still limited to 1 percent of Gross National Product (GNP). Perhaps China's leaders, guided by their own ideology and practice, could not imagine that successive governments of a country as developed and technologically adept as Japan with a history of militarism could deliberately and with the full support of its people eschew strategic independence and a military capability commensurate with the high levels of its other capacities.

Similarly, Japanese showed little understanding of the Chinese determination to become strong given the depiction of its modern history as one of victimhood and humiliation heaped on a once great country that had been unjustly laid low by a succession of modern aggressors culminating in the most cruel and extensive aggression by Japan. If Chinese emotional nationalism was intensified by a change of generations, the significance of generational change was also true of Japan, but without a similar emotional intensity. By the 1990s the generation that had been active in the war and in the occupation of China had more or less passed from the scene. The generation born after 1945 did not share their parents' experience or sense of guilt and they were more wedded to the democratic values developed since the end of the American occupation in 1952. The new patriotism that emerged in China under the aegis of the CCP evoked more alarm than sympathy, especially because of its anti-Japanese character. The continual Chinese quest for atonement and the refusal to take note of the many Japanese expressions of regret (by one account these were expressed on at least thirty-nine separate occasions between the 1950s and the 2010s)[34] were seen as no more than cynical attempts to extract concessions from Japan and even as interference in Japanese domestic affairs.[35]

Attempts by the Japanese Ministry of Education to inculcate pride in "Japaneseness" among the young made it all the more difficult for the younger generation to respond sympathetically to Chinese concerns. Younger Japanese tended to show more sympathy for the democratic transition taking place in Taiwan than for the travails of authoritarian China. If younger Chinese were inculcated with a sense of historic victimhood, so were their Japanese counterparts. The latter saw themselves as having risen from the ashes of Hiroshima and Nagasaki and from the destruction of their country at the end of the war in 1945. A succession of Chinese acts beginning with nuclear testing in May, August and September of 1995 and even in 1996, continuing with the bracketing of Taiwan with missiles in March 1996 and subsequent intrusions into Japanese air and sea spaces, including exploration for oil near the median-line in the East China Sea, all contributed to a growing distrust of a rising China by the Japanese.[36]

At the same time apologies by Japanese leaders for the war (many of which were the product of negotiations between the two sides) were perceived in China as limited and insincere, especially in view of occasional, but persistent statements of denial of wartime aggression by individual Japanese ministers. The fact that they invariably were forced to resign made little difference to the Chinese judgment, as they were seen to be representative of an incipient revival of militarism. Whereas within Japan people were getting weary of the Chinese government's continual harping on the theme and suspected the Chinese of ulterior motives. As we have seen, opinion polls among younger people in both countries reflected the growing antagonism between them. A Chinese survey taken even after the American intervention in the Taiwan crisis in 1996 found that Japan with 47 percent was the most disliked country followed by the US with 37.7 percent.[37] In the same year the number of Japanese who felt no affinity for China for the first time exceeded those who felt an affinity.[38]

The change of generations among the leadership in both China and Japan also contributed to the souring of relations. Deng Xiaoping's generation shared the intellectual milieu of those such as Zhou Enlai and China's leading modern writer, Lu Xun, who as young men had spent time in Japan before the First World War to learn from the first modern Asian state and who had some understanding of Japanese life and sensibilities. Deng's successor, Jiang Zemin, and his generation had no such experience of Japan and their formative years were shaped by Japanese aggression and its occupation of China. Jiang Zemin was known for his antipathetic feelings towards Japan.[39] According to accounts in China, members of Jiang's immediate family had been victims of Japan's aggression, which he had witnessed first hand, being twenty-one years old when the war ended in 1945. This has been disputed from outside China by claims that far from being a victim, Jiang's family had prospered under the Japanese occupation.[40] Be that as it may, Jiang played a prominent part in the official criticisms of Japan, especially for its alleged failure properly to address its historical guilt. Jiang had blamed the Americans for failing to de-militarize Japan after the war, leaving the Japanese ignorant of their own history and regarding themselves as victims of atomic warfare.[41] It has been suggested that this was a deliberate attempt to bolster his patriotic credentials in response to criticisms from Premier Li Peng and others to his policies of reform and opening up, which deepened the disruptive impact of globalization and tied the country too closely to the United States.[42] Matters came to a head during Jiang's visit to Japan in 1998, the first by a Chinese head of state. Jiang was disappointed by Japan's failure to issue a formal written apology for its wartime behavior. He had been led to believe that one would be forthcoming, especially as the Japanese government had just issued one for the new South Korean President Kim Dae Jung. Moreover Jiang was also irked by Japan's failure to follow US President Clinton in adopting a "Four Noes" policy towards Taiwan.[43] As a result Jiang spent the rest of his visit publicly and undiplomatically criticizing the Japanese for not addressing their history "correctly." Japanese were particular offended by his doing this at a ceremonial meeting with the emperor.[44]

The simultaneous change of generations in the Japanese leadership saw the disappearance of many of those associated with the opening of relations with China in 1972. These had been people who had served in the war or in occupied China and Manchuria, who, in the words of Michael Green, "equated Japan's militarism with its mistreatment of China, ... [and] who wanted to make amends." Prime Minister Tanaka, who had officiated at the ceremonies of recognition in 1972, had been a sergeant in the Kwantung Army and after 1972 he developed close personal relations with China's leaders. As the leader of the most powerful faction in the LDP, he and his colleagues cultivated what was later called "friendship diplomacy with China," which was notable for its sensitivity to Chinese sensibilities. By the mid-1990s that generation was replaced largely by men who lacked those emotional and personal ties to Beijing. In 1996 Prime Minister Ryutaro Hashimoto and opposition leader Ichiro Ozawa, who hailed from the Tanaka faction, were both regarded in Beijing as dangerous nationalists. Even the *Asahi Shimbun*, that used to echo Chinese criticisms of Japanese nationalism, prominently editorialized against China's nuclear tests.[45]

Not surprisingly, the two sets of leaders did little to bridge the gap between the two sides. Ironically, pragmatic officials of both sides had prepared a new statement on the relationship, calling it the "Building of a Partnership of Friendship and Cooperation for Peace and Development." The highlight of this consisted of twenty-eight major projects that Japan would build in China within the next two years. But the generational change and the hardening attitudes towards China contributed to a purging of the Japanese Ministry of Foreign Affairs of many officials associated with pro-China positions. That contributed to the deterioration of relations. On the Chinese side, however, officials who were more pragmatic in their nationalism were keen to bring the relationship back on course. They contributed greatly to the success of Premier Zhu Rongji's fence-mending visit to Tokyo in October 2000 in which he avoided the mentioning of history. But the true flavor of the predominant view towards Japan within the Chinese leadership was perhaps better reflected by a front-page article in *The People's Daily* on the day after Zhu's departure from Japan, which sharply criticized alleged Japanese militarism.[46] At the same time it was possible to interpret the difference between Zhu and the Party newspaper as reflecting divisions in the leadership.[47]

What is clear, however, is that as the 1990s unfolded, the relationship between China and Japan deteriorated. For the first time in their long history as neighboring countries they had become great powers at the same time with neither regarding the other as superior. Yet they were unable to build on the relatively good relations of the 1980s. One of the major reasons for that was the way their evolving identities contributed to the distrust and rivalry between the two countries. The particular direction taken by the development of Chinese patriotism painted Japan in dark colors. Japanese attempts to establish a more active and prominent international position, while maintaining the alliance with the United States, were perceived in China as attempts to limit China's rise. The Japanese felt under increasing diplomatic and military pressure from China as the decade came to an end. The Chinese in turn felt that Japan was assuming a more active military role in the region designed to contain China.

Notes

1 For excellent analysis and further details on the issues discussed in the last two paragraphs see, Joseph Fewsmith, *China Since Tiananmen: the Politics of Transition* (Cambridge: Cambridge

University Press, 2001), Part One, pp.21–71. For details of Deng's "southern tour" and of his success in overcoming the resistance to accelerating economic reform and economic growth see, Ezra F. Vogel, *Deng Xiaoping and the Transformation of China* (Cambridge, MA: Harvard University Press, 2011), Chapter 23, "Deng's Finale: The Southern Journey," pp.664–90.

2 For extended discussion see, Fewsmith, pp.75–131. See also, essays by Chinese intellectuals in the following: Chaohua Wang (ed.), *One China, Many Paths* (London and New York: Verso, 2003), Xudong Zhang (ed.), *Whither China? Intellectual Politics in Contemporary China* (Durham, NC: Duke University Press, 2001) and Wang Hui (trans. and ed. by Theodore Huters), *China's New Order: Society, Politics and Economy in Transition* (Cambridge, MA: Harvard University Press, 2003).

3 See the discussion in Suisheng Zhao, *A Nation-State by Construction: Dynamics of Modern Chinese Nationalism* (Palo Alto, CA: Stanford University Press, 2004), pp.214–17.

4 Ibid., Chapter 6, "The Rise of State-Led Pragmatic Nationalism: An Instrumental Response to the Decline of Communism in China," pp.209–47.

5 For details see, ibid., pp.218–47. For the enduring effect on younger people see, Zheng Wang, *Never Forget National Humiliation: Historical Memory in Chinese Politics and Foreign Relations* (New York: Columbia University Press, 2012).

6 Jun Saito, "Electoral Foundations of Japan's Foreign Policy Choices," *Foreign Policy Research Institute*. fpri@fpri.org. Accessed August 1, 2008.

7 See the discussion in Michael J. Green, *Japan's Reluctant Realism: Foreign Policy Challenges in an Era of Uncertain Power* (New York: Palgrave, 2001, for the Council on Foreign Relations), pp.18–29.

8 For analysis of the debates and developments in the early 1990s see ibid., Chapters 1 and 2, pp.11–76.

9 Don Oberdorfer, *The Two Koreas* (Reading, MA: Addison-Wesley, 1997), pp.318–20.

10 Reinhard Drifte, *Japan's Quest for a Permanent Security Council Seat: A Matter of Pride or Justice?* (New York: St. Martin's Press, 2000), p.130.

11 Senator Tsongas cited by Maureen Dowd, "The 1992 Campaign Memo: Voters Want Candidates to Take a Reality Check," *New York Times*, February 17, 1992.

12 Laura Hein and Akiko Takenaka, "Exhibiting World War II in Japan and the United States since 1995," *Japan Focus*, July 23, 2007, p.2. http://japanfocus.org/products/details/2477. Accessed July 23, 2007.

13 Richard J. Samuels, *Securing Japan: Tokyo's Grand Strategy and the Future of East Asia* (Ithaca, NY: Cornell University Press, 2007), pp.117–19.

14 See the discussion in Kenneth B. Pyle, *Japan Rising: The Resurgence of Japanese Power and Purpose* (New York: Public Affairs, Perseus Books, 2007), pp.286–89.

15 Green, *Reluctant Realism*, pp.31–32.

16 Samuels, *Securing Japan*, p.112.

17 Drifte, *Japan's Quest*, Chapter 2, pp.52–111.

18 Fewsmith, *China Since Tiananmen*, p.203.

19 Annual poll by the Japanese Prime Minister's Office, cited in Ming Wan, *Sino-Japanese Relations: Interaction, Logic and Transformation* (Washington, DC: Woodrow Wilson Center Press / Palo Alto, CA: Stanford University Press, 2006), pp.68–69.

20 Allen S. Whiting, *China Eyes Japan* (Berkeley: University of California Press, 1989), pp.127–28.

21 Interviews in Beijing, August 21–28, 1996.

22 Cited in Ming Wan, *Sino-Japanese Relations*, p.71.

23 Michael Pilsbury, *China Debates the Future Security Environment* (Honolulu: University Press of the Pacific, 2005, reprinted from the 2000 edition), pp.113–38.

24 Gerald L. Curtis, "Institutional Reform: Back to Basics." Discussion Paper No. 33, *Discussion Paper Series* APEC Study Center, Columbia Business School, September 2004.

25 Fewsmith, *China Since Tiananmen*, pp.154–56.

26 See Peter Hays Gries, *China's New Nationalism: Pride, Politics and Diplomacy* (Berkeley: University of California Press, 2004) for an extended discussion of what are called China's "fourth generation nationalists."

27 According to Richard Rigby, a former senior Australian diplomat and Director of the Australian National University (ANU) China Institute, at a seminar in the East–West Center, Washington,

DC, July 18, 2008. http://www.eastwestcenter.org/ewc-in-washington/events/previous-events-2008/july-18-2008-australian-perspectives-on-china-and-northeast-asian-security/. Accessed April 7, 2013.

28 Michael Leifer, "China in Southeast Asia: interdependence and accommodation," in David S.G. Goodman and Gerald Segal (eds.), *China Rising: Nationalism and Interdependence* (London and New York: Routledge, 1997), pp.172–91.

29 Michael Yahuda, "How much has China learned about interdependence?" in Goodman and Segal, *China Rising*, pp.6–26.

30 Avery Goldstein, *Rising to the Challenge: China's Grand Strategy and International Security* (Palo Alto, CA: Stanford University Press, 2005), Chapter 2, "China Adjusts," pp.118–35.

31 Fewsmith, *China Since Tiananmen*, p.174.

32 Green, *Reluctant Realism*, pp.104–05.

33 David Finkelstein, *China Reconsiders its National Security: "The Great Peace and Development Debate of 1999"* (Alexandria, VA: CNA Corp., 2000).

34 See *Wikipedia*, "List of war apology statements issued by Japan," cited by Ming Wan, *Sino-Japanese Relations*, p.157 and p.280. http://en.wikipedia.org/wiki/List_of_war_apology_statements_issued_by_Japan. Accessed March 27, 2013.

35 Ming Wan, *Sino-Japanese Relations*, p.157 and p.280.

36 Green, *Reluctant Realism*, pp.80–88.

37 Green, *Reluctant Realism*, p.96.

38 Cited in Ming Wan, *Sino-Japanese Relations*, p.71.

39 Ming Wan, *Sino-Japanese Relations*, p.144. I was also told this by one of China's most prominent specialists on Japan, who had also served as a policy adviser.

40 Christopher R. Hughes, "Japan in the politics of China's leadership legitimacy: recent developments in historical perspective," *Japan Forum* Vol. 20, No. 2, p.255.

41 See his "Fazhan zhong-ri guanxi bixu zhengquechuli lishi wenti he Taiwan wenti" ("To develop Sino-Japanese relations it is imperative to handle correctly the victory problem and the Taiwan problem"), *Jiang Zemin Wenxuan (Jiang Zemin Selected Works)* Vol. 2 (Beijing: Renmin Chubanshe, 2006), pp.241–49. Cited in Hughes, "Japan," p.255.

42 Hughes, "Japan," pp.254–55.

43 During his visit to Beijing earlier in the year Clinton had publicly confirmed to the Chinese that the US would not support Taiwan membership of any organization where sovereignty was a condition of membership. This was the fourth "no" added to the standard three of opposing the independence of Taiwan, two Chinas, or a one-China-one-Taiwan solution to the Taiwan problem.

44 Several Japanese, both official and academic, interviewed in Tokyo in April 1996, were particularly taken aback by what they saw as Jiang's televised deliberate *lèse-majesté* before an emperor, whose protocol would not allow him to respond.

45 Green, *Reluctant Realism*, pp.82–83.

46 Ibid., p.107.

47 Zhu's standing in the leadership had been considerably weakened towards the end of the previous year. See, Finkelstein, *China Reconsiders its National Security*.

Chapter 3

China's rise and Japan's decline 2000–12

The contrast between the dramatic rise of China and the relative decline of Japan is best captured in figures. In the year 2000, according to the IMF, China's GDP was $1.198 trillion and Japan's was $4.667 trillion. By 2010 China's had reached $5.879 billion and Japan's $5,474 billion.[1] In other words, from being a quarter of the value of Japan's economy in 2000 the Chinese economy had grown to exceed that of Japan in the space of ten years and become the world's second largest economy. The economic achievement was also accompanied by a sharp rise in China's military capabilities that was marked especially by an unprecedented active naval presence in seas close to its neighbors.

Much patriotic pride was on display in the opening ceremony of the summer Olympic Games held in Beijing on the auspicious day and time of 08/08/08 at 08 PM.[2] Chinese self-confidence was further boosted by the way it overcame the international financial crisis of 2008/09 in contrast to the enduring economic difficulties encountered by the languishing American and European economies. That doubtless contributed to China's exceptionally assertive international behavior in 2009 and 2010.[3]

Yet this self-confidence was also accompanied by continuing anxiety and self-doubt, as has been apparent all along and in particular since the end of the Cold War. Embedded in the education in patriotism is the presentation of China as a victim of a hundred years of humiliation by Western and Japanese imperialism and the legacy of that sense of victimhood was evident in the adverse reaction to criticism in the Western media to Chinese harsh treatment of Tibetans in the spring of 2008 and in Chinese anger at protests in Western cities against the Olympic torch bearers en-route to Beijing.[4] In the first decade of the twenty-first century the long-standing issue of how to balance adherence to state-party ideology with the demand for openness and further market-based reform was reflected in both domestic and external challenges. Among the former were the resistance to Chinese rule in Tibet and Xinjiang, deepening economic inequalities, corruption, political uncertainties about reform and so on. The perceived external vulnerabilities included ideological subversion and threats to China's "core national interests" as these expanded to include claims in the South and East China Seas. In addition there was a new consciousness of Chinese vulnerabilities of maintaining access to trade routes on which the economy had come to depend. The peculiar mixture of Chinese self-confidence and anxiety is reflected in continuing debates within China about how to understand developments in the outside world and about the direction China should take both at home and abroad.

The Chinese official announcement that Japan's GNP had been surpassed did not in itself immediately generate a sense of triumphalism in China. The senior Chinese economic official who first announced the news, cautioned that in terms of per capita

GDP China was more than ten times behind Japan and that China still had "a long way to go." He added, "China is still a developing country, and we should be wise enough to know ourselves."[5]

However, his caution was not echoed by other more nationalistic figures, who claimed that after the international financial crisis of 2008 China emerged as the rising global power confronting a declining American superpower.[6] In fact the rapidity of China's rise and the speed with which it has acquired global interests found its leaders and main writers on international affairs unready and divided on how to meet the new challenges and opportunities. They differed on whether the late Deng Xiaoping's advice to keep a low profile still applied, on whether the relative decline of the US was temporary or structural and so on. In other words the arguments about China's identity have become more open as China has emerged more clearly as a major country of global significance. Meanwhile the making and implementation of China's foreign policy became more complex as the number of actors, or stakeholders, with different interests and approaches increased.[7]

China's rapid rise deepened the sense of malaise in Japan and it increased the country's anxiety about China. However, Japanese domestic concerns went beyond those associated with its economic stagnation to include dissatisfaction with the failure to carry out political reform. The seeming resurgence of more conservative elements in the LDP associated with Prime Minister Junichiro Koizumi and his two lieutenants, Shinzo Abe and Taro Aso, failed to build on the momentum to revise the peace constitution and Koizumi was unable to bring about fundamental political change during his five years in office (2001–06) despite having engineered a massive electoral victory before leaving the leadership. His short-lived successors starting with Abe reverted to traditional factional politics and not even the victory of the opposition DPJ (Democratic Party of Japan) in 2009 was able to bring about a political revival of the country even though it was the first time in more than fifty years that an opposition party had been able to defeat the LDP in a general election.

Japan's immediate readiness to support the American wars in the greater Middle East in the wake of 9/11 may have drawn the US and Japan closer together, but coming on the back of new security guidelines between the two that were endorsed by the Japanese Diet in 1999, the Japanese unprecedented dispatch of naval vessels to the Indian Ocean to provide logistical support to American forces in Afghanistan accentuated Chinese concerns about the direction the Japanese–American alliance was taking. The long-standing debates in Japan about how to balance its identity as an Asian country with its Western style modernization and the alliance with the United States resurfaced. Some prime ministers, such as the LDP's Yasuo Fukuda (September 26, 2007–September 24, 2008) and the DPJ's Yukio Hatoyama (September 16, 2009–June 2, 2010) favored moving closer to China to balance the alliance with the United States, but their successors pushed Japan back closer to the United States. Similarly, the debate as to whether Japan should seek to provide leadership to others as a pacifistic nation or identify itself with like-minded democracies and seek security relations with them was also affected by the perceived need to remain close to the US. It was, however, the unrelenting military and diplomatic pressure from China, which weakened the position of those Japanese who sought to tilt towards their giant neighbor and which had the effect of moving Japan towards a policy of seeking to balance against it, which of course weakened the position of the contrary arguments of the pacificists and the Asianists.

Notwithstanding the latest evidence of its relative decline, Japan remains a highly developed country, and a major economy of regional and international significance. Japanese debates about their country's identity continue to have strategic significance for the development of the Asia-Pacific as a whole and more particularly for its relations with China. Nevertheless the huge loss by the LDP to the DPJ, which then formed a government in 2009, was a monumental change in Japanese politics even though the new governing party was constrained by inexperience and internal divisions suggesting that like the previous LDP government it would prove unable to tackle Japan's problems at home and abroad despite the shadow of rising China, which for the first time was officially said to be a cause of "concern" for Japan's security.

As in the previous chapters, the evolution of the respective identities of the two countries and how they were affected by the conduct of relations between them will be addressed chronologically. The period 2000–05, which may be characterized as the Jiang–Koizumi years, saw the political relationship descend to its lowest point, only to be recovered by the joint efforts of new leaders in the years 2006–08, and then to fall back again in 2009–10, with signs of readjustment in 2011, only to deepen again in 2012. The underlying tensions have been mitigated by the interdependence of the two economies and by the recognition by the two sets of leaders of the need to keep their differences within bounds. Nevertheless much has depended upon the course of their respective domestic politics. The way in which the evolving identities of the two countries affected their respective perceptions of the other continued to contribute significantly to the difficulties of the leaders in managing the relationship. Overall relations improved following the departure of Koizumi and Jiang, particularly through attempts to institutionalize relations together with South Korea. But the improvement was not sustained, primarily because of the continuing rise of China's military power and the rapid changes of prime ministers in Japan.

The slip towards an abyss (2000–05)

It was not immediately obvious in the year 2000 that the relationship would deteriorate. The Chinese side attempted to improve ties after the upset of Jiang's 1998 visit. For example, Jiang and Premier Zhu spoke positively about the relationship in 2000, without referring much to the question of history and the Chinese side reacted fairly mildly to a new textbook problem and to the visit to Japan by Taiwan's former President Lee Teng-hui.[8] For its part, the Japan side in July 1999 gave its approval to China's accession to the World Trade Organization. Prime Minister Koizumi met President Jiang in Shanghai in October 2001 and in April 2002 Koizumi stated at China's Bo'ao Forum that (contrary to many views expressed in Japan) China's economic rise was an "opportunity and not a threat" for Japan.[9]

However, there were also signs of continuing distrust and apprehension on both sides. In 2000 Japan expressed its concern about Chinese naval and maritime research activities in disputed areas in the East China Sea and in waters near Japan including its Exclusive Economic Zone (EEZ). The July 2001 Defense White Paper for the first time stated that China's military expansion exceeded what was needed for defense. The Chinese side not only rebuffed the statement, but also expressed its own concerns about Japan's recent security measures and the expansion of its military activities. The Chinese noted with concern Japan's passing of new laws (in response to American calls after 9/11) in 2001, allowing its forces to operate far beyond its shores, for the first time since 1945, in order to contribute ancillary services to the American-led wars in Iraq and Afghanistan.

The distrust between the two sides was evident from interviews I conducted with leading Chinese scholars, with whom I discussed Sino-Japanese relations in July 2010. They all agreed that the passing of the older generation of leaders on both sides was significant, as they had experience of the war, knew each other and respected each other's culture. Whereas they felt that the new generation of leaders in Japan, especially, had less respect for and sensitivity to Chinese concerns and tended to see more significance in China's lack of democracy. Most agreed that Japan too had declined in Chinese estimations because of the bursting of the bubble economy and the uncertainties of its politics. Japan was no longer regarded as a model from which Chinese could learn, although two of the eight interviewed expressed admiration for Japan's technological achievements and one even praised Japan for having developed a democratic system since the end of the war. Nearly all, however, said they distrusted Japan because it had not come to terms with its history and because it was too closely aligned with American interests. That was why, they claimed, few in China thought Japan could become a partner of China despite their close economic relations. The Chinese scholars also argued that the Chinese government was constrained in its dealings with Japan by the intense anti-Japanese sentiments of young Chinese people in particular. All asserted that Japan's publicly stated interest in working with the US to develop a theater missile defense system was directed against China, even though Japanese claimed that it was in response to the North Korean missile that passed over Japan in 1998. The Chinese scholars claimed that the Chinese government did not want bad relations with Japan, but it nevertheless remained suspicious; it did not want Japan to develop too independent a political role; and it was opposed to Japan becoming a permanent member of the UN Security Council. They expected that Japan would either remain quiet as still a major economy or that it might become more active, but only in close partnership with the United States. In any event China's leaders wanted their Japanese equivalents to pay heed to Chinese concerns.[10]

A similar visit by me immediately afterwards to Japan confirmed the sense of mutual suspicion. Japanese scholars and officials complained that their Chinese equivalents seemed to think that because of past Japanese history of militarism in the 1930s a revival of that could happen now and happen quickly. It was as if the Chinese scholars took no account of the very different democratic and peace-oriented system that had taken root in Japan in the more than fifty years since the end of the war. They hoped that the rise of China would lead to stability in the country and in the region, but the emergence of China's military, its lack of transparency and the recent Chinese naval activities in waters near Japan raised doubts. They argued therefore that while Japan had to engage China, it also had to hedge against it through the alliance with the United States. Like their Chinese counterparts, they felt that the change of generations was significant as the younger generation was no longer willing to treat China as an exceptional country, to whom allowances should be made and they tended to pay more attention to its lack of democracy. Additionally, there was growing impatience in Japan with the Chinese emphasis on history, which was seen as politically inspired, and there was concern about the expanding influence of anti-Japanese sentiments among the young in China. There was a predominant view that no apology would ever be acceptable to the Chinese side. There was the expectation that relations would continue to go up and down and there were complaints that despite many exchanges at bilateral and multilateral levels, those involving the military or discussions of strategic issues were of very limited value. My Japanese interlocutors claimed that it was easier for both the Chinese and Japanese sides to discuss weighty matters with the United States than it was with each other. They gave the examples of Taiwan and Korea, as issues, which were important to Japan's sense of security, which Beijing was willing to discuss, if at all, only in terms of high principle, but which the Japanese felt was discussed in closer detail between China and the US.[11]

It will be seen from a comparison of these views that mutual suspicion ran deep and that each side sensed that the other did not respond to its concerns. As Richard Bush observed, the distrust took place against the structural context of a rising China and a Japan that was in relative decline.[12] If China's search for status as a global power was fueled by its sense of grievance against foreign powers and especially Japan in the previous 150 years, Japan was seeking to find a new political identity as a different major power in the post-Cold War world. But neither was willing or able to envision a regional order which was acceptable to the other. That put a premium on how the two sets of leaders could manage relations so as to limit the possibilities of the eruption of tension between them.

It was at this point that exigencies of domestic politics came into play. In 1999 a series of events, including the attacks on ethnic Chinese in Indonesia, the bombing of the Chinese embassy in Belgrade and Lee Teng-hui's statement about there being "two states" across the Taiwan Strait, combined to bring to the fore young nationalists as new players in the domestic/external political arena in China. They were able to communicate through the new technologies of the Internet, cell phones, texting and so on. They were also sensitive to differences that had emerged in the leadership over retaining China's political identity under Communist Party rule and the need to become strong through economic development under conditions of globalization.[13] The nationalism that had been inculcated in the young at all levels of the education system had emphasized patriotism as the key to linking policies of economic development, national unification and foreign relations. It had become both a constraint on policy-makers and an instrument that top leaders could use against foreign adversaries. But it was an instrument that had to be used with care: since the turn of the twentieth century Chinese history is strewn with examples in which nationalistic campaigns which began by demonstrating against foreign adversaries ended up by criticizing leaders at home for not doing enough to rebuff the foreign "enemy."[14] As already noted, Japanese actions since 1993 in particular were seen as an affront to Chinese nationalists. These included the alleged refusal to acknowledge its past aggression and to make appropriate apologies, accusations about its supposed combining militarily with America to restrict China in the region, and charges that it was obstructing China's unification by interfering in the Taiwan issue and by denying Chinese sovereign rights to islands in the East China Sea.

Following the conclusion of the 1999 debate in favor of re-emphasizing the significance of external economic linkages, the policy of cultivating good relations with neighbors was reconfirmed. Experts in the Ministry of Foreign Affairs and others in the Chinese government argued that Japan was an important neighbor, which was playing a major role in the modernization of the Chinese economy, and it made little sense to demonize it, especially as that would push it closer to the United States.[15] But this expert bureaucratic view, which might have prevailed in earlier times, had to contend with the intense nationalist currents that were increasingly in evidence in China. If the approach of the Foreign Ministry were to prevail it would have required a response from Japan that was sensitive to the new Chinese nationalist sensibilities. That was true for Jiang Zemin personally, who was known to harbor ill will towards Japan.[16] Nevertheless Jiang, who had played the decisive role in concluding the national security debate in favor of the openness associated with the slogan "peace and development," put his personal stamp on improving relations with Japan by giving a positive speech to a 5,000 strong Japanese delegation in May 2000. Premier Zhu Rongji visited Japan in October 2001 and made a point of thanking his Japanese hosts for their economic assistance. Neither Chinese leader dwelt on the history issue. In fact China's leaders continued to seek better relations with Japan for the next two years.[17]

It was the way in which domestic politics in Japan developed at this time that played a major part in the deterioration of Sino-Japanese relations. Prime Minister Junichiro Koizumi (2001–06) was regarded as particularly offensive by China's leaders for his insistence on attending annually the Yasukuni Shrine – home to the spirits of Japanese soldiers killed in war since 1868, which also included those of fourteen who had been condemned as Class A war criminals. From 2002 they refused to hold summit meetings with him and Sino-Japanese relations spiraled downwards. Koizumi had been an unlikely choice for leadership of the ruling LDP as he was something of an outsider who belonged to a minority faction. But in the context of the loss of Japanese confidence in their traditional elite and in Japan's major institutions there was general support in the country for major reform in order to recover from the lost decade. A deflated LDP was prepared to risk reforming itself in order to retain power.[18] Koizumi appealed to the rank and file, promising to "destroy the LDP" (meaning its traditional factions and politicking). Unlike some right-wingers in his party he was not necessarily opposed to China and its rise. His otherwise puzzling readiness to offend Chinese sensibilities and risk confrontations with China had its origins in domestic Japanese politics. In his rise to power as an outsider he cultivated the support of the Japanese Association of Bereaved Families (JABF), which held a significant number of votes in the LDP, by promising to attend the Yasukuni Shrine every year if elected. The leader of the majority faction, former Premier Hashimoto, who had twice been chairman of the JABF, was in trouble with the Association for yielding to Chinese pressure by refusing to go to Yasukuni again after his visit there in 1996. Subsequently, the main political opposition in Japan to Koizumi's repeated visits from 2001 to 2006 came from Hashimoto and his faction, which Koizumi was determined to destroy, and he would have weakened his hold on the premiership had he conceded.[19] For his part, Koizumi was not known to have visited Yasukuni before becoming prime minister and therefore he could not be said to be attached to the shrine, unlike the more nationalistic wing of the LDP. Koizumi maintained that he went there to pray for peace and that Chinese objections to his visits amounted to interference in Japan's domestic affairs.

Koizumi's visits to Yasukuni enraged China's leaders and Jiang Zemin in particular, who refused to hold summit meetings with him after 2002. Only two previous Japanese prime ministers (Nakasone and Hashimoto) had visited the shrine since 1985 and they both desisted after their first visit because of Chinese protests. But Koizumi alone ignored all objections by the Chinese side. The deterioration of political relations sparked many anti-Japanese incidents in China especially by the young.[20] Japanese public opinion reacted adversely to several highly publicized incidents of Chinese expressions of hostility in often-violent fashion towards Japan and Japanese people. Although a majority was unhappy with Koizumi's visits to Yasukuni, more than half of Japanese polled consistently perceived Chinese demands over the shrine to be unjustified.[21] Relations apparently reached their lowest point in 2005, when a number of Japan related events coincided to arouse nationalist ire in China: in February a joint US–Japanese statement on strategy included for the first time a reference to Taiwan; Japan (as well as the US) pressed the EU not to lift the embargo on arms sales to China; Chinese anger about Koizumi's visits to the shrine were enhanced by yet another approval of a right-wing textbook by Japan's Education Ministry; and finally, Chinese were apparently outraged by Japan's attempt to become a permanent member of the UN Security Council (supported by the UN Secretary General, Kofi Annan) as the UN debated the question of its own reform. Demonstrations and riots broke out in major cities in China, notably in Shanghai in April 2005, where Japanese property was damaged.[22]

However, by this stage Chinese politics had begun to change. The formal leadership of Jiang Zemin had given way to that of Hu Jintao, who had taken over the last of Jiang's posts as head of the Central Military Commission in 2004. Hu, who was born in 1942, did not have the same experience of suffering from the Japanese invasion as his predecessor who had been born sixteen years earlier, and Hu seemed to be more amenable to the views of different ministries, notably that of Foreign Affairs, who sought a more balanced relationship with Japan.[23] It was noted in Japan that Hu had worked closely with the late liberal-minded leader, Hu Yaobang, in seeking closer relations with Japan and that it was he who had organized the visit of 3,000 youth from Japan in the 1980s.[24]

There was also official concern that the anti-Japanese demonstrations had gone too far and there was fear that they could turn against the government for allegedly being too soft on Japan.[25] The Propaganda Department of the CCP ensured that newspapers, television and radio did not report the demonstrations in detail and it moderated its earlier inflammatory language about Japan. Immediately after the attacks on Japanese property in Shanghai the authorities used the cell phones and other IT instruments of communications (which had been used by protesters to organize demonstrations) to issue orders to forbid further demonstrations.[26]

Perhaps alarmed by the downturn in relations, described by a Chinese vice foreign minister as their most serious challenge since diplomatic relations were normalized in 1972, the two leaders Hu and Koizumi agreed to meet on the sidelines of the Afro-Asian summit in Indonesia on April 23. Koizumi issued an apology for Japan's past wrong doings and militarism a day earlier. Hu then expressed his wish to improve relations and proposed five points as a basis for doing so.[27] This led to a series of lower level exchanges between the two foreign ministries about the terms on which the two states could create a better basis for the relationship.

In the event this turned on two major political changes in both countries in September 2006. In China Hu Jintao deposed the Party Secretary of Shanghai, Chen Liangyu, who was one of the stalwarts of the so-called Shanghai faction of Jiang Zemin. Chen, who had earlier openly criticized one of Hu's policies, was accused of corruption, but more to the point his ousting was a major blow to Jiang Zemin's remaining power and influence behind the scenes. It should be noted that one of the peculiarities of the current Chinese political system is that the appointments to the leading bodies of the ruling CCP are made in effect by the outgoing leader and his associates. The new leader then has five years before the next Party Congress to build his own power base. Chen Liangyu's dismissal was therefore a major step in Hu Jintao's assertion of his own leadership and authority. Senior Japanese diplomats in Beijing interpreted the dismissal as opening the door to a reconciliation between China and Japan due to the ending of what they saw as Jiang Zemin's capacity to obstruct it.[28]

The major change on the Japanese side was the ending of the Koizumi premiership and the election of Shinzo Abe to the presidency of the LDP on September 20 and his becoming prime minister on September 26. Abe belonged to the conservative right of the LDP, who rose to prominence as the leading advocate on behalf of those abducted by North Korea and was a strong proponent of making Japan a "normal" country by revising the pacifist clause of the constitution. Yet ironically, it fell to him to make the opening to China. It should be noted, however, that Abe was a realist as far as China was concerned and, unlike Koizumi, belonging more to the mainstream of the LDP, he enjoyed greater flexibility with right-wing groups on the Yasukuni issue. In fact as we shall see, in February 2006 top diplomats of each side began talks that were to lead to a breakthrough in relations once the new Japanese prime minister took office. Moreover much as Abe stood for tightening security relations with the United States, there was a growing political interest in the LDP and beyond about improving relations with China to which it made sense for him to respond.[29] The attempts by both Chinese and Japanese officials to set out terms for improving relations acquired a new urgency and by October 6 Abe was able to make his first visit to Beijing and agree to a new statement that both sides regarded as the "breaking of the ice" between them.

Koizumi's impact on Japan

Koizumi was by far the longest serving prime minister in the more than two decades since the end of the Cold War. He came to office determined to bring about fundamental reform in the way the country was governed and to prepare the basis for a Japanese economic recovery. In the event the country did undergo important changes during the Koizumi premiership. The economy moved out of its slump to register modest growth and a large part of that was due to the growth of economic relations with China. But the promised political change was more apparent than real. Koizumi's pledge to destroy the LDP and transform Japan seemed on its way to being fulfilled when his personal popularity and his campaign to privatize the post office led the LDP to an immense victory in the lower house elections in 2005, only to disappoint in the end. He had brought in some twenty-five celebrities and unconventional candidates to replace LDP diehards who had resisted his reforms. But when his own preferred successor became prime minister, Shinzo Abe made his peace with the ousted politicians, and politics in the LDP reverted to type, while little came of the post office reforms. More significant, however, was the fallout from Koizumi's attempt to change the character of Japan's society by seeking to make its members more self-reliant and to introduce greater competitiveness, without at the same time introducing a social safety net for those who could no longer attain permanent employment. The growing inequalities in Japan were later blamed on his policy of encouraging what he called "self-reliance," as was the decline in the sense of commonality that rightly or wrongly had been a feature of the "Japanese miracle" before the economic meltdown, which began in early 1991. One of the effects of the economic stagnation had been the end of the "salary-man model" for graduates of universities. Many found that they had to take temporary appointments with lower incomes and without the benefits that accrued to permanent employees. Unemployment rose to over 5 percent, which for Japan was a very high level. Koizumi's projected reform of major institutions in the end proved to be limited.[30] In effect considerable social change took place during the Koizumi prime-ministership that was not accompanied by the promised political reform.

As against that rather bleak view of domestic developments during the Koizumi years, Japan became more active militarily in the international arena and within the region by tightening its security relations with the United States. Building on the reinvigoration of the alliance in the 1990s, Koizumi continued Japan's participation in developing missile defense systems with the United States and perhaps more significantly, he was able to pass legislation through the Diet very quickly after 9/11/2001 that enabled him to dispatch members of the SDF to Iraq and Afghanistan and to send naval ships to the Indian Ocean to help refuel mainly American ships bound for the Afghan war.

However, the enlargement of the sphere of operations of the SDF encountered sufficient opposition in Japan to weaken its larger significance. The dispatch of an SDF contingent to Iraq never enjoyed popular support and there was sufficient opposition to the idea of Japan signing up to the concept of collective security to prevent that from going forward as a policy proposal. Moreover opinion polls consistently showed that there was not a sufficient majority in favor of revising the peace article 9 of the constitution although there was a majority for changing other aspects of the constitution to bring it more up to date and to give it more of a Japanese as opposed to the American flavor of the original. But the perceived threat from North Korea beginning in 1998 and the reaction to China's growing military power had brought back the revision of the constitution on to the current political agenda.[31] A former vice foreign minister noted in December 2002, "pacifism is in retreat now … One shot [the missile test by North Korea] in 1998 over Japan knocked down three taboos, namely, missile defense, satellite reconnaissance, and areas surrounding Japan."[32] At the same time Koizumi's resistance to Chinese pressure on Yasukuni resonated with a Japanese public that was increasingly resentful of what were seen as Chinese attempts to manipulate domestic Japanese affairs.

In other words, the Koizumi years had a mixed effect on Japan's identity. The proposed domestic reforms did not bite sufficiently deep as to lift the economy and society out of the slump of the 1990s, but they did have the effect of moving the country away from its collectivist myth. Considerable social change was taking place, involving more career opportunities for women, less full-time work opportunities for young men and a lower fertility rate as the society continued to age. The sense of malaise continued. Internationally, Japan's profile was raised by Koizumi's successful efforts to have units of the SDF participate in American-led (as opposed to only UN-mandated) military action. Much of that, however, still remained symbolic, as the Japanese participation did not involve engagement in actual military combat. Japan still maintained the asymmetric alliance with the United States, by which it relied for its defense on US forces based in Japan, while abjuring rules for offensive engagement. This added up to no more than up-dating the Yoshida Doctrine.[33]

Fence-mending 2006–08

The breakthrough of October 2006 was the product of political changes in both China and Japan. Hu Jintao was keen to build a new relationship with Japan.[34] In 2006 China's leading foreign policy official, State Councilor Tang Jiaxuan, led a "small working group" on policy towards Japan, which concluded that relations should be improved, but no compromise could be made on the Yasukuni issue. Moreover from about February 2006 the two Foreign Ministries, conscious of the impending conclusion of Koizumi's premiership, began preparatory work for a possible summit between Hu and Koizumi's successor. As noted earlier, the desire to rein in from the brink of April 2005, when relations appeared to be spiraling downwards out of control, was a contributing factor. Domestic politics in Japan were an important consideration for Abe. As leader of the LDP his future depended on a successful outcome to the elections to the upper house due the following year and to a certain extent that hinged on establishing better relations with China. Japanese public opinion may have favored standing up to Chinese pressure on the Yasukuni issue, but it also strongly favored improving relations with China. Amid intensive negotiations between Tokyo and Beijing in the days after his becoming prime minister Abe reconciled his nationalist conservative credentials (which favored his visiting Yasukuni) with his need to resurrect relations with China, by seizing on the formula that he would not commit himself either way about going to the shrine.[35]

Abe duly visited Beijing August 8–9, 2006. The summit was hugely important as a symbol of a new era in Sino-Japanese relations. The Chinese officially called it "ice-breaking" and added significance was given to the event by holding the summit meeting at the same time that Communist Party leaders from throughout the country were in Beijing for a meeting of the Central Committee. This ensured that all the leading elements in the Party were associated with the summit.

The significance of the summit, however, went beyond the merely symbolic. The Joint Press Statement that was issued on October 8 involved changes of formulations by both sides designed to create a better atmosphere so as to move relations forward. The Chinese side was pleased with the commitment to "operate the two wheels of politics and economics," as they had long complained that "economics were hot and politics cold." The Statement went on to specify areas for cooperation including those such as energy and environmental protection, in which Japan was a leader in high-technology. The Chinese were also pleased with the formulation (which according to a Japanese diplomat, came from the Japanese side) about their "striving to build a mutually beneficial relationship based on common strategic interests." The formula was to be repeated as a standard template in future joint statements. The Japanese side was particularly pleased that the Chinese had for the first time formally acknowledged that Japan had consistently pursued the path of peace for the past sixty years. It also noted approvingly that the Chinese side formally supported reform of the UN Security Council. Additionally the history issue, which had long been used by the Chinese side to excoriate the Japanese, was now to be taken out of the realm of politics and be devolved to a joint group of scholars to research. In other words, history was to be left to the historians.[36] According to a senior Japanese diplomat, the text had been agreed in advance, apart from the clause noting Chinese "positive appreciation" of Japan being a peaceful country, which was added at the last minute – meaning that it had Hu Jintao's personal imprimatur.

Despite the positive character of the Abe–Hu summit, distrust and suspicion was still evident on both sides. No mention had been made of Taiwan, notwithstanding Chinese desires for reassurance about Japanese intentions following their apparent agreement with the Americans to play a more active military role in the region, their development of ballistic missile defense (which could cover Taiwan, even though it was formally aimed at North Korea) and their stated common strategic interest with the US in a peaceful settlement of the Taiwan issue. The Chinese side did not get a firm commitment from Abe that he would not visit Yasukuni and it feared that he might do so if his domestic political position were to be strengthened by possible LDP success in the elections to the upper house due the following year in 2007. On the Japanese side, it was noted that nothing was said about military questions and the Chinese lack of transparency. Little progress was made on territorial issues between the two sides, which were limited to an agreement to consult further on the possibility of joint development in the East China Sea.[37]

However, the two sides were brought together by their outrage at North Korea's first nuclear test, announced on October 9. Such fears that the Chinese may have had as to whether Japan or South Korea might decide to go nuclear too were at least partially assuaged by the immediacy with which the US assured its allies that the American extended nuclear deterrence still applied to them. Moreover such improvement in relations as was achieved was only at the elite level. Public opinion polls in both countries still showed that large majorities had unfavorable opinions about the other.[38]

The alacrity with which Prime Minister Abe had chosen to visit Beijing must also be seen in the context of relations with the United States. The Bush administration had been displeased with the breakdown earlier of relations between the Chinese and Japanese leaders and had discretely sought to persuade Koizumi to stop provoking the Chinese by his visits to Yasukuni. Thus Abe's hurriedly arranged summit in Beijing also served to cement relations with Washington, as became evident from his successful meeting with President Bush when he visited the US the following month, on November 17.[39]

It soon became clear, however, that Abe's agenda remained that of what Richard Samuels called "a normal nationalist." He upgraded the Self Defense Agency into a full-blown Ministry, pushed through legislation promoting patriotic education and established legal guidelines for holding a referendum on revising the constitution. Abe also developed what he called a "value based diplomacy." On a visit to India in August 2007 he urged New Delhi to join Tokyo in the creation of "an arc of freedom" incorporating the US and Australia. China was clearly excluded and Australia soon indicated that it would not participate in any such arrangement precisely because it seemed to be aimed at China.

Notwithstanding Abe's evident lack of warmth towards China, China's Premier, Wen Jiabao, visited Japan April 11–13, 2007, which he dubbed in advance as "ice melting" – building on Abe's "ice breaking" visit to China in October. Progress was made especially on the economic front. Agreements were made to institutionalize a high level dialogue and to begin exchanges between the two sets of military. However, no progress was made on sharing resources in the East China Sea, or in developing further the promotion of "shared strategic interests." Once again the history issue was downplayed by the Chinese side, but Chinese concerns about Taiwan and possible visits to Yasukuni were made clear. Wen expressed understanding for Japan's commitment to settling the question of those abducted by North Korea. Wen addressed the Diet – a first for a Chinese prime minister – and he also displayed a personal touch in carrying out morning exercises with Japanese people.[40]

Hu Jintao evidently regarded the improvement of relations as a major policy issue and little was made officially of Abe's "value based diplomacy," which at other times might have been denounced as being aimed at the encirclement of China. As one Chinese diplomat observed privately, "Jiang Zemin had made his mark by improving relations with the United States and Hu Jintao wished to do likewise with regard to Japan."[41] Perhaps that explained why Beijing made far less than politicians in Washington of Abe's evasions regarding Japan's wartime responsibility for "the comfort women" who had been coerced to provide sexual services to the Japanese Imperial Army.[42] The fact that as early as the summer of 2005 (i.e., immediately after the riots) the Chinese media began to report more positively about Japan may be seen as another indication of the determination of Hu Jintao to enhance relations, by trying to reduce popular hostility towards Japan.[43] Doubtless this played a part in an improvement in the image Chinese urbanites had of Japan that was shown in opinion polls conducted in 2008 both before and after Hu's visit in May. It should be noted that the improvement was from a very low level; that 70 percent of one poll thought Japan did not accord China sufficient respect and another poll showed that less than half thought relations were "good or relatively good"; and, significantly, that it was up by 34 percent on the previous year.[44]

If Shinzo Abe belonged to that wing of the LDP which sought to transform Japan into a more "normal country," by revising the constitution, promoting patriotism, strengthening the military and legitimating collective defense so as to work more closely with the United States, his successor Yasuo Fukuda was more to Chinese liking. He may have favored the adoption of collective defense back in 2003, but in June 2006 he was one of the lawmakers who proposed a secular alternative to Yasukuni and he had long emphasized the importance of building strong ties with China and the rest of Asia. He quickly made clear his opposition to a value based diplomacy. At the same time he was regarded as a moderate, as he also favored continuing the deployment of Japanese ships in the Indian Ocean to help supply fuel to the American mission in Afghanistan. In other words, unlike Abe or Koizumi, Fukuda belonged to the tradition in Japanese politics that sought to balance its Asian and American orientations.[45] For all the apparent freshness of his vision Fukuda's elevation was a product of traditional LDP factional political maneuvering, signifying that the return to old-style LDP politics had been firmly re-established after Abe had reversed Koizumi's attempt to transform it.[46]

Far from seeing the US alliance as an obstacle to the improvement of relations with China, Fukuda saw it as the lynchpin of Japanese foreign policy, providing the necessary ballast on which Japan could reach out to China. Hence he first visited Washington in November and only then visited China in late December. He was accorded warm personal hospitality and pleased his hosts by saying at the outset that he opposed Taiwanese attempts to enter the UN and Chen Shui-bian's attempts to change the status quo in cross Strait relations. Fukuda's speech at Peking University on December 28 was particularly noteworthy as it stressed the importance of "making efforts to understand the other country in a true light" and discussing the issues that divide them, while keeping in mind their shared interest in cooperating to resolve regional and international issues. He identified three pillars on which the mutually beneficial strategic relationship could be built: cooperation (e.g., energy and conservation), understanding (e.g., exchanges of youth, intellectuals and the military) and contributions to international society (e.g., against terrorism, climate change, issues involving North Korea, UN reform and African development). Although a measure of idealism can be identified in Fukuda's approach, it nevertheless provided a demonstration of where progress could be made in developing a more workable and a less tension ridden relationship.[47] The Chinese dubbed the visit as "Spring heralding."

Fukuda's visit was followed in May 2008 by a visit to Japan of President Hu Jintao, which the Chinese called "Spring warming." Hu saw the visit as an important event in the context of the 2008 Olympic Games due to be held in Beijing three months later. The

Olympics were regarded as the supreme symbol of China's ascent onto the global stage and a mark of what was officially called "China's Renaissance." Fukuda promised to attend the opening ceremony and Hu made much of the significance of the "mutually beneficial strategic interests" to which the leaders had agreed at the previous three summits by declaring that "the revival of Asia cannot happen without cooperation between China and Japan." This suggested a new vision of the evolution of Asia that would have accorded with the views of Fukuda and with those in China who sought to cultivate cooperative relations with neighbors to demonstrate China's peaceful rise, while simultaneously reducing the incentives for those neighbors to align militarily with the United States.[48]

The Joint Statement that was issued was notable for avoiding any mention of apologies when it touched on the history issue and for sketching out seventy joint projects in which Japanese knowhow and high-tech in particular could help China tackle environmental problems – something that would resonate in Japan, as pollution from China had been reaching Japan for some time. Unlike the Statement issued on the occasion of Abe's visit, this time the Japanese side reaffirmed its 1972 position (which included Japan's "acknowledgment" – but not recognition – of Beijing's claim to Taiwan) at the time when relations were normalized. As a signal of Chinese pleasure and goodwill, Hu also offered Japan a panda to replace the one that had died in Tokyo's zoo. Agreements were reached to extend military confidence building measures, such as naval port visits. Some progress was registered on the thorny dispute of joint development of energy resources in the East China Sea, but not as much as had been anticipated.

However, the visit was marred by continuing popular Japanese distrust of China as a result of its continuing failure to acknowledge responsibility for the poisonous dumplings imported in February. Japanese public opinion also reacted adversely to Chinese repression in Tibet later that month and it also bristled at the hostility of Chinese reactions to worldwide protests at the processions of the Olympic torch. As against that, Chinese responded favorably to Japanese assistance to victims of the Sichuan earthquake, which was much applauded by the official Chinese media. For their part Chinese experts were concerned by the drop of Fukuda's popularity to around the 20 percent mark from the 60 percent he had enjoyed on attaining office. A Chinese scholar commented to the effect that the enthusiasm at the official level contrasted with the suspicion at the popular level and that this constituted a structural flaw in the relationship. Japanese scholars too tended to be cautious in their assessment of Sino-Japanese relations. It seemed as if Hu Jintao had sought to take advantage of Fukuda's prime-ministership to formalize the highpoint of relations since the nadir of 2005.[49] However, the closeness of the relations between Hu and Fukuda also illustrated the inherent difficulties in establishing a true partnership between these two very different nations. Obviously it was important for the leaders of the two divided countries to have good working relations, but if Sino-Japanese relations were to be fundamentally improved in the longer run such personal high level relations would have to be matched by institutionalizing the relationship at all levels and by each side paying closer attention to the major interests of the other.

If the Hu visit may be described as the high point in Sino-Japanese relations it was not without its limitations. As already noted, on the Japan side Fukuda's declining popularity at home and the difficulties in dealing with a divided legislature in which his party, the LDP, did not have a majority in the upper house, meant that its two-thirds majority in the more important lower house could not continually override the vote of the upper one.[50] But developments in the domestic politics of China also constrained what Hu could achieve in Japan. In the absence of a generally commanding overall leader such as a Mao Zedong or a Deng Xiaoping, the top leaders had to operate by consensus while competing bureaucratic interests became more entrenched. For one thing, the top leaders were not united in their approach to Japan. Some put a higher priority on the nationalistic agenda and in ensuring that China's claims in the East China Sea were upheld to the full. Others had particular interests in the economic aspects of the relationship with Japan, such as the Ministry of Commerce in Beijing and several of the eastern provinces, which were centers of Japanese investment. Others were not so inclined, such as elements in the military, who were also to the forefront in arguing that China's national interests required a capability to defend the seas around China and to extend its military reach to defend the sea lanes for China's trade. China's oil companies sought to restrict Japanese access to the oil and gas fields in the East China Sea and China's Coast Guard, which was under the Public Security Bureau's Border Troops, had their own concerns. Thus the failure to translate into operational terms the Hu–Fukuda agreement in principle of June 18 on jointly developing oil and gas in the East China Sea owed a great deal to the difficulties of coordinating the different interests on the Chinese side.[51]

The replacement of Fukuda in September 2008 by the hawkish Taro Aso did little to enhance relations even though he took a more pragmatic approach as prime minister than he had as foreign minister 2005–07.[52] At that time he had even suggested that the emperor should visit Yasukuni and said that the Chinese should "stop complaining." However, once he became prime minister Aso talked up the importance of Sino-Japanese cooperation to tackle global environmental problems, to deal with the financial crisis and to advance Asia's potential as a growth center for the twenty-first century. But he rather spoilt his copybook with China, by sending a symbolic plant to Yasukuni for the spring festival in April 2009. The Chinese side registered its objection without transforming the issue into a cause célèbre. Aso duly held a summit meeting in Beijing at the end of April 2009 and both sides spoke about the importance of relations, but no substantive progress was made.

In sum, within the context of a Hu Jintao leadership that favored more cooperative relations and the deepening economic partnership between the two sides, it was the different visions of successive Japanese prime ministers that shaped not only the tone of relations, but the degree to which the two sides could cooperate. Abe may have "broken the ice," but that breakthrough had been determined in advance of his becoming prime minister and his diplomacy towards India and his denial of official responsibility for the "comfort women" limited the scope for relations with China despite the latter's efforts to minimize their disquiet in public. By contrast his successor, Fukuda, openly sought to cultivate China as a balance to his embrace of the United States. His "Asianism" was appreciated by the Chinese side and Hu Jintao over-rode domestic opposition to offer his administration the prospect of joint development in a gas field in the disputed East China Sea. However, the prospect was not pursued with his successor, Aso, who did not share the outlook of Fukuda. Meanwhile the Japanese public was less enamored of a China that was blamed for exporting poisoned dumplings to Japan and for making the situation worse by seeking to evade legal responsibility. The episode conjured up for many in Japan a vision of a China that was careless, callous and lawless. Whereas Japan was seen at the time by many Chinese to be excessively fastidious.[53] In other words issues of identity continued to plague relations between the two East Asian giants.

The advent of the DPJ

In September the unpopular Aso led the discredited LDP into a huge electoral defeat for the lower house, thus leading to a sea change in Japanese politics in which the LDP for the first time in fifty years (apart from a brief hiatus in 1995) no longer held the reins of government, which were now held by the opposition DPJ (the Democratic Party of Japan) with a large majority in the key lower house and as the biggest party in the upper house, but just short of a majority. This constituted the biggest change in Japanese government in fifty-five years, breaking the near monopoly held by the LDP. The DPJ, formed in 1996, was a relatively new party, not to be confused with the party of the same name that joined with the Liberal Party to form the LDP back in 1955. The new DPJ was made of diverse groups, including disenchanted members of the LDP and a variety of smaller parties. It has been described as center-left. The chief architect of its victory in 2009 was Ichiro Ozawa, a former major figure in the LDP, who resigned from the LDP in the early 1990s and was the originator of the phrase "normal nation," which he understood required the strengthening of the military, but limiting its external operations to UN (rather than US) command.[54] Ozawa was a master of the arts of LDP style politics and would have led the DPJ to power had he not been accused of corrupt politicking and had to pass on the leadership to Yukio Hatoyama in May, just before the elections in September, allowing the latter to become the DPJ's first prime minister. Yet as General Secretary of the DPJ, Ozawa was considered to be the main center of power and was dubbed the "Shadow Shogun."

The DPJ had an ambitious electoral manifesto that included changing the long established nature of governance, by having politicians rather than bureaucrats make policy as well as carrying out new policies aimed at reforming the economy and society. It also sought what it called a more "equal" relationship with the United States and a reorientation of the country more towards Asia.[55] Like most of his colleagues, the new Prime Minister Hatoyama had no experience in government and had few personal connections with either American or Chinese elites. Moreover, by downgrading the role of senior civil servants the DPJ ministers deprived themselves of those with experience and expertise. On taking office in September 2009 Hatoyama chose well-known idealistic Asianists from the 1990s to be his key advisors.[56] This idealistic regard for Asia reflected a deep-seated tendency by many Japanese to reach out to China as a measure of its Asian identity, but it soon foundered on the harsher realism represented by China's inexorable rise and by American strategic demands of Japan.

From the outset Hatoyama found himself caught in a bind between competing obligations to the American ally and to the people of Okinawa. This stemmed from his election promise to agree to the transfer of an American marine base from its urban setting to a less populated area of Okinawa only with the agreement of the people of Okinawa. The problem was that the transfer of the base had been formally agreed by the previous Koizumi and Bush administrations in May 2006. The Obama administration refused to renegotiate the agreement, especially as it had yet to establish the kind of ties and connections with Hatoyama and most of his colleagues that Washington had long enjoyed with the outgoing LDP. On a visit to Japan barely a month after the DPJ took office US Secretary of Defense Robert Gates uncompromisingly insisted that the agreement on the base reached with the previous LDP government should be implemented. The DPJ fared better with China: Ozawa and his team of about a hundred and forty lawmakers and more than four hundred businessmen were feted in Beijing by Hu Jintao in January 2010 and Vice President Xi Jinping was allowed on a protocol-breaching short notice to have an audience with the emperor in Tokyo. Washington sensed that the new government was beginning a tilt towards China. Hatoyama's problems with the American government were not helped by the vagueness with which Hatoyama promoted what he called "yuai (fraternal or community) diplomacy" so as to bring the East Asian countries closer together without American participation.[57] Although Hatoyama had found favor with China's leaders they did not adopt his new and rather vague concept, as they had already promoted the ASEAN Plus Three and, more pertinently, the institutional cooperation of China, Japan and South Korea as the best means of developing an East Asian community. Indeed as we shall see in the next chapter, the three countries had already arranged meetings and reached agreements to enhance economic and social interaction.

Although Hatoyama claimed that relations with the US formed the foundation of a foreign policy that enabled him to reach out to China, his relations with Washington were soured over the base issue. Moreover he had little to show for his warmer relations with China. Despite several meetings between him and Chinese leaders, no substantive progress was made on settling the question of joint development in the East China Sea and new tensions arose over China's increasingly assertive naval activities near Japanese islands in the Okinawa chain. Meanwhile, as prime minister, Hatoyama proved unable to impose discipline on his ministers, who often advanced contradictory policy positions. Amid declining popularity (public support for his government had fallen to 17 percent), he eventually acceded to the American position on the base and promptly resigned in June 2010 after less than nine months in office. Within less than a year of replacing the LDP the DPJ too seemed incompetent with internal divisions crippling its capacity to govern.[58]

Hatoyama's replacement, Naoto Kan, was held responsible for a loss of seats by the DPJ in the elections to the upper house in September, for having made a gaffe about the raising of the sales tax. But he was still able to defeat Ozawa's challenge to his leadership later that month. However, Ozawa still retained a following among DPJ members of the Diet capable of blocking the passage of bills by Kan's government. Moreover the LDP used its majority in the upper house to obstruct bills passed by the DPJ in the lower house where it still had a majority. In view of his low popularity in the polls, Kan's position was not strong and he was in danger of becoming the fifth Japanese prime minister in succession to lose office within a year.

This did not mean that Kan was unable to leave his mark on foreign affairs. He dropped his predecessor's pursuit of a new East Asian community, mended relations with the United States and made it clear that he favored an active military role for Japan's armed forces. Although he was unable to overcome Okinawan resistance to the relocation of the American base there, he nevertheless established much better working relations with the United States than his ill-starred predecessor.

China's new assertiveness and its aftermath 2009–11

Alone of the major powers China had emerged from the global financial crisis of 2008–09 with its economy virtually unscathed. Its stimulus package enabled the economy to sustain its high growth rates of around 10 percent per annum. The US by contrast appeared to be in decline. Many in the Chinese elite began to exude an air of triumphalism, despite acknowledging that the country still had many deep-seated problems. This led to a new assertiveness in the conduct of relations with the outside world.[59] President Obama got a first whiff of this in his visit to China in November 2009, which was followed by his being treated with a degree of disrespect at the UN climate change conference in Copenhagen, where the Europeans also complained of Chinese rudeness. The Chinese reaction to Obama's meeting with the Dalai Lama and to his authorization of an arms sale to Taiwan was seen as excessive. Within the region the Chinese in May 2010 extended what they claimed as "core interests" from Tibet and Taiwan to include the South China Sea and they objected strongly at an ASEAN meeting in July that year to American indications of support for the wish of resident states to have the maritime territorial disputes settled on a multilateral basis. At one point the Chinese foreign minister berated an ASEAN minister saying, "China is a big country and other countries are smaller, and that's just a fact." Like their ally, the United Sates, Japan's principal interest was in ensuring the unfettered freedom of navigation in the South China Sea. But Japan also had an interest in resisting Chinese attempts to dominate their Southeast Asian neighbors and to that end it considered offering to supply patrol ships.[60] Perhaps more troubling to Japan was China's apparent support for North Korean military provocations in sinking a South Korean naval ship and in shelling an island occupied by civilians.[61]

However, the turning point for Japan was a clash with China over an incident on September 7 between a Chinese fishing boat and Japanese Coast Guard vessels near the Senkakus in which the boat's drunken captain apparently rammed two of the Coast Guard's patrol boats. The boat's captain and his crew were first detained and the captain arrested. The Chinese response was fierce and uncompromising: all high level contacts with Japan were suspended, exports of much needed rare earth to Japan were suspended or delayed and four Japanese were arrested on charges of espionage. As tensions rose the Japanese side suddenly released the captain without trial. The Senkaku incident brought to a head underlying distrust between the two sides and the gap between popular and official perceptions on both sides. If the Japanese warned about growing Chinese military maritime assertiveness, the Chinese complained that the Japanese had suddenly changed the rules of the game, as previously they quietly detained and then released Chinese fishermen near the Senkakus. Only a few months earlier the crew of a Taiwanese vessel was detained and then sent quietly back to Taiwan. Moreover the Chinese regarded the detention of the captain within the framework of Japanese domestic law as a provocative attempt to ratchet up Japanese claims to sovereignty of the islands. For their part the Japanese saw the Chinese response as excessive and unwarranted. The offending captain had deliberately rammed two Japanese Coast Guard patrol vessels and had been treated lawfully. The official Chinese account of the incident was misleading. The arrest of the four Japanese was seen as politically inspired and the delays in shipping rare earth as an unwarranted use of economic pressure. The Chinese demand for an apology and for compensation that followed after the release of the captain was regarded as outrageous. Yet at the same time both sides took steps to keep control of the situation. The Chinese authorities used their security forces to prevent major demonstrations against Japan, while the Japanese government attempted to prevent the incident from escalating by releasing the Chinese captain, even though it opened itself to widespread criticism for being too soft. The incident, however, led to a sharp deterioration of Japanese views of China. The annual Japanese Cabinet opinion polls showed that 88.6 percent felt that relations with China were not good (an increase of

33.4 percent on 2009) and 77.8 percent felt no affinity with China (an increase of 19.3 percent).[62]

Once the episode was over officials on both sides sought ways to reduce the tension and resume productive ties. Perhaps the most significant on the Chinese side was the response of Vice President Xi Jinping (Hu Jintao's expected successor) to the visiting head of New Komeito on December 16, 2010. Xi stated that "the common interests of the two countries are greater than the differences of views between the two sides" and while acknowledging that the Senkaku/Diaoyu incident had damaged the "national sentiments of both sides" China regarded Japan as "a partner and not a rival."[63] This suggested that China's leaders had begun to respond to the adverse reactions caused by their new assertiveness. For its part the Japanese government also indicated a desire to improve relations, despite the continuing popular distrust of China. In contrast to their Western counterparts, who condemned Beijing for its harsh treatment of Liu Xiaobo, the new recipient of the Nobel Peace Prize, Japanese leaders were careful to avoid open criticism of Beijing.[64] In January 2010 Japanese leaders said they looked forward to meeting China's leaders later in the year.

The more sober official Chinese reaction to the news that the Chinese economy had passed that of Japan may also be seen as indicating the abandonment of Chinese hubris. Indeed the authoritative *People's Daily* carried the revealing headline "China Surpassing Japan to Become World's Second Biggest Economy – But not The Strongest."[65] The contradictory nature of Chinese nationalism was yet again evident even as China reached a milestone in its yearning to be acknowledged as a great power. The call by Western governments for China to take on what they called "international obligations" commensurate with its newfound significance was treated with suspicion as designed to subordinate China to a Western agenda. Far from being welcomed as a sign of the new respect accorded to an ascendant China, the call was portrayed as an alleged attempt by the West to exaggerate China's role so as to "slow down and check China's development."[66] In effect the official response placed the Western call on China to play the role of a great power within the context of the narrative of its education in patriotism going back to the Opium War some 160 years earlier. The suspicion of the outside and the implied vulnerability of China suggested by this sat oddly with the nationalist grandeur claimed for the Beijing Olympic Games in 2008 and the global fair in Shanghai in 2010. It suggested that at a time when China's leaders exuded pride in the supposed superiority of their system over that of the Western democracies and of that of the US in particular they were still haunted by anxieties about their perceived vulnerabilities.

Nationalism in Japan was altogether more subdued. Nationalistic sentiments about the lack of responsibility for aggressive wars and for the forcible sexual enslavement of foreign women for the Japanese military (the so-called "Comfort Women") tended to be voiced by right-wing leaders without much support among the general population. The textbooks, which downplay or deny Japanese responsibility for the wars in Asia and which are the subject of widespread nationalist anger in China, have been used in less than 2 percent of Japanese schools. The overwhelming majority of Japanese do not support these right-wing positions.[67] As we have seen, opinion polls show a growing distaste for China, which is perhaps best understood as a reaction to Chinese growing political and military pressure on Japan, combined with a deepening of the interactions between the two societies, which is having a negative effect. After all, the two have sharply different political and judicial systems. Japanese nationalism is more evident in the tenacity with which successive governments stick inflexibly to the sovereign claims of islands disputed with Russia, South Korea, as well as China. But this should be distinguished from the extreme emotionalism of Chinese nationalism as often encouraged by Chinese leaders and as evident in Chinese history textbooks, which are compulsory reading material in all schools.[68]

Sino-Japanese relations soured again in September 2012, again on the question of sovereignty over the Senkaku/Diaoyu Islands, which Japan claims as indisputably its own and therefore not subject to dispute with China. In April the right-wing nationalist governor of Tokyo, Shintaro Ishihara, who had long been known for his anti-China views, announced that he was raising funds to purchase some of the islands from the Japanese family who rented them out to the Japanese government. Fearing the consequences of the purchase of the islands by Ishihara, who promised to build structures to emphasize Japan's sovereignty, Prime Minister Noda purchased the islands on behalf of the Japanese government. Hu Jintao rejected Noda's explanation that the purchase was to uphold the status quo and saw it instead as an unacceptable ratcheting up of Japan's legal claim to the islands. Although the purchase made no difference to the legal basis of Japan's claims to the islands and it was designed to prevent any change to the status quo of Japan's administration (as would have happened had the anti-Chinese mayor of Tokyo, Shintaro Ishihara, bought them), Hu Jintao nevertheless called the purchase "nationalization" and insisted that it was a provocative act. He and the other leaders then encouraged huge demonstrations that broke out in up to one hundred Chinese cities in mid-September that in many cases led to the destruction of Japanese property and attacks on Japanese and even Chinese using Japanese made cars. The demonstrations abruptly came to an end after September 18, the anniversary of Japan's 1931 invasion of Manchuria – presumably at the insistence of the Chinese authorities.

The Chinese side maintained diplomatic pressure, threatened economic consequences and even tried to win over the US to the Chinese view that Japan had swung dangerously to the right and that it constituted a threat to regional and international order.[69] The Japanese side supported by public opinion refused to back down and the US government repeated its commitment to the defense of the islands even as it stated that it took no view as to who held sovereignty. It urged both sides to "cool down." The immediate problem was that neither government sought to escalate the conflict, but neither was prepared to back down and the two governments seemed unable to come up with an acceptable formula which would enable them to put the dispute to the side so that they could focus on more important matters. Not only were the two governments subject to popular pressure to stand up to the other side, but each one also faced imminent changes of leadership, raising the costs to the contenders for high office of appearing to be weak on the sovereignty question. Once again domestic politics and each country's view of its standing relative to the other were having deleterious effects on their relationship.

Problems of governance

The early years of the second decade of the twenty-first century suggested that these two great regional powers were in the grip of deep-seated problems of governance. These arose primarily from domestic sources and it is difficult to discern their precise impact on foreign policy-making, although they doubtless affected the implementation of policy. The problems of governance had been building up for a few years in each country, but they became more apparent in the new decade. In China the collective system of government had replaced that of the strong leader, epitomized by Mao and Deng. Arguably, Jiang Zemin was able to continue their legacy to a certain extent, but Hu Jintao's leadership was more circumscribed. The nine members (reduced to seven in November 2012) of the Standing Committee of the Political Bureau represented special bureaucratic interests and political power had become more fragmented, presenting new difficulties in coordinating policy between provinces, ministries, state-owned companies and so on. The difficulties in arriving at consensus have delayed needed reforms as advocated by the World Bank and China's government linked Development Research Center.[70]

Meanwhile at home the academic debates between the "New Left" and the "Liberals" reflected differences at the highest levels between those associated with the domestic security organizations, the military and the propaganda organs on the one hand and those more concerned with the running of the economy. These differences were greatly affected by the jockeying for position within the higher reaches of the party in the build-up to the leadership changes announced at the national Congress of the Party held in November 2012. These problems did not make it any easier for China's leaders and public intellectuals to come to terms with China's rise. Had the balance between China as a great power and as a developing country changed? Had relations with neighbors to be adjusted? How should China position itself following the American "pivot to Asia" announced in November 2011? Differences were apparent between some of the military and the civilian intellectuals, raising questions about the degree of control the party-state had over actors in foreign affairs.

If the Chinese were uncertain how best to adapt to their ascendancy and about which policies should be pursued, the Japanese were divided about how to manage the consequences of their decline. Some saw it as an opportunity to promote a new kind of Japan, that accepts its diminished status as a "middle power" and seeks political cooperation with others and focus on its remaining economic and soft power capabilities, while remaining allied to the US.[71] Others argued for a more vigorous response in which Japan reinvigorated the alliance with the US as the "corner stone" of peace and security in the Asia-Pacific, with Japan playing an important role in bringing together other Asian countries committed to democracy, the rule of law and following the rules of market economies so that together with the United States it would shape a new order in the Asia-Pacific. This entailed, however, opening up Japan's traditionally protected domestic markets and especially overcoming the protection of the politically powerful agricultural sector so as to join the projected Trans Pacific Partnership and to make Japanese more internationally minded.[72] There were differences between those who argued for the centrality of China for the Japanese economy and those who argued that Japan should cultivate a more diverse range of economic partners in Asia.[73]

Arguably the Japanese sense of decline arose more from domestic factors than from being overtaken by China to become the world's third economy. First, is the impact of the economic stagnation on the young, many of whom can no longer look forward to the full-time employment and social benefits of the "salary man" and instead face the prospect of temporary employment at lower rates of pay and without social benefits. This has had dire social effects alongside the perceived shift from a communal society towards one that emphasizes more individual and lonely responsibility, with a consequential rise in a sense of malaise among the young.[74] Second, the Japanese population is aging and shrinking. Its fertility rate is 1.3 (2.1 is the rate necessary for population replacement) and as of 2009 23 percent of the population was over sixty-five (compared to about 13 percent in the US) with children constituting only 13 percent of the population. The number of workers supporting each retiree shrank from 10 in 1950 to 3.6 in 2000 and will reduce to 1.9 by 2025. While this may be seen as a looming time-bomb it can be argued that the effects may not be so dire, as the demographic predicament is known well in advance and policies can be adjusted appropriately.[75] Nevertheless, that has raised the broader issue of immigration. However desirable that may seem in principle so as to bring in needed labor and caregivers, resistance is deep on the grounds that it would dilute the Japanese character and culture. There is therefore a profound contradiction between the aspiration to play a more active role abroad even as a civil power and the inward-looking parochial character of Japanese society, which unlike the globalist tendencies of students elsewhere in East Asia has actually seen the number drop of Japanese studying abroad.[76]

Yet the triple disaster of March 2011 showed a divergence between a cohesive and resilient Japanese society and a dysfunctional government. Japanese communities affected by the disaster reacted calmly and with great fortitude as different elements of civil society and indeed individuals helped each other in the absence of an efficient government response.[77] This sense of a Japanese governmental system that was unable to deal with disasters at home or resolve its financial and fiscal problems was enhanced by its failure to respond effectively to the demands of its ally and protector, the United States.

This sense of a declining Japan as faced by a rapidly rising China may be seen as providing a structural framework against which to consider their changing identities and their respective debates about questions of identity. The Senkaku/Diaoyu incidents of 2010 and 2012 showed how quickly tension and putative conflict between the two sides could erupt. Nevertheless both governments quickly sought to prevent an escalation of the conflict and effectively restored a workable relationship in 2010, and they have displayed a degree of caution in the 2012 crisis. For example, their deployment of ships to challenge each other's positions on the disputed islands was confined to their respective Coast Guard vessels rather than elevated to the more war-like level of deploying actual naval forces.[78] Nevertheless Chinese Coast Guard vessels and aircraft have continued to patrol waters close to the islands in a bid to undermine in practice Japanese claims to administer them. China's actions fitted into a pattern established by its behavior in the South China Sea, which has been described as "reactive assertiveness". In response to what Beijing perceived as provocations (earlier by the Philippines and in this case by Japan in nationalizing three of the islands) China's maritime forces took strong counter-measures, which in effect changed the status quo in its favor.[79]

In December 2012 the LDP won back power with a huge electoral victory in the lower house. It was recognized by the incoming leader, the former prime minister, Shinzo Abe, that the victory was due principally to the failings of the DPJ government and that he and his new government faced a huge task to try and revive the economy and recapture the confidence of Japanese people in their political system. Initial indications were that he would soften his nationalist stance regarding China and that the Chinese in turn were cautiously optimistic that he would bring a new approach that would help de-escalate the conflict over the Senkaku/Diaoyu islands.[80]

Notes

1 Mure Dickie, "China Economy overtakes Japan," *Financial Times*, February 14, 2011. See also, "It's (Almost) Official: China's No. 2," *Wall Street Journal*, January 20, 2011.

2 For an account of the symbolism and meaning of the Chinese display see, William Callaghan, *China, the Pessoptimist Nation* (Oxford: Oxford University Press, 2010), pp.1–11.
3 For analyses see, Michael D. Swaine, "China's Assertive Behavior – Part One 'Core Interests'," *China Leadership Monitor* No. 34, February 22, 2011 (Palo Alto, CA: Hoover Institution, Stanford University) and Thomas J. Christiansen, "The Advantages of an Assertive China: Responding to Beijing's Abrasive Diplomacy," *Foreign Affairs*, March–April, 2011, pp.54–67.
4 Suisheng Zhao, "The Olympics Chinese Nationalism," *China Security* Vol. 4, No. 3, Summer 2008, pp.48–57.
5 Yi Gang, Deputy Governor of China's central bank and head of the State Administration of Foreign Exchange, also cited in *Xinhua*, August 4, 2010.
6 For further details and analysis see, David Shambaugh, "Coping with a Conflicted China," *The Washington Quarterly*, Winter 2011, pp.7–26.
7 Linda Jakobson and Dean Knox, *New Foreign Policy Actors in China (SIPRI Policy Paper No. 26)* September 2010.
8 Ming Wan, *Sino-Japanese Relations: Interaction, Logic and Transformation* (Washington, DC: Woodrow Wilson Center Press / Palo Alto, CA: Stanford University Press, 2006), pp.130–31.
9 See his "Press Conference, April 12, 2002," in Japan's Ministry of Foreign Affairs website. http://www.mofa.go.jp/announce/press/2002/4/0412.html#1. Accessed March 27, 2013.
10 Interviews conducted in Beijing, July 10–20, 2010 with scholars from the Chinese Institute of Contemporary International Relations, various institutes of the Chinese Academy of Social Sciences, The National Defense University, Peking University, Tsinghua University and the Chinese People's University.
11 Interviews conducted in Tokyo, July 31–August 4, 2010 with scholars and officials from the Ministry of Foreign Affairs, The Intelligence and Analysis Bureau of MOFA, the Japan Institute of International Affairs, the Institute for Defense Studies and various universities.
12 See Richard C. Bush, *The Perils of Proximity: China–Japan Security Relations* (Washington, DC: Brookings Institution Press, 2010), Chapter 4, "Explaining the Downturn," pp.23–40.
13 David Finkelstein, *China Reconsiders its National Security: "The Great Peace and Development Debate of 1999"* (Alexandria, VA: CNA Corp., 2000).
14 For an excellent analysis of the contradictions inherent in the nationalism developed in China since the Tiananmen disaster, see Christopher R. Hughes, *Chinese Nationalism in the Global Era* (London and New York: Routledge, 2006).
15 Private discussion with a well-connected Chinese researcher on Sino-Japanese relations, Beijing, October 10, 2006.
16 Ming Wan, *Sino-Japanese Relations*, p.144. A leading Chinese researcher on Japan told me in Beijing on October 9, 2006, that Jiang still bore the scar on his leg from the bite of a Japanese military dog.
17 See ibid., pp.130–32 for official Chinese attempts to improve relations with Japan.
18 See the discussion in Jeff Kingston, *Contemporary Japan: History, Politics and Social Change since the 1980s* (Chichister, West Sussex, UK: John Wiley, 2011), pp.117–21.
19 See, Mong Cheung, "Personal survival and the Yasukuni controversy in Sino-Japanese relations," *The Pacific Review* Vol. 23, No. 4, September 2010, pp.527–48.
20 For details and analysis of this new manifestation of popular nationalism see, Peter Hays Gries, *China's New Nationalism: Pride, Politics and Diplomacy* (Berkeley: University of California Press, 2004).
21 Mong Cheung, "Personal survival," p.537.
22 For details see, Robert Ash, "Quarterly Documentation and Chronicle," *China Quarterly* Issue 183, September 2005, pp.762–63.
23 Interviews with two Chinese notable academic experts on Sino-Japanese relations, October 10, 2006.
24 Interview with Professor Ryosei Kokubun, Tokyo, October 14, 2006.
25 See the discussion in Bush, *The Perils of Proximity*, pp.207–10.
26 Ibid., p.210 and Danila Stockman, "Who Believes Propaganda? Media Effects during the Anti-Japanese Protests in Beijing," *The China Quarterly* Issue 202, June 2010, pp.269–89.
27 Ming Wan, *Sino-Japanese Relations*, p.144.
28 Interview with a senior Japanese member of the embassy, Beijing, October 10, 2006.

29 Mong Cheung, "Personal survival," pp.539–42, points out that Abe had the support of the majority Mori faction in the LDP and that important sections of the Party, the bureaucracy, the business community and the general public favored better relations with China and South Korea.
30 This account relies heavily on Jeff Kingston, *Contemporary Japan*, especially, Chapter 5, "Jobs at Risk," pp.84–123.
31 Tobias Harris, "Constitution revision back on the agenda," Japan Observer (blog). http://www.observingjapan.com/2009/04/constitution-revision-back-on-agenda.html. Accessed March 27, 2013.
32 Ming Wan, *Sino-Japanese Relations*, p.161.
33 For further discussion and analysis, see, Richard J. Samuels, *Securing Japan: Tokyo's Grand Strategy and the Future of East Asia* (Ithaca, NY: Cornell University Press, 2007), especially pp.94–107.
34 Interview with senior Chinese scholar, Beijing, October 10, 2006.
35 For detailed analysis see, Alan D. Romberg, "Politicians Jockey for Position in Taiwan's 2007–8 Elections, While Japan Jockeys for Position Across the Strait," *China Leadership Monitor* (Hoover Institution, Stanford University) No. 20, Winter 2007, pp.1–36.
36 See the website of the Ministry of Foreign Affairs of Japan, October 8, 2006 for the text of the Joint Press Statement. www.jamestown.org/programs/chinabrief/single/?tx_ttnews%5Btt_news%5D=4633&tx_ttnews%5BbackPid%5D=168&no_cache=1. Accessed April 7, 2013.
37 Much of this paragraph is drawn from my discussions with academics and officials in Beijing and Tokyo in October 2006. See also Bush, *The Perils of Proximity*, Chapter 4, "Explaining the Downturn," pp.23–40.
38 Ibid.
39 Michael J. Green and Shinjiro Koizumi, "U.S.–Japan Relations: Abe Shows the Right Stuff," *Comparative Connections* (Hawaii, CSIS) Vol. 8, No. 4, January 2007.
40 For details see, James J. Przystrup, "Japan–China Relations: Wen in Japan: Ice Melting But … ," *Comparative Connections* (Hawaii, CSIS) Vol. 9, No. 2, July 2007.
41 Conversation with senior Chinese official, Ministry of Foreign Affairs, Beijing, September 25, 2007.
42 Ming Wan, *Sino-Japanese Relations*, p.161.
43 This was noted by interviewees in both Beijing and Tokyo in October 2006.
44 See Zhang Haizhou, "Chinese view Japan more positively," *China Daily*, May 7, 2008; and Nie Ligao, "Survey: Sino–Japanese relationship improving," *China Daily*, September 8, 2008.
45 See, Samuels, *Securing Japan*, p.99 and Norimitsu Omishi, "Yasuo Fukuda, a moderate, is chosen to lead Japan," *New York Times*, September 23, 2007.
46 Kent Calder and Min Ye, *The Making of Northeast Asia* (Palo Alto, CA: Stanford University Press, 2010), pp.213–14.
47 For an account of the visit in the context of the Sino-Japanese relationship see, Kazuyò Kato, "China-Japan Rapprochement in Perspective," *Jamestown Foundation*, China Brief: Volume 8 Issue 1, February 4, 2008. http://www.jamestown.org/single/?no_cache=1&tx_ttnews[tt_news]=4633. Accessed March 27, 2013. For the text of Fukuda's speech at Peking University see, http://www.mofa.go.jp/region/asia-pacifi/china/speech0712.html. Accessed March 27, 2013.
48 For the significance of the Olympics in China see, Callaghan, *Pessoptimist Nation*, pp.1–8.
49 For a representative of mainstream Chinese thinking on the relationship at this point see, Jin Xide, "Hu Jintao's visit to Japan and New Trends in Sino-Japanese Ties," *International Review* (Institute of Japanese Studies, Chinese Academy of Social Science, Beijing), May 2008, pp.26–38. See also the discussion published just before the Hu Jintao visit between the Chinese and Japanese experts on Sino-Japanese relations, Feng Zhaokui and Okabe Tatsumi, "Sino-Japanese Relations: Pursuing Mutual Benefits," *Japan Echo* Vol. 35, No. 3, April 2008, pp.30–35.
50 Masamo Ito and Reiji Yoshida, "Fukuda announces resignation," *Japan Times*, September 2, 2008.
51 For an analysis of the diffusion of foreign-policy making in China at this time see, Jakobson and Knox, "New Foreign Policy Actors in China." For a thorough account and analysis of the dispute see, Reinhard Drifte, "Japanese–Chinese territorial disputes in the East China Sea – between military confrontation and economic cooperation," Working Papers, Asia Research Centre, London School of Economics and Political science, London, UK, 2008.
52 See, "Aso's behavior Does Not Match Rank of Japanese Foreign Minister," *Xinhua News Agency*, March 18, 2006.

53 Rumi Aoyama, "Changing Japanese Perceptions and China–Japan Relations," in Gerald Curtis, Ryosei Kokubun and Wang Jisi (eds.), *Getting the Triangle Straight: Managing China–Japan–US Relations* (Tokyo: Japan Center for International Exchange, 2010), pp.262–63.
54 Samuels, *Securing Japan*, p.124.
55 See, Daniel Sneider and Richard Katz, "The New Asianism," *Foreign Policy*, October 20, 2009.
56 Michael J. Green, "Japan, India and the Strategic Triangle with China," in Ashley J. Tellis et al. (eds.), *Strategic Asia 2011–2012: Asia Responds to its Rising Powers – China and India* (Seattle, WA: National Bureau of Asia Research, 2011), p.153.
57 Martin Fackler, "In Japan, U.S. Losing Diplomatic Ground to China," *New York Times*, January 24, 2010.
58 Blain Harden, *The Washington Post*, June 2, 2010.
59 Michael D. Swaine, "Perceptions of an Assertive China," *China Leadership Monitor* Vol. 32, Spring 2010. www.hoover.org/publications/china-leadership-monitor/3601. Accessed April 7, 2013. For the views of British, Indian, Japanese and American senior diplomats see, Ewen MacAskill, "WikiLeaks cables: Aggressive China losing friends around the world," *The Guardian*, December 4, 2010. http://www.guardian.co.uk/world/2010/dec/04/wikileaks-embassy-cables-diplomacy-china. Accessed March 27, 2013.
60 D.J. Yap, "Japan eyes maritime aid for Philippine defense," *Global Nation*, May 18, 2012. globalnation.inquirer.net/37235/japan-eyes-maritime-aid-for-philippine-defense. Accessed June 4, 2012.
61 For more examples of Chinese assertiveness, see June Teufel Dryer, "Grimm Foreign Policy?" *The Diplomat*, February 2011.
62 For careful accounts of the episode, see Mike Mochizuki, "China over-reached," Q&a, *Oriental Economist* Vol. 78, No. 10, Japan Watchers LLC, October 2010; Wenran Jiang, "New Twists over Old Disputes in China–Japan Relations," *Jamestown: China Brief* Vol. 10, Issue 20, October 8, 2010; and Akio Takahara, "Japan–China Relations and the Implications for the United States and Okinawa," paper presented to the conference, "The Okinawa Question: Regional Security, The US–Japan Alliance and Futenma" held at the Sigur Center for Asian Studies, The Elliott School, George Washington University, September 19, 2011. For a broader context see, Michael D. Swaine and M. Taylor Travel, "China's Assertive Behavior Part Two: The Maritime Periphery," *China Leadership Monitor* No. 35, September 21, 2011 (Hoover Institution, Stanford University).
63 James J. Przystup, "China–Japan Relations: Troubled Waters, Part II," *Comparative Connections* (Hawaii, CSIS) Vol. 12, No. 4, January 2011; and Michael Bristow, "China–Japan row reveals deep-seated differences," *BBC News: Asia-Pacific*, September 21, 2010.
64 BBC, "Japan says release of China's Liu Xiaobo 'desirable'," October 14, 2010. http://www.bbc.co.uk/news/world-asia-pacific-11539333. Accessed March 27, 2013.
65 Chester Dawson and Jason Dean, "Rising China Bests a Shrinking Japan," *Wall Street Journal*, February 14, 2011.
66 David Shambaugh, "Beijing, a global leader with a 'China First' Policy," *Yale Global Online*, June 29, 2010. http://yaleglobal.yale.edu/content/beijing-global-leader-china-first-policy. Accessed March 27, 2013.
67 Sven Saaler, *Politics, Memory and Public Opinion: the History Textbook Controversy and Japanese Society* (Munich: Iudicium Verlag, 2005). See also Madoka Futamura, "Japanese Social Attitudes Toward the Tokyo Trial: A Contemporary Perspective," *The Asia Pacific Journal, Japan Focus* Issue 29, No. 5, July 18, 2005.
68 Zheng Wang, *Never Forget National Humiliation: Historical Memory in Chinese Politics and Foreign Relations* (New York: Columbia University Press, 2012).
69 As told to me by an American official who claimed to be knowledgeable about the meeting between Xi Jinping and American Defense Secretary Panetta, which took place that September.
70 "The politics of economic reform," *The Economist*, March 3, 2012.
71 A position long held by Soeye Yoshide, but also argued by others. See, Samuels, *Securing Japan*, pp.127–31.
72 Seiji Maehara, Minister for Foreign Affairs of Japan, "Opening a New Horizon in the Asia Pacific," Speech delivered at CSIS, Washington, January 6, 2011. http://www.mofa.go.jp/region/n-america/us/juk_1101/speech1101.html. Accessed March 27, 2013.

73 See, for example, the argument of Kaoru Yosano, Economic and Finance Minister, *Kyodo News*, "Japan as No.3 views neighbor as benefactor," *Japan Times*, February 19, 2011. For the argument against dependency on China see, Akao Nobutoshi, former chief negotiator in the Uruguay Round of GATT and former ambassador to Thailand, "Promoting Japan's Participation in the TPP," Japan Forum for International Relations, *JIFR Commentary*, February 10, 2011.

74 Kingston, *Contemporary Japan*, Chapter 5, "Jobs at Risk," pp. 84–100. See also, Michael Zielenziger, *Shutting out the Sun: How Japan Created its own Lost Generation* (New York: Vintage Books, 2006).

75 Kingston, *Contemporary Japan*, Chapter 3, "Defusing the Demographic Time Bomb," pp.41–65.

76 Japan's Foreign Minister, Seiji Maehara, has complained both of the drop in the number of Japanese students in the US (his January 6, 2011 speech, "Opening a New Horizon") and of the difficulties in recruiting foreign workers (*The Japan Times*, February 17, 2011).

77 Lucy Birmingham and David McNeill, *Strong in the Rain: Surviving Japan's Earthquake, Tsunami and Fukushima Nuclear Disaster* (London and New York: Palgrave Macmillan, 2012).

78 IISS, *Strategic Comments*, "Island dispute stirs Sino-Japanese tensions," September 28, 2012.

79 International Crisis Group, "Dangerous Waters: China–Japan Relations on the Rocks," *Asia Report No. 245*, April 2013.

80 George Nishiyama, Alexander Martin and Fred Dvorak, "Japan's New Government Vows Quick Action," *The Japan Times*, December 26, 2012; and AFP, "[Chinese] Foreign Ministry calls for effort to put ties back on track after confirmation of Japan's new PM," *South China Morning Post*, December 27, 2012.

Chapter 4

The politics of Sino-Japanese economic interdependence

The vast scale of the economic relationship between China and Japan ensures that it will greatly influence the evolution of relations between the two countries. A country's economic wellbeing has become a key element in the political success of democratic countries as well as in dictatorial China. Much of the political malaise in Japan stems from the sluggish performance of the economy since the bursting of the financial bubble in the early 1990s; and China's leaders believe that their very legitimacy depends on their continuing to deliver high economic growth. Notwithstanding Japan's relatively sluggish economic growth its trade with China has grown by leaps and bounds. Since 2007 China has become Japan's largest trading partner, outstripping the United States for the first time, and the gap in China's favor has continued to grow.[1] Japan is China's second most important trading state partner. Beginning in the 1980s, but accelerating into the 1990s and the first decade of the twenty-first century, various major and increasingly medium and even small Japanese business enterprises have established mutually dependent economic relations with Chinese counterparts. Complex chains of production have given both sets of companies enduring stakes in the interdependent character of the economies of both countries. Japan provides the high-tech, design and chief managerial dimensions of the production chain and China the rest. These links have been reinforced by sister type relations between regions and more than 300 cities in each country. Japan is the third largest investor in China with more than 22,000 companies employing more than 10 million Chinese workers. More recently, China has begun to invest in Japan too.[2]

The political significance of their economic interdependence should be seen not only in the context of their bilateral relationship, but also in the context of regional and international developments. If Japan was the main economic hub of the East Asian region in the 1970s and 1980s, it was replaced by China in the 1990s and the first decade of the twenty-first century, when China became a major player in the international economy. Moreover in the first decade of the twenty-first century America found that it was being replaced by China as the leading economic partner not only of Japan, but also of Korea, Taiwan, Australia and practically all its other allies and partners in Asia. This has brought about a disjunction between the economic and strategic orders in East Asia. If the United States still provides the security of the region through its bilateral alliances (the so-called "hub and spokes system") and, as a result, the public goods for maritime trade on which the countries of the region (including China) depend, it is increasingly China which has become the economic center on whose economic dynamism the regional countries depend for economic development and growth. If Japan leans more towards

China for escaping its economic doldrums, Japan turns to the United States to meet the growing military challenge from China.

Having discussed previously how the evolution of their respective national identities has deepened the discord between these two great powers of East Asia, the question arises as to how far the economic interdependence of China and Japan has helped to mitigate their differences or, alternatively, whether the economic relationship has served to highlight some of those differences. In other words, does the closer engagement of the two economies and societies contribute to increasing mutual understanding and better relations between these two very different societies and economies, or to the contrary, drive them further apart? Economic relations and trade necessarily generates disagreements between countries. For example, even close allies with similar systems such as the EU and the US often dispute aspects of the terms of trade and the nature of their economic competition. However, the broader issue, especially as far as Japan is concerned, is whether closer interactions with China might increase the latter's attractiveness as a partner or generate distaste. Instead of bringing about harmony, could greater closeness lead to conflict? Alternatively, it may be argued that given the expansion of China's military power as well as its economic significance, Japan may be faced with having to rethink its strategic position. Should it seek to modify its strategic dependence on America by reaching out more to China? Should it seek to bandwagon with China in some way? Or alternatively, even think in terms of developing its own independent military power, including consideration of the nuclear option?

The relationship between economic interdependence and conflict has been the subject of enduring debate as it pits the two major schools of International Relations, Liberalism and Realism, against each other. In the Liberal view economic interdependence reduces the risk of armed conflict and encourages peaceable relationships as ties develop between different groups and interests in both countries and procedures are developed to manage disputes and disagreements. Indeed, expanded more broadly, interdependence between states leads to the establishment of regimes with agreed procedures to regulate a growing range of functional issues. At an even more advanced level it may be possible to reach a stage of complex interdependence, when governments may find it difficult to differentiate between the relative importance of competing interests.[3]

In the Realist view economic interdependence is either altogether separate from the high politics of security, or it may even lead to conflict as an outgrowth of disputes over trade and other matters. Both schools of thought have been able to cite historical evidence in support of their positions. The difficulty in disentangling these contrasting intellectual approaches is compounded in the case of China and Japan by the fact that the management of their respective economies is deeply integrated with the conduct of high politics in each country. In China, it is the state, and behind that the Communist Party, which directly controls much of the economy; and the survival of Communist Party rule is seen to depend on providing continuous rapid economic growth, which alone is seen as ensuring social stability. In Japan, where strategic security has been provided by the United States, the main business of government both at home and abroad has been the management of the economy. Even at the height of its power at the end of the 1980s Japan's international significance was measured exclusively in economic terms.

A recent study of the significance of economic interdependence in the region, focusing especially on China, Japan and South Korea, argued that its importance arose from the extent to which it was bringing about regional integration and from the way this encouraged the three to deepen their engagement in the international economy including its rules and incentives. Their economic interdependence, it was argued, provided the basis for a newly emerging Northeast Asian regionalism. The study did not go so far as to claim that military conflict had been superseded but it argued that the incipient conflicts between the three had been muted.[4] Another recent study of the international political economy of the region argued that the domestic systems of the relevant countries changed to meet the norms and rules of the regimes of the international economy.[5]

I shall argue that the sheer complexity of Sino-Japanese relations does not allow for any clear or definitive resolution of the relationship between their economic interdependence and their propensity for armed conflict. There are wider strategic issues to be taken into account. For example, it can be argued that the absence of armed conflict between the two countries may be ascribed not only to the huge scale of their economic interdependence and the enormity of the costs of conflict to their respective economies, but also to the uncertainties of the political costs to each one in the domestic arena and in its relationships with the wider world, which armed conflict might entail.[6] But the absence of armed conflict may also be ascribed to Japan's security alliance with the United States, which not only obliges the latter to defend Japan, but also has enabled Japan to abjure offensive military capabilities that could threaten neighboring countries. More recently, the alliance may also be said to act as deterrence against China's growing military might and assertiveness.

The interdependence of the two economies arises out of their complementarity and their proximity. Before 1945 Japanese leaders argued that the prospects for their economy depended on guaranteed exclusive access to Chinese resources and to the Chinese market. In the 1950s Prime Minister Yoshida still thought that economic engagement with China was important for Japan. However, by the 1960s and 1970s access to the Chinese economy was no longer seen as a priority, given the economic orientation of Japan to the United States and to maritime Southeast Asia. But Japan became China's most important trading country after the Chinese break with the Soviet Union in the late 1950s. The ties, however, were limited because of the character of China's command economy and the Chinese emphasis on self-reliance. Even after the establishment of diplomatic relations in 1972 trade expanded considerably, but it did not really take off, primarily because of political uncertainties in China and the consequence of Mao's refusal to consider accepting Japanese reparations at the time of normalizing relations in 1972.

Trade and economic relations did in fact expand rapidly in the 1980s and Japan became the major external contributor to Deng Xiaoping's efforts to modernize the Chinese economy.[7] From a Japanese perspective, over and above commercial considerations, it was important to ensure that China's modernization should not fail lest the country return to angry isolation and perhaps even disintegration. The balance of economic power began to change in the 1990s, when the Japanese economy began to stagnate and the Chinese economy began its meteoric rise. Nevertheless the two economies became more interdependent as complex chains of production and distribution emerged between them (and others too). It is important to recognize that although China's overall GNP overtook that of Japan in 2010, becoming second only to the United States, Japan's per capita GNP was ten times greater than China's. More significantly, Japan was far ahead of China in terms of advanced technology and in innovative capacity and it will take China at least fifteen years to catch up.[8]

The development of close economic relations between China and Japan has always involved politics in one form or another. However, the pattern has changed much over the years – from a time when Japan was the colonial power and then the marginal niche player for China in the early years of the Cold War to its becoming a key player in the opening up of the economy to finally becoming a partner in a deepening economic interdependency in the post-Cold War period. I shall first look briefly at the periods before the end of the Cold War as these provide a perspective within which to gauge the shift of economic advantage in China's favor.

Economic relations during the Cold War

The Japanese invasion and occupation of much of China in the 1930s and early 1940s was designed in part to gain access to Chinese resources initially to prepare for waging war on the Soviet Union and later to serve as an economic base for the conduct of the wider war in Asia. It was seen as the key for establishing a new order in Asia, the so-called "Asia Co-Prosperity Sphere." It was in Manchuria in particular that the Japanese built a capitalist command economy.[9]

After Japan's defeat the legacy of the importance of access to the Chinese economy lingered on in the minds of Japan's conservative elite and there were still those who wished to retain aspects of Japan's Asian identity despite American efforts to transform the country into an anti-communist bastion. Thus in June 1952 an agreement was signed between the Chinese side and three prominent Japanese to conduct barter trade until the end of that year. Nominally this involved the separation of economics from politics, but this was politically significant for both sides and it was not long before politically important figures on both sides participated in the yearly negotiations. On the Japan side this constituted an open break with the American embargo on trade, with China coming barely after the suspension of hostilities in Korea and against the background of the Sino-Soviet treaty of 1950, which had singled out Japan by name as an adversary. Moreover the American alliance system, on which the security of Japan depended, was directed against China as well as the Soviet Union. The 1952 agreement was followed up the following year by the decision to exchange resident trade missions, who were then granted diplomatic privileges in 1956. Although the trade was modest, accounting for less than 5 percent of each other's total foreign trade, its significance was that it took place at all.[10] The Chinese used the trade negotiations to try and make political points, especially as some prominent conservative leaders of the LDP made overtures to the KMT leaders in Taiwan with whom they had ties going back to the war years in China.

China's break with the Soviet Union opened the door to deeper economic ties with Japan and a memorandum to that effect was signed in 1963. Given the structure of the Chinese command economy, foreign trade was limited. Even so Japan was China's leading trade partner in the 1960s and 1970s. The trade was relatively modest in terms of value, but it was important for China as the imports from Japan filled gaps in its self-reliant command economy.[11] The Japanese government saw the trade as contributing to China's economic development and to the prevention of a possible social and political collapse of its giant neighbor, which would end up damaging Japan too. For their part the Chinese sought to use the economic relations for political purposes, for example by setting conditions, which Japanese companies had to meet and by attempting to use the trade as a lever against more right-wing Japanese Prime Ministers such as Nobusuke

Kishi in the late 1950s, who was seen to be too close to Chiang Kai-shek and other KMT leaders in Taiwan. A decade later Chinese ire was directed against Prime Minister Eisaku Sato for similar reasons and it was only after he resigned that it become possible to proceed towards the normalization of relations in 1972. In fact Zhou Enlai had indicated that Sato was not acceptable as an interlocutor. Zhou was able to take advantage of the urgency with which major Japanese business people sought to normalize relations lest they lose out commercially to European and other competitors, who had already established diplomatic relations with Beijing.[12] As will be shown later, this was to be the precursor of Chinese attempts to identify Japanese politicians with whom they would or would not engage. However, it will be recalled that one of the more remarkable aspects of the normalization of relations was Mao's refusal to contemplate any form of reparations for Japanese war depredations. Doubtless he had in mind Chiang Kai-shek's refusal back in 1952, when his government was eager for international recognition and when he knew the United States had left Japan no option but to do so. Mao too had his reasons for playing down potential discord with Japan, as he sought to include Japan in his attempt to establish an anti-Soviet coalition. His successors were later to regret his "generosity."

It is important to recognize that although the normalization of Sino-Japanese relations in 1972 followed on from the rapprochement between China and the United States, Japan did not base its own rapprochement with China on the kind of grand international strategic calculations that brought Nixon and Mao together. It arose rather from its long-held desire to deepen economic relations with China despite the Cold War security structure and its own alliance with the United States.[13] For the first time since 1949 Japan found no contradiction between maintaining security relations with the US and developing relations with China. A further instance of the Japanese desire to be free of the broader international security context was its resistance to Chinese pressure to target the Soviet Union in the prolonged negotiations over a peace and friendship treaty. The Japanese did not want to be caught up in the Sino-American anti-Soviet alignment, especially as they still entertained hopes of reaching an understanding with Moscow over claims to the disputed islands to the north of Hokkaido. Additionally, they did not want to foreclose the prospects of access to Russian far eastern energy resources. In the end, the 1978 Treaty duly included the anti-hegemony clause, but it crucially also stated that the treaty was not directed against any third country. The Chinese had wanted to add to that the words "that did not practice hegemony." This time it was the Chinese side which was anxious to conclude the negotiations quickly in view of the imminent conflict with Vietnam, hence they did not insist on including their wording in the final document of the treaty. Meanwhile Deng Xiaoping, who had visited Japan to negotiate the conclusion of the treaty, was so impressed by Japan's modernity and its economic methods that he regarded it as a model for China's own economic modernization.[14]

If the Chinese and Americans (and for that matter the Soviets too) thought and acted in terms of grand international strategy, the Japanese did not.[15] For example, in late 1978 Japan went against the policies of its ally, the US, and its new friend, China, to try and wean Vietnam from its deepening strategic alliance with the Soviet Union by encouraging it to develop relations with ASEAN. Not surprisingly, the attempt failed as the drift to confrontation between Vietnam (and its Soviet ally) on the one side and China (and its strategic partner, the US) was sharpening to the point of open warfare with the Vietnamese invasion of Cambodia in December 1978 and the Chinese attack on Vietnam in February

1979. From a Chinese perspective both the recognition in 1972 and the 1978 Treaty were a component of the goal of establishing an international anti-Soviet front. The Japanese, however, saw the Treaty in much narrower terms and did not see themselves as having been caught up in the Chinese net, even though Moscow saw the Treaty in those terms. Tokyo still entertained hopes of reaching understandings with Moscow over claims to disputed islands and over agreements about access to Soviet energy resources in East Asia.[16]

By 1982 Chinese concerns about the Soviet threat had abated and China's leaders felt more assured about their country's security, as was demonstrated by the declaration of the adoption of an "independent foreign policy" at the 12th CCP Congress of that year. Deng's willingness to target Japan in 1982 over alleged textbook history revisionism also suggested that he was no longer seeking to lure Japan into joint opposition to the Soviet Union.

Such differences as did arise in Sino-Japanese relations in the period from 1972 until the end of the Cold War were strictly bilateral in nature. These included Japanese treatment of the Taiwan issue and problems of history, disputes over the Senkaku/Diaoyu Islands, Chinese fears of an allegedly newly militarizing Japan and various trade and commercial problems.

Although the massive expansion of economic relations between the two countries took place only after China embarked on the course of reform and opening in the 1980s, significant changes did take place after the establishment of diplomatic relations in 1972. The two reached a comprehensive trade agreement and agreements on aviation and fisheries. The last set out the parameters for fishing in the Yellow and East China Seas. In the 1970s the value of trade expanded six fold from $1.1 billion in 1972 to $6.6 billion in 1979. However, the trade became a point of contention in China between the leftists and the reformers while the ever-suspicious Mao was still alive. Zhou Enlai and Deng Xiaoping were criticized during the ascendancy of the "Gang of Four" in 1975–76, among other things, for the "selling out of China's oil resources to foreign exploiters."[17] It was only with Mao's death, followed by the arrest of the "Gang of Four," that such criticisms came to an end. This was soon followed by a grandiose scheme of modernization, which turned out to exceed China's capacity to implement. In the process, however, several Japanese companies were caught up in Japan's first bout of "China fever." On finding that their contracts were abruptly canceled some were able to negotiate a measure of redress, but the affair left a cloud of suspicion about Chinese business practices.[18] It was only after Deng finally established his predominance in late December 1978 that China finally embarked on a more successful road of economic reform and openness.

The first reform period 1979–89

As already noted, the Sino-Japanese Treaty of Peace and Friendship was signed in Beijing on August 12, 1978 after Deng Xiaoping accepted the Japanese draft stating that it was not directed against any third party. If the Chinese side saw the significance of the Treaty primarily in strategic terms, the Japanese side saw it primarily as an opportunity to cement ties for commercial reasons. But it was also seen in Japan as an opportunity to overcome the bad historical legacy of Japanese aggression with China without arousing the enmity of the Soviet Union. Deng Xiaoping then visited Japan October 19–28, 1978 to raise the relationship to a new level. As the first Chinese leader ever to visit Japan in over

2,000 years of contact between the two countries, Deng made a huge impression and he was received with great honor. He in turn was greatly impressed with the modernity of the country, its advanced technology (the kind of which he had never seen before) and its highly efficient systems of management. He spoke frankly about China's relative backwardness and said that China should learn from Japan. Many Japanese felt that helping China to modernize would contribute to mitigating their historic guilt.[19]

The improved atmosphere between the two countries led to new economic agreements including one, which was to be renewed over the years, of grants and soft loans from Japanese Official Development Assistance (ODA) that helped to establish infrastructure, modern factories, new training in modern industrial skills and management that were to be the foundation for the modernization of the economy. In the words of one of America's leading experts on both Japan and China: "During Deng's years at the helm, no country played a greater role in assisting China build its industry and infrastructure than Japan."[20] These years also coincide with what in Japan was considered its "friendship policy" towards China.

The development of close economic relations between China and Japan served the political objectives of both sets of governments, even as these objectives may have changed over time. From the Chinese perspective the economic exchanges with Japan have contributed greatly to rapid economic development and to the consolidation of the peaceful international environment, from which China has benefited greatly. Both of these have been central drivers of China's rise and, by helping ensure relative domestic stability, they have proved to be essential for the maintenance of Communist Party rule in the post-Cold War period. From a Japanese perspective the economic engagement with China has served the political goal of helping prevent a breakdown of order in that country and of giving the Chinese elites a stake in mitigating popular nationalist hostility against Japan. It was also a means by which Japan could give expression to the Asian dimension of its identity. At the same time the 1980s was also the decade in which the United States went out of its way to engage China and consequently there was no difficulty for Japan in relating to both the major powers, which were at the center of its foreign policy concerns. In fact Japan experienced more problems in conducting relations with the United States because of what were regarded as its unfair economic policies.

However, there was also a darker side to the Sino-Japanese relationship in these years. Given the centrality, the depth and complexity of Sino-Japanese relations it is not surprising that the respective elites of the two countries often disagreed among themselves about various aspects of the conduct of relations with the other side on matters that have also included economics. In China Deng Xiaoping, who had initially encouraged his people to learn from Japan, found reason to be more critical of Japan later in the 1980s. In 1982 he played a part in urging that Chinese people should be educated in patriotism. Although this arose mainly from the domestic shift of emphasis away from socialism as a basis for appealing for the loyalty of Chinese people, it was triggered by reports of a new Japanese school textbook that reportedly whitewashed Japan's past aggression against China.[21] A few years later when he was angered over Japanese foot-dragging over ODA he described Japanese aid as something to which China was entitled because it did not insist on reparations at the time of normalizing relations. Relations with Japan continued to arouse controversy at the highest political levels in China. For example, the fall in 1987 of Hu Yaobang, the Secretary General of the CCP, which was due primarily to his more liberal policies, was also related to his pro-Japanese views. He looked upon Japan as a possible economic model for China and his ideologically conservative opponents took that as further evidence of his inclination to what was called "bourgeois liberalization."[22] Sino-Japanese relations remained a contentious issue between leaders on both sides. As noted in earlier chapters, the top leaders Jiang Zemin and Hu Jintao held different views about the significance of past history in the conduct of current relations. Japanese political leaders have also disagreed about the significance to be attached to China. Two early post-Second World War prime ministers, Shigeru Yoshida and Nobusuke Kishi, for example, differed on the respective weight to be attached to China and Taiwan. Contending LDP factions linked to different key ministries of Finance and Trade took divergent views on the significance of relations with China, which had an impact on economic policy towards the region including China.[23] Similarly divergences between different bureaucratic interests existed in China with regard to Japan.[24]

In fact the first hurdle to be overcome after the signing of the 1978 Treaty and the Long Term Trade Agreement, also in 1978, arose after the change of direction of the Chinese economy from the ambitious targets pursued by the Hua Guofeng leadership before the ascendancy of Deng Xiaoping in late 1978. In February 1979, China requested the suspension of many of the business contracts signed earlier, notably that for the Baoshan Steel complex near Shanghai, and in January 1981 abruptly canceled them. The unilateral cancelation shocked Japan and dampened the so-called "China fever."[25] Nevertheless at the request of the Chinese, during this period of relative disenchantment the Japanese granted ODA in 1981 to the value of Yen 300 billion for the period 1978–83 together with loans on preferential terms to build huge infrastructure projects including ports, railways and hydro-electric power. Additional Japanese aid flowed to China throughout the rest of the 1980s, which provided much of the infrastructural basis on which the Chinese were able to expand their economy so rapidly in the 1990s.

Despite the ebb and flow of domestic politics, China's strategic position continued to improve in the second half of the 1980s, especially as the advent of Gorbachev reduced tension and therefore the prospect of conflict with the Soviet Union. At the same time relations with the United States had improved markedly. But from a Chinese perspective problems had developed in relations with Japan. This was less because of economic issues as such than because of Chinese concerns about Japan's emergence as a "political power" and even possibly a military power. Chinese sensitivity was also occasioned by domestic political differences highlighted by the dismissal of Hu Yaobang in 1987. This was the point at which Deng Xiaoping chided the Japanese government over its failure to do something about a dormitory that a Japanese court had ruled belonged to Taiwan rather than China. He went on to criticize Japan for exceeding the 1 percent ceiling of the defense budget as that would fuel Japanese militarism. He then observed that Japan should do more to assist Chinese development, adding "to be frank, Japan is the country in the world most indebted to China: we did not demand war reparations at the time of diplomatic normalization."[26]

The twenty years from 1972 to 1992 saw the total value of Sino-Japanese trade leap from $1.038 billion to $25.38 billion. The total amount of Japanese ODA, loans and grants extended to China came to Yen 1,394.22 billion. Moreover as a sign of things to come the balance of Chinese exports to Japan began to shift towards manufactured goods.[27] This was also a period of learning for both sides, as the two had to find ways to overcome the difficulties posed by the enormous divergence in their economic and political systems. If the Japanese found that the cultivation of personal ties helped to overcome some of the problems associated with the Chinese bureaucracies and competing levels of officialdom, the Chinese found that they had to pay great attention to Japanese commercial laws and codes of behavior rather than rely upon attempts to exploit perceived differences between Japanese politicians or competing Japanese business people. However, many of the problems were eased by the ties between Chinese and Japanese leaders that had been forged ironically during the times of strife between the two countries in the first half of the twentieth century.[28]

The time from the Tiananmen massacre of June 4, 1989 until the end of 1992 may be regarded as one of transition towards the post-Cold War era, when both sides reassessed their domestic and external identities in the entirely new international circumstances. But even before that there were signs of growing unease between the Chinese and Japanese arising from changes in the balances of their relative power. As already noted, towards the end of the 1980s Chinese leaders became more confident of their strategic position and they became more suspicious of a Japan that seemed to be rising inexorably to replace the United States as the leading economy. As noted earlier, Japan was increasingly seen as a "political power" and potentially a "military power." Deng's strictures of 1987 to the Japanese to recognize their obligations to China should be seen in this light. A leading Japanese China scholar, Eto Shinkichi, had earlier observed, "there are signs that the Japanese are taking a high-handed attitude toward the Chinese because of their technological supremacy and powerful economy."[29]

Although Japan joined the rest of the Group of Seven in imposing sanctions on China in the immediate aftermath of June 4, it did so reluctantly and it soon played the leading role in bringing the economic and political ones to an end. Notwithstanding the drop of Japanese esteem of China as expressed in opinion polls, from 80 to 50 percent, the Japanese government took steps to alleviate the diplomatic and economic isolation of China. It did so less out of economic calculations of costs and benefits or under the influence of economic interdependence and more because of the long-standing Japanese concern about isolating China and about the possible negative consequences to itself and the region from instability in its huge neighbor. This led to what Michael Green has called "an artificial honeymoon."[30] In June 1991 Tokyo resumed aid, in August that year Prime Minister Kaifu Toshiki became the first leader of the Group of Seven to visit China after Tiananmen, and in April 1992 General Secretary Jiang Zemin visited Japan to be followed in October by Emperor Akihito making the first ever imperial visit to China. By 1993, however, the effects of the new post-Cold War international environment became evident when the Japanese prime minister and foreign minister for the first time pressed Beijing publicly for greater military transparency.[31]

In conclusion it may be argued that the ebb and flow of Sino-Japanese ties were dictated by changes in Chinese and Japanese appreciations of their country's international situation. For China this applied especially in the context of its position in the strategic triangle involving the United States and the Soviet Union, and its pursuit of an "independent foreign policy" after 1982 as the perceived threat from the Soviet Union diminished. For Japan the key change followed the Sino-American rapprochement, which allowed the country simultaneously to cultivate China economically and to maintain the strategic alliance with the United States. Sino-Japanese economic ties served an important political purpose for China by contributing greatly to its embarkation on what turned out to be in the 1980s a tortuous path to economic modernization. The Japanese government's role in extending ODA and encouraging Japanese companies to engage China served the

Japanese goal of contributing to the domestic stabilization of China. If the ties came under strain in the late 1980s it was due to Chinese worries about growing Japanese political power as an outgrowth of its rapidly rising economy and to Japanese pretensions of superiority. To be sure their economic ties had become more important to both sides, but they were seen certainly by the Chinese side less in terms of mutual interdependence and more in terms of concern about a possible dependency on Japan.

Cold politics and hot economics, 1993–2005

Any such hopes as Japanese leaders may have entertained about using their economic power to influence Chinese politics and foreign relations soon faded. The end of the Cold War and the dissolution of the Soviet Union was a strategic boon to China, as it no longer had any lingering fears of attack or invasion from the north while giving it greater strategic latitude in the long neglected maritime regions to the east and south. At the same time the adoption of patriotism as the basis for the CCP's appeal to its people led to a new emphasis on a historic narrative of renewal and recovery from a hundred years of victimization by foreigners culminating in fifty years of Japanese aggression. This meant that Japan had to deal with a more assertive China that was bent on eliciting ever more fulsome apologies from the Japanese for their past aggression. It also resulted in greater insistence by China's leaders in demanding Japanese economic assistance as of right, as a kind of reparation for the wartime devastation.

Japan too was trying to come to terms with the new international environment, but it was overwhelmed by the collapse of its economic bubble in 1991 and by the end of the so-called San Francisco political system, which undermined the previous balance between the ruling conservative LDP and the opposition leftist JSP. The Japanese adjustment was not helped by the expectations of its strategic ally, the United States, on whom Japan continued to depend, that Japan would contribute more to regional and international security in military as well as in financial terms. Pressure built up on Japan as it was found wanting for contributing only financially to the American-led first Gulf War of 1990 and not at all to the first nuclear crisis with North Korea in 1993/94. In fact Japan claimed it could not even prevent the transfer of funds from Japan to North Korea. During this time, as we have seen in chapter 2, the Japanese, to simplify grossly, were debating as to whether they should seek to be the Great Britain or the Switzerland of East Asia.

It was in this context that the Japanese found that they totally failed in an attempt to use their economic leverage to persuade China to desist from carrying out nuclear tests, which were resumed on May 15, 1995 at a time when the Comprehensive Test Ban Treaty was about to come into force and when the other declared nuclear powers (with the notable exception of France) had already stopped carrying out such tests. Tokyo suspended a symbolic $75 million of grant assistance, only to be reprimanded by Beijing: how could Japan the historic aggressor have the temerity to protest at what the Chinese claimed was purely a defensive move on their part? The Chinese then proceeded to carry out two more tests in August and September. Outraged members of the LDP in the Diet called for the suspension of ODA, but the Ministry of Foreign Affairs was faced with Chinese angry objections that the loans were not Japan's to suspend. MOFA told the LDP that the ODA was still "the main pillar of Japan's China policy." In July 1996 China carried out its last nuclear test before acceding to the CTBT. It will be recalled that prior to this in 1995 and 1996 China fired missiles in the seas off Taiwan as exercises in coercive diplomacy.[32] These events spelled the end of what Japan called its "friendship diplomacy" towards China.

Yet economic ties continued apace. By 2004 the value of Sino-Japanese trade had grown exponentially to $167 billion from the $25 billion of 1992. Throughout the years 1994–2003 Japan maintained its place as the leading trade partner of China, until it was replaced in 2004 by the EU (with its ten new members). During this time China was Japan's second largest trader. Such dips in economic relations as did take place from time to time were caused by strictly economic considerations. For example, Japan ranked second as an investor in China until 1995, when Beijing reduced the preferential treatment for foreign firms so that Japan dropped to fifteenth place by 1999. In the year 2000 Japan's FDI grew in anticipation of China's joining the World Trade Organization, lifting its ranking to sixth. In 1997 Sino-Japanese trade declined in response to the Asian Financial Crisis of that year and in 1978 Japan found itself the object of criticism by China for having earlier changed the value of Yen to the cost of countries in the region. As China embarked on its remarkably high-growth trajectory so its economic ties with the rest of the world deepened and expanded, thereby weakening its former dependence on Japan even though its actual trade with Japan continued to expand. For example, the EU and the US also became key suppliers of high-technology to China.[33]

Neither exchanges between the two sets of people, nor intergovernment agreements to establish institutions to mediate trade problems or to facilitate cultural exchanges modified the poor opinions that the two populations held of each other. Japanese constituted the largest national group of visitors to China accounting for about 20 percent per annum in this period. For example in the roughly representative year of 2001 Japanese visitors numbered 2.38 million (20 percent), South Koreans 1.79 million (15 percent) and Americans 1.01 million (8.5 percent). In this period Chinese visitors to Japan numbered about a fifth of Japanese who visited China. Japanese students in China numbered second only to South Koreans (in 2003, 12,765 as against 35,353 respectively). Nevertheless throughout this period both Chinese and Japanese consistently expressed a lack of affinity and distaste for each other by wide margins in opinion polls. The Tiananmen massacre left an indelible mark on Japanese thinking about China that no amount of economic and other exchanges could obliterate. Prior to 1989 70–80 percent of Japanese felt affinity for China, but thereafter the number fell sharply to less than 50 percent and in 2004 it dropped to 37 percent. Chinese polling figures also displayed strongly negative views of Japan. A 2004 poll in China showed that 6.3 percent felt close to Japan as opposed to 53.6 percent who did not.[34]

During this period, as noted in the previous chapter, the Chinese emphasis on Japan's failure to atone for its war of aggression and the reactions to various incidents which took place both in China and in Japan, combined with a deteriorating security situation between the two sides, soured the atmosphere between China and Japan. Clearly, whatever else the evidence of mutual distrust may suggest, it does not indicate that the growing economic ties have done much to overcome the otherwise deepening divide between them. The Chinese then coined the phrase "economics hot, politics cold" to characterize their relations at that point. This was the period when Japan's Prime Minister Junichiro Koizumi had so angered the Chinese leaders by his annual visits to the Yasukuni Shrine that they severed high level contacts between the two countries. Nevertheless commercial relations between the two countries did not seem to have been affected as their trade grew more than two and a half times during the Koizumi years (2000–06) from $86 to $227 billion.[35]

However, it may be argued that the divide between the two countries would have been even worse were it not for the growing economic and social ties between them. Indeed many in their respective official circles decried the deterioration of their relations. In China the Ministry of Foreign Affairs was known to endorse the call for new thinking on relations with Japan that was made in public by a prominent editor of the *People's Daily* and by a leading International Relations scholar.[36] But interestingly, the call for "new thinking" stressed diplomatic and political needs without much mention of economic imperatives. Hu Jintao and Wen Jiabao, the two leaders who took over power beginning in 2003, recognized the damage that popular nationalist anti-Japanese sentiments and demonstrations were doing to China's foreign relations and to those with Japan in particular. The demonstrations of April 2005, which turned into riots directed against Japan, were a turning point. Thereafter Japan began to be presented in a more positive light in the official media and as discussed in the previous chapter, the strengthening of Hu Jintao's political position at home and the replacement of Prime Minister Koizumi in Japan by Shinzo Abe, provided the opportunity to "break the ice" in October 2006.

Arguably, the amelioration of relations could be said to be due to the high cost of discord at a time of economic interdependence. Perhaps that is why the pressure to improve relations came from elite sources, which were better placed to appreciate the damage caused by deteriorating relations. The opaqueness of the Chinese political decision-making process does not allow for examination of whether regional or functional groups within China connected with the economic exchanges with Japan pressed the leaders to change course. But it is known that relations with Japan figured in high-level political disputes. On the Japan side business representatives were known to have pressed Koizumi to refrain from going to the Yasukuni Shrine, which they saw as a needless provocation to China. However, Koizumi was able to resist such pressure by playing on Japanese resentment of what they saw as Chinese use of the history "card" to interfere in Japan's domestic affairs.

Doubtless economic ties helped to ameliorate relations but the available evidence suggests that it was mainly political and strategic factors that drove both the Chinese and the new Japanese leader to try and reach a new understanding. Within Japan there had long been a view that the country had to balance its Western orientation, as expressed in the alliance with the United States, with an Asian orientation that would not be possible as long as it was ostracized by China. Moreover Japan's ally the United States had indicated to Japanese leaders it did not like to see bad relations and tension between the two great powers of East Asia. From a Chinese perspective the negative relationship with Japan ran counter to China's proclaimed "good neighbor" policies, threatening regional peace, which was deemed essential for the national priority of economic development. Besides which, it did no good to Chinese interests to drive the other great power of the region into an ever closer military alliance with the United States.

The economic balance shifts towards China 2005–11

China's emergence as a major global economic power and as the regional economic hub of East Asia during this period transformed the economic significance of Japan. Japan ceased to be the key economic player, along with the United States, in shaping the region's trade and economic relationships. The effect on the balance of Sino-Japanese economic bilateral relations was dramatic. In 2005 China (+ Hong Kong) replaced the United States as Japan's leading trading partner and in 2007 it did so alone. By the end of 2010 the value of Japan's trade with China exceeded that of its trade with the US by a staggering 40 percent ($301.85 billion to $203.9 billion) and by 2012 Japan's trade with China had grown to around $340 billion, while that with the US remained at about the $200 billion mark. Even though Japan remained an important player at the high-tech end of the chains of production involving China, the change in the relative significance of the one to the other may be gauged from the fact that the value of Japan's trade with China accounted for 22 percent of Japan's total world trade, whereas Japan's trade with China accounted for only 10 percent of the Chinese equivalent. At the same time the proportion of Japanese trade taken up by the US was progressively declining. For example in the year 2000 the US accounted for 25 percent of Japan's trade and ten years later it had declined to 18 percent.[37]

These figures may underestimate the importance of Japan to the Chinese economy: first, they constitute part of chains of production in which goods have been manufactured in China by Japanese companies who supplied the more high-tech designs and so on from products imported from abroad and to which the total added value by the Chinese side may be only a small proportion of the amount registered in the trade figures. Second, a great deal of what is recorded as inter-state trade is really economic exchange between different branches of huge multinational companies such as Canon, Mitsui, Matsushita, Honda and Toyota, who run large manufacturing plants in China.[38] These qualifications, however, may also be seen as illustrative of how deeply enmeshed or interdependent the two economies had become.[39]

Yet, as we have seen it is hard to argue that it was the growing economic interdependence between the two countries that drove the two to improve their diplomatic and political relations in October 2006. The key points of the Joint Statement were political rather than economic. For example, the key commitment was to build a "mutually beneficial relationship based on common strategic interests." The two sides attempted to diffuse the political dimensions of the question of history that had increasingly bedeviled the relationship by passing it on to a joint committee of historians to report three years hence. Japanese diplomats attached importance to the Chinese formal acknowledgment of Japan's economic contribution to Chinese efforts at reconstruction as they hoped it would help to improve their country's image in China. For the same reason they regarded it as highly significant that the Chinese government for the first time publicly acknowledged Japan's commitment to peace since 1945. They hoped that it would remove from the table the Chinese charge that Japan was about to return to the path of militarization. Both sides agreed that their relationship was "important" and that they would operate on the "two wheels of politics and economics." Up to that point the Chinese charged that "economics were hot and politics cold" and the new phrasing reasserted the need to cultivate the political dimension too. Similarly they agreed to promote exchanges in all areas at all levels.

It was not until the political framework had been settled that the economic dimensions began to be fully addressed by the two governments, especially in the course of the subsequent visits to Japan by Premier Wen Jiabao in 2007 and President Hu Jintao in May 2008. The last in particular spelled out a range of economic agreements in which Japan could contribute to projects designed to improve Chinese energy efficiency and reduce pollution. Additionally, a raft of agreements was signed to facilitate the exchange of communication technology, to improve conditions for investment, finance, food and product safety. It was agreed that joint projects would be established to promote farming, forestry and fishery. Educational exchanges would be promoted as would tourism. Finally, intellectual property rights would be better protected. The particularly forthcoming approach of the Chinese leaders owed more to their desire to respond favorably to Prime Minister Yasuo Fukuda who, alone among the three prime ministers who followed Koizumi in quick succession, truly favored cultivating relations with Asia and especially with China. An example of the favorable Chinese disposition towards Fukuda was the readiness to agree in principle at least that joint development of oil and gas fields might be possible in disputed areas of the East China Sea.[40] All this suggested that the key to a significant upgrade in the character of economic relations depended on the mending of political relations. At the same time it was also apparent that in the absence of substantive agreements to improve security relations the most public and effective ways to demonstrate that the meetings of leaders had made a positive difference was to reach a large number of agreements about economic and cultural relations.

Fukuda, who was regarded favorably by the Chinese side, resigned in September 2008 after barely a year in office and before his closer relationship with Chinese leaders could bear fruit. Also the context of Sino-Japanese relations changed as the impact of the international financial crisis of 2007/08 was felt. Unlike their Japanese partners, the Chinese emerged notably stronger and more successful. The rise of their international economic stature was recognized at the meetings of the G-20 and was reflected by increasing their voting rights at the IMF. Their economy also helped regional economies to weather the crisis better than the developed countries of Europe and indeed the US itself. By comparison Japan continued to stagnate and its GNP was duly passed by China, whose economic output was exceeded only by the US.

The deepening economic interdependence of the two countries, however, was not enough in itself to overcome some of the long-standing sovereign and political issues that remained between them. Indeed in some respects it added to them, by drawing attention to the distrust between the two peoples arising from their divergent identities and different political systems. For example, in February 2008 a batch of dumplings imported from China was found to have been poisoned and it took two years before the Chinese side eventually identified a culprit in China who allegedly bore a grudge against the Chinese producers. But the manner in which the investigations were conducted and the Chinese instinctive reaction to cast blame on Japan first, cast the Chinese authorities in a bad light in Japan. The Chinese for their part found cause to retaliate against the Japanese attempt to protect certain agricultural products from Chinese competition.[41] The significance of these Sino-Japanese trade differences was that they illustrated how commercial disputes spilled over into the political arena, rather than being regarded as an understandable friction between close economic partners.

Given China's new-found relative economic strength it is perhaps surprising that China did not respond more warmly to the newly elected DPJ government in Japan, which had overwhelmingly defeated the more conservative LDP in September 2009 and which favored better relations with Asia and China. Hu Jintao did not respond warmly to the proposal of a "Yuai" (friendship) based Asia Community advanced by the new Prime Minister Yukio Hatoyama. Perhaps Hu regarded the concept as too vague, especially because of its Japanese authorship. In any event Hu indicated a preference for the already functioning institution of the Northeast Asian three (China, Japan and South Korea), which had grown out of the ASEAN Plus Three.[42]

The DPJ had started with a strong pro-China tilt. China was the first country visited by Hatoyama, who was quickly followed to Beijing by the DPJ's political strongman, Ichiro Ozawa, accompanied by 143 members of the Diet and about 470 secretaries, political supporters and businessmen. The new approach to China was confirmed by the visit a day later of Vice President Xi Jinping to Tokyo, where, against strict protocol, he had an audience with the emperor.[43] By contrast Hatoyama's relations with the United States could not have started off on a worse footing because of the disagreement about relocating the marine base in Okinawa. Far from using the opportunity of the bad blood between the Obama administration and Hatoyama to build on new opportunities suggested by the tilt towards Beijing by the DPJ leaders, China's leaders allowed relations with Japan to falter. Their failure to respond more positively to the DPJ government's early initiatives does not suggest that the value of interdependence with their key economic partner rated highly as a driver of Chinese policy.

Notwithstanding continued high level exchanges of government, military and other leaders, political, defense and sovereignty issues had begun to rapidly cloud the relationship. Disputes arose over sovereign claims in the East China Sea and over whether the Japanese-owned Okitinori reefs in the Pacific constituted island territory in international law. The Japanese demanded greater military transparency from China, particularly after a flotilla sailed close to Japanese islands, and they objected to their ships monitoring the Chinese naval exercise being buzzed too closely by Chinese helicopters. The Chinese in turn objected to their exercises being monitored by Japanese ships and aircraft. The two sides also differed over North Korea and its role in the torpedoing of a South Korean vessel and in firing upon a civilian occupied island.

As noted in the previous chapter, matters came to a head in September 2010 after Japan arrested the captain of a Chinese fishing vessel who had rammed two Japanese Coast Guard ships. The Chinese response was vitriolic and it included the arrest of four Japanese nationals and the effective suspension of the export to Japan of rare earth metals on which China had a near monopoly. Japan relented and released the ship's captain before completing the pre-trial procedures. The episode led to shrill anti-Japanese demonstrations in a number of Chinese cities and a smaller number of well-behaved Japanese counter demonstrations in Tokyo and elsewhere. The Japanese government was accused within Japan of having meekly succumbed to Chinese pressure. Public opinion in both countries swiftly plumbed new depths of opprobrium for the other country. The result was that Japan became more closely aligned with South Korea and the United States in response to what each saw as unusually assertive, if not actually aggressive behavior by China. Despite China's apparent attempt to use its near monopoly of rare earths to punish Japan, broader Sino-Japanese economic relations were apparently unaffected, suggesting that they operated on a separate plane from the main thrust of political and diplomatic relations between these two great powers of East Asia. As outlined in the previous chapter, another round of vitriolic and violent demonstrations took place in China over the Senkaku/Diaoyu islands two years later in September 2012, which were also suddenly brought to a halt. But on this occasion some Japanese factories closed down because of the violence. In response to vague warnings from a Chinese minister about economic consequence, the Japanese prime minister, Noda, warned the Chinese leaders against the use of economic measures against Japan lest they rebound to hurt the Chinese economy, which he judged to be fragile.[44] In other words, their economies had become genuinely interdependent so that one could not be hurt without damaging the other and indeed the repercussions could even spread to the international economy.

Notwithstanding these disputes and the growing disenchantment of the two populations with each other, China and Japan together with South Korea intensified the institutionalization of a range of trilateral meetings between them to facilitate the conduct of commercial exchanges. Beginning in 2008, summit meetings have been held annually and they have focused on economic cooperation and disaster relief. In 2011 a Trilateral Cooperation Secretariat was established in Seoul and in May 2012 it was agreed to begin preparations for establishing a free trade agreement (FTA) between the three leading economies of East Asia. This may be seen as building on the long gestation of an agreement to establish a currency swap facility in 2010, known as the Chiang Mai Initiative, which began with a reserve pool of $120 billion that two years later in 2010 was extended to $240 billion. In 2012 Japan and China also agreed to use their own currencies in the conduct of bilateral trade. This is in alignment with the Chinese objective of reducing the international role of the US dollar, but it suited the Japanese side as it reduced the transaction costs of their economic exchanges. The details of these institutionalized arrangements will be examined more closely in the next chapter. Some have seen these developments as evidence of the regionalization of Northeast Asia.[45] But in the absence of the establishment of agreed mechanisms to avoid or mitigate conflicts, it would seem that it is premature to claim that regionalization has taken place.

In conclusion it would seem that the deepening economic interdependence between China and Japan has not brought about a resolution of the deep political and security divisions between the two. Nor would it seem to have increased mutual trust and understanding between the two peoples. Yet the bureaucratic and business elites of both countries have successfully intensified their mutually dependent economic relations to the extent that neither side has allowed mutual antipathies to stand in the way of their economic exchanges, despite occasional threats to boycott the other side's products. Moreover, both sets of governmental leaders have been conscious of the potential economic and political costs of a major breakdown of relations. In China's case the economic consequences could threaten social stability and even Communist Party rule.

Notes

1 See *China Daily*, May 5, 2008, for the Chinese account of China's GDP surpassing that of Japan. For the widening of the gap between Chinese and American trades with Japan, compare the value of Japan's trade with China in 2010 of $301.9 billion with its trade in the same year with the US of $268 billion. See *Jetro*, February 23, 2011 (www.jetro.go.jp/en/news/releases/20110512035-news, accessed March 27, 2013) for the first; and for the second, see William H. Cooper, "U.S.–Japan Economic Relations: Significance, Prospect and Policy Options," *Congressional Research Service*, February 14, 2011.

2 Theresa M. Greaney and Yao Li, "Assessing Foreign Direct Investment Relationships Between Japan, the People's Republic of China and the United States," Asian Development Bank Institute: *ADB Working Papers* No. 161, November 2009.

3 Robert O. Keohane and Joseph Nye, *Power and Interdependence* (Summit, NJ: Longman Classics in Political Science, 4th edition, 2011); and for discussion of Liberal internationalism see, David Baldwin (ed.), *Neorealism and Neoliberalism: The Contemporary Debate* (New York: Columbia University Press, 1993) and the more recent, Edward D. Mansfield and Brian M. Pollins, "Interdependence and Conflict: an Introduction," in their (eds.), *Economic*

Interdependence and International Conflict: New Perspectives on an Enduring Debate (Ann Arbor: University of Michigan Press, 2009).

4 Kent Calder and Min Ye, *The Making of Northeast Asia* (Palo Alto, CA: Stanford University Press, 2010).

5 Scott L. Kastner, *Political Conflict and Economic Interdependence Across the Taiwan Strait and Beyond* (Palo Alto, CA: Stanford University Press, 2009).

6 Historical experience suggests that close economic interdependency in itself is no guarantee against the outbreak of even the most highly destructive wars. The clearest example is the First World War, which broke out despite the intensity of economic globalization especially between the principal parties. The depth of their economic interdependence was so great that Norman Angell's *The Grand Illusion* of 1910 famously ruled out the possibility of war in Europe.

7 Ezra F. Vogel, *Deng Xiaoping and the Transformation of China* (Cambridge, MA: Harvard University Press, 2011), Chapter 10, "Opening to Japan, 1978," pp.294–310.

8 Claude Meyer, *China or Japan: Which will Lead Asia?* (New York: Columbia University Press, 2011), pp.116–19.

9 For accounts of this period see, W.G. Beasley, *The Modern History of Japan* (London: Weidenfeld and Nicolson, 1964), Chapter 14, "An Empire Won and Lost, 1937–45," pp.258–78; and Marius B. Jansen, *The Making of Modern Japan* (Cambridge, MA: Harvard University Press, 2000), Chapters 17 and 18, "The China War" and "The Pacific War," pp.576–674.

10 Chae-Jin Lee, *China and Japan: New Economic Diplomacy* (Palo Alto, CA: Hoover Institution, Stanford University Press, 1984), p.3.

11 This is an argument of Alexander Eckstein, *Communist China's Economic Growth and Foreign Trade: Implications for US Policy* (New York: McGraw-Hill, 1966).

12 Wolf Mendl, *Issues in Japan's China Policy* (London: Macmillan, 1978), pp.60–61.

13 Ibid., pp.58–59.

14 Vogel, *Deng Xiaoping*, pp.304–05 and pp.455–64.

15 Soeye Yoshide, "Japan's Relations with China" in Ezra F. Vogel, Ming Yuan and Akihiko Tanaka (eds.), *The Golden Age of the U.S.–China–Japan Triangle, 1972–1989* (Cambridge, MA: Harvard University Press, 2002), pp.210–26.

16 Michael Yahuda, *The International Politics of the Asia-Pacific* (London and New York: Routledge, revised 3rd edition, 2011), pp.171–72.

17 Thomas Fingar, *China's Quest for Independence: Policy Evolution in the 1970s* (Boulder, CO: Perseus Books, 1979).

18 Lee, *China and Japan*, pp.20–29; and Ryosei Kokubun, "The Politics of Foreign Economic Policy-making in China: The Case of Plant Cancelations with Japan," *The China Quarterly* No. 105, March 1986.

19 This paragraph draws heavily on Vogel, *Deng Xiaoping*, Chapter 10, "Opening to Japan," pp.294–310.

20 Ibid., p.310.

21 Caroline Rose, *Interpreting History in Sino-Japanese Relations* (London and New York: Routledge, 1998), especially Chapter 4, "Background to the Textbook Issue: Domestic issues in the 1970s and 1980s," pp.59–79.

22 On Hu Yaobang see, Richard Baum, *Burying Mao: Chinese Politics in the Age of Deng Xiaoping* (Princeton, NJ: Princeton University Press, 1994), pp.206–08 and Zhao Ziyang, *Prisoner of State* (New York: Simon & Schuster, 2009), pp.161–82. See also the discussion in Calder and Min Ye, *The Making of Northeast Asia*, pp.212–22.

23 My interviews with officials and scholars in Beijing, May 2004 and August 2006.

24 Lee, *China and Japan*, Chapter 2, "Steel Industry: The Baoshan Complex," pp.30–75.

25 Allen S. Whiting, *China Eyes Japan* (Berkeley: University of California Press, 1989), p.158.

26 Zhang Tuosheng, "China's Relations with Japan," in Vogel et al. (eds.), *The Golden Age*, p.193.

27 For accounts of these ties see the various chapters in Mendl, *Issues in Japan's China Policy*, and Lee, *China and Japan*.

28 Cited in Lee, *China and Japan*, p.144.

29 Michael J. Green, *Japan's Reluctant Realism: Foreign Policy Challenges in an Era of Uncertain Power* (New York: Palgrave, 2001, for the Council on Foreign Relations), p.78.

30 Ibid., pp.80–82.

31 Much of the substance of the above two paragraphs is drawn from Ming Wan, *Sino-Japanese Relations: Interaction, Logic and Transformation* (Washington, DC: Woodrow Wilson Center Press / Palo Alto, CA: Stanford University Press, 2006), pp.45–65.
32 Mike M. Mochizuki, "China–Japan Relations: Downward Spiral or a New Equilibrium," in David Shambaugh (ed.), *Power Shift: China and Asia's New Dynamics* (Berkeley: University of California Press, 2005), pp.135–38.
33 This paragraph draws on Hideo Ohasi, "China's Regional Trade and Investment Profile," in Shambaugh, *Power Shift*, pp.71–95.
34 The statistics are drawn from Ming Wan, *Sino-Japanese Relations*, "Bilateral Sociocultural Interaction," pp.63–79.
35 WTO statistics on merchandise trade. www.wto.org/english/res_e/statis_e/its2011_e/its11_appendix_e.htm. Accessed March 27, 2013.
36 See Christopher R. Hughes, *Chinese Nationalism in the Global Era* (London and New York: Routledge, 2006), "Japan: popular nationalism and elite discourse," pp.146–51.
37 All figures were drawn from data of the Japanese Ministry of Finance and the US Census Bureau, Foreign Trade Division, Data Dissemination Branch.
38 For accounts of the operations of these companies in China see, Calder and Min Ye, *The Making of Northeast Asia*, p.10 and more generally, Chapter 6, pp.129–62.
39 See, Hugh Patrick, "Japan's foreign economic relations," *East Asia Forum*, October 31, 2010.
40 For details of these and related disputes see, the articles by James J. Przystup on Japan–China relations in *Comparative Connections*, for the years 2008–10.
41 For details see, ibid., January 2010.
42 Calder and Min Ye, *The Making of Northeast Asia*.
43 Banyan, "The Shogun and the Emperor", *The Economist*, December 10, 2010.
44 Tony Sekiguchi and George Nishiyama, "Japan's PM warns China on Dispute," *Wall Street Journal*, September 25, 2012.
45 Richard C. Bush examines a whole range of dysfunctional institutional arrangements that need to be addressed if China and Japan are to overcome the obstacles to reducing tensions, let alone overcoming their rivalry in his *Perils of Proximity: China–Japan Security Relations* (Washington, DC: Brookings Institution Press, 2010).

Chapter 5

Partnership and rivalry in regional institutions

The regional institutions of East Asia are often regarded as being relatively soft in character. Unlike those associated with the Western variety, they are not based on legally binding rules and procedures. They operate by consensus and such resolutions as they may produce are not binding on member states. These institutions are designed to enhance statehood and sovereignty, unlike say the African Union, which regularly sends troops into the countries of fellow members to uproot terrorism as in Somalia, or to help overcome violence against civilians as in Sudan, let alone the EU, whose member states "pool sovereignty." Instead the East Asian regional organizations operate on the principle of non-interference in each other's domestic affairs. Many of them are based on, or linked to, ASEAN (the Association of Southeast Asian Nations) founded in 1967 – the only multilateral regional organization from the Cold War period to survive. Such economic integration as has taken place in the region owes little to formal multilateral intergovernmental organizations. Rather it has been driven by businesses of various kinds that have built up across border chains of production and other economic linkages.

It is the relative looseness of these regional institutions that has made them attractive to both China and Japan. Neither has been willing to alter what each has regarded as the fundamentals of its domestic system to meet the demands of other states. China in particular has resisted external pressure, which its leaders sense might threaten Communist Party rule. Japan with its neo-mercantilist economy has also been resistant to external pressure to change some of its key features. However, the approaches of China and Japan towards regional institutions have been quite different. As a relatively isolated country that was still constrained diplomatically in the region because of the legacy of its aggressive wars, Japan sought to embed itself in East Asia through soft regional institutions and enhance its economic and political influence. China, on the other hand, valued membership of regional institutions as they provided a means to assuage fears of China's rise, to promote regional stability and expand Chinese influence.

It was not until the latter half of the 1990s that it became apparent that China and Japan became rivals as well as partners in these regional organizations and in the region as a whole. Until then Japan was able to pursue an informal leading role as the so-called head of a flock of flying geese. But after the bursting of its economic bubble in 1991 and its failure to recover, the luster of its economic model was lost. As Japan turned more inward it lost much of the vitality it had hitherto displayed in Southeast Asia in particular. Ironically it was just at this time that China began its new policy of cultivating its neighbors, especially those in Southeast Asia. In comparison with an apparently stagnant Japan, China was visibly the major country on the rise. It was this sense of a rising China and a stagnating Japan that set the stage for an emerging rivalry between the two even though they were also partners in many respects.

They became competitors for influence and status as each sought to use its largely economic assets to gain advantage. However, each of the two great regional powers carried a mixed baggage of assets and liabilities in their dealings with the region. In addition to the long shadow cast by China's past imperial attempts to impose its superiority over the region's centers of authority, contemporary China had encouraged subversion during the Maoist period and it had territorial and maritime disputes with several counties in Southeast Asia. China had also resorted to the use of force several times in support of its claims. The ethnic Chinese resident in Southeast Asia has been both an asset and a liability. On the positive side, they have been China's principal economic interlocutors in the region as well as the providers of needed investment. Against that they have sometimes been seen as less than fully loyal to their countries of residence and in that sense they have sometimes been liabilities for the Chinese mainland, which has then faced the dilemma of either supporting fellow ethnic Chinese and risking good relations with the relevant Southeast Asian state, or of favoring relations with the state and thereby risking the wrath of nationalists back home.

China's main assets were its growing significance as the dynamic economic hub for the region and its rising power. As the major regional power China was able to ensure that no Southeast Asian state challenged its position on Taiwan or on other key interests that did not involve regional states directly. China was also able to take advantage of the desire of ASEAN states to engage with it and to socialize it into accepting regional norms of cooperation and conflict avoidance. The regional engagement of China also had the effect of imposing on China reciprocal obligations since it was effectively faced with the alternatives of gaining the trust of resident states or of dealing with a situation in which they would seek to balance against its power by looking to the United States and to Japan. From about 1995 until the aftermath of the 2008 financial crisis China did in fact seek to cultivate ASEAN countries with much success, but following the crisis China became more assertive in the region in 2009–10 with the result that most of the ASEAN countries sought to balance against it with the United States and Japan. However, the ASEAN states did not wish to see a confrontation between the two giants in which they had to choose between them. By this stage China had become their most important economic partner and it was well understood that China was a permanent geographical presence, whereas the United States, on the other side of the Pacific, could choose to place less emphasis on Southeast Asia.

Unlike China, Japan had no territorial disputes or maritime claims in Southeast Asia. But it did have such disputes with each of its neighbors in Northeast Asia, which as we shall see in the next chapter, constrained its diplomatic maneuverability considerably. Similarly, the historical memory of Japan's wartime aggression was less of an obstacle to the cultivation of good relations in Southeast Asia than in Northeast Asia. Thus Japan encountered less distrust in its dealings with Southeast Asian countries than China. However, in the 1960s and 1970s Japan tended to be regarded with a degree of suspicion, as its major companies appeared focused entirely on their own interests, leading to the charge that the Japanese were "economic animals." It was not until Prime Minister Takeo Fukuda's visit in 1977 (after the communist victories in Indo-China) when he committed Japan to building "heart to heart" understandings with the ASEAN countries that Japanese diplomacy began to respond more actively to their interests.[1]

Japan's main assets in Southeast Asia lay primarily in the economic realm where it became the promoter of economic development and its economic system was widely seen as a model. Japanese investment in the region including the transfer of manufacturing capacity and trade increased markedly after the abrupt increase in the value of its currency in 1985. However, once Japan came to be seen as economically stagnant in the early 1990s it lost much of the attractive gloss it once had. To be sure Japan remained a leading trade partner and a major source of investment, and a key source for the transfer of advanced technology and managerial knowhow, but the general impression was that its influence had decreased. Japan clearly lacked the historical standing and political/strategic weight of the Chinese giant. Nevertheless Japan offered a useful economic balance against dependence on China. At the same time the logic of the economic links forged through chains of production ensured that Sino-Japanese competition in the region was tempered by the need to promote common economic interests and to establish institutional mechanisms of cooperation. After all, their economies were complementary rather than competitive. But in reaction to Chinese military pressure over the disputed Senkaku/Diaoyu Islands the Japanese sought to deepen ties in Southeast Asia with countries who were subject to similar pressure. In particular it agreed to transfer patrol boats to the Philippines. Thus Sino-Japanese regional competition is being extended to the geopolitical arena.

Japan's early leading role

The early stages of the Japanese economic "miracle" relied heavily on privileged access to the American market, while protecting its own market through a mixture of tariff and non-tariff barriers. By the 1960s Japan began to emerge as an economically developed country, but one that was nevertheless relatively isolated. Japan had already developed important economic relations with Southeast Asian countries in which they had gone beyond trade in Southeast Asian raw materials for Japanese manufacturers to more complex economic exchanges involving Japanese investment and the setting up of industrial enterprises.

Lacking organized links with countries other than the United States and still faced with a legacy of hostility in the larger East Asian region arising from its recent history of aggression in the 1930s and 1940s, Japan had to approach the building of regional institutions with a degree of caution. Japanese began the active pursuit of establishing regional organizations, which would mark their acceptance as a legitimate fully fledged player in regional community building by focusing initially on non-intergovernmental sectors such as business corporations, academics, journalists and officials acting in a non-official capacity among other developed economies in the Pacific. These included the business oriented Pacific Basin Economic Council established in 1967, for the then five Pacific members of the Organisation for Economic Co-operation and Development (OECD): Japan, Australia, New Zealand, Canada and the United States. The following year the organization of Pacific Trade and Development (PAFTAD) was established primarily for academics under the sponsorship of Foreign Minister Takeo Miki. A major breakthrough in relations with Southeast Asian countries occurred in 1977 when Prime Minister Takeo Fukuda visited the region in the wake of criticism of the hard-nosed economic behavior of Japanese companies. He stressed Japan's commitment to peace and committed Japan to support the region as an equal partner with ASEAN and indeed ODA to Southeast Asian countries was doubled in the next five years. The new partnership with ASEAN was facilitated by Japan's security alliance with the United States particularly as the Southeast Asians sought assurance after the victories of the communist forces in Indo-China in 1975, following the American withdrawal from Vietnam two years earlier.[2]

It was not until 1980, when Japan had become the economic hub for the region, that it was able to establish the Pacific Economic Cooperation Council (PECC), which included officials as well as academics and business people. But it too did not involve the formal participation of governments and, however useful it may have been for networking and for the generation of ideas and blueprints through study groups, none of the resolutions or recommendations was binding on governments. However, in most cases their respective governments funded the unofficial national committees that represented their countries. By this stage the primary reason for the failure to develop an Asian-Pacific intergovernmental organization was the resistance of the ASEAN countries. As less developed countries, they feared being overwhelmed by the developed ones and they were also afraid that their relatively weak grouping might be weakened still further. At the same time the OECD members of the Asian-Pacific economies, which collectively were becoming more significant in the world economy, did not want to appear to be forming a rich man's club by setting up an economic grouping without the less developed countries of the region. However, there was a growing sense that all the countries would benefit from a grouping in which they could consult each other and examine ways in which they could coordinate trade and other related activities.

The PECC seemed to provide a perceived need and it was boosted by China's membership in 1985. This was the first regional grouping that China joined. In a pattern that was to be repeated, the Chinese side insisted as a condition of its membership that Taiwan be represented in such a way as not to undermine the claim that Taiwan was a part of China. However, it was precisely because PECC was technically a non-governmental organization that the two committees of Taiwan and China could attend as nominal equals.[3]

The first intergovernmental region wide organization was the Asia-Pacific Economic Cooperation (APEC) forum. First mooted in January 1989 as a response to the fear of emerging trade blocs in Europe and in North America, both of which were perceived as having a negative effect on the East Asian economies for which they were the most important markets. It was this fear that helped overcome the reservations of ASEAN members. But they insisted that the governance of the proposed APEC be modeled on that of the ASEAN Way, which meant in effect that its findings or resolutions would not be binding on members.

Ostensibly it was created in November 1989 at the initiative of the Australians, but the key movers behind the scenes were the Japanese in the shape of the Ministry of International Trade and Industry. It was they too who facilitated the entry of China, together with "Chinese Taipei" and (the British colony) Hong Kong in 1991. China was still technically subject to sanctions by several of the Western members of the organization. For its part China was happy to join under these conditions as part of its rehabilitation after the Tiananmen massacre of June 4, 1989. But it was precisely the consensus-based decision-making process and the non-binding character of its resolutions that appealed to the Chinese side. It ensured that the other members could not "gang-up" on China as it meant in effect that the Chinese would not be made to accept policies against their wishes, while at the same time they could benefit from being accepted into the regional community, and from such programs of trade facilitation as APEC had to offer. From a Japanese perspective it was important to bring China in as a member in the expectation that it would absorb the market friendly practices of the other members and help integrate the huge country into the region.[4]

Japan was also instrumental behind the scenes in encouraging the establishment of the region's main security organization, the ASEAN Regional Forum (ARF). It stemmed from the Post Ministerial conference of an ASEAN meeting in 1993 (at which China was not present) and the inaugural meeting of the ARF, which took place the following year, included China as a founding member. The objectives outlined by its first chairman were consultative in nature: (1) "To foster constructive dialogue and consultation on political and security issues of common interest and concern"; and (2) "to make significant contributions towards confidence-building and preventative diplomacy." A "concept paper" was adopted in the following year, 1995, which emphasized the centrality of ASEAN and its norms. It sketched three stages for its evolution: beginning with confidence-building measures, proceeding from there through preventative diplomacy (a mechanism to identify potential points of conflict so as to minimize them), to ultimate conflict resolution mechanisms. The last was seen by the Chinese side as a bridge too far and, at its insistence, it was amended to read as the "elaboration of approaches to conflict." Although not all the major powers were happy with placing ASEAN in the driving seat, China was, as this was better for the pursuit of its interests than any other available leadership. The Chinese were also particularly pleased with the adoption of the ASEAN practice of ensuring that all participants were "comfortable" with the process and the speed of the consultation process. Japan and other members of the region accepted these arrangements, even though it meant at that point excluding collective discussion of all the conflicts to which China was a party, notably, Taiwan, the North Korean issue and sovereignty disputes in the East and South China Seas.[5]

A tacit bargain had been reached between China and the countries of the region whereby China would give up its great power advantage of dealing with them on a bilateral basis in return for gaining acceptance as a non-threatening member of the region. Other members of the region hoped that by inducting China for the first time into a multilateral regional security grouping it would become more attuned to the security interests of others in the region and become more socialized in the conflict avoidance norms of ASEAN in particular. From a Chinese perspective membership of the ARF would allow it to better cultivate its neighbors in order to advance its national interests and to prevent developments that may harm those interests.

Given that Japan's interests in the region and in Southeast Asia in particular were primarily economic and in avoiding any disruption of regional order that might threaten those interests, Japan clearly stood to gain from embedding a rising China in the multilateral groupings of the region. The expectation was that a China that was more closely engaged with the region would be less likely to be disruptive. By the same token, Japan had supported the participation of a potential rival in regional affairs. Japanese encouragement of Chinese membership of regional groupings took place in a period in which Japan was seen as the senior partner pursuing "friendship diplomacy" designed to encourage Chinese prosperity and stability. By the mid-1990s Japanese attitudes began to change as a more assertive China tested nuclear weapons and fired missiles across the Taiwan Strait.

China had its own interests in Southeast Asia during the Cold War era in which these were largely subordinated to its larger problems with the two superpowers. These were reflected in the Maoist era in part by the support of revolutionary movements in some Southeast Asian countries and in part by its opposition to the establishment of bases in the region at first by the United States and later by the Soviet Union. China attacked Vietnam briefly in 1979 to "teach it a lesson" for seeking to dominate Indo-China with the support of the Soviet Union, thereby contributing to China's sense of encirclement. In the 1980s China and the ASEAN countries became virtual diplomatic allies in opposition to Vietnam and the regime it had imposed on Cambodia. Related to that, China in this time used force to occupy disputed islands with Vietnam in 1974 (the Paracels, then occupied in part by the soon to be defunct South Vietnam) and in 1988 (eight islands in the Spratlys). However, after the Tiananmen disaster and the disintegration of the Soviet Union, China reached out to the Southeast Asian neighbors as part of its new good neighbor policies. It also began to take an interest in ASEAN itself, becoming a founding member of the ARF in 1994. Although its military were found to have occupied a reef (ironically named "Mischief Reef") in the Spratlys, within 120 miles of the coast of the Philippines (well within its EEZ), the Chinese took care not to take over any others after that.[6]

China was also guided by other major considerations, which shaped its policies independently of the potential competition with Japan. These included the determination to ensure that Southeast Asian states should not challenge Beijing's position on Taiwan and that they should not carry out policies that were inimical to China's basic national interest. In the case of the former, Beijing objected to attempts to allow formal Taiwanese representation in regional bodies and to any discussion of security issues involving the island, which it defined as China's domestic affair. As China's power and influence grew it also insisted that no visits should take place between Taiwanese and Southeast Asian leaders even on an informal basis. Beijing also objected to the establishment of American bases in the sub-region after the withdrawal from its bases in the Philippines in 1992.[7] In other words, Southeast Asia and its various countries were important for China's direct security concerns. Japan by comparison saw the region as important for its security in a less direct way. In addition to such economic interests as it had, Japan saw the maintenance of order and the freedom of navigation through the region as of major strategic significance. Thus neither China nor Japan was prepared to concede to the other dominance or hegemony of Southeast Asia.

The beginnings of Sino-Japanese regional rivalry 1995–2000

Despite remaining as the most or second most important economic partner for the majority of the East Asian economies, Japan had lost much of its attractiveness.[8] This coincided with the emergence of a more nationalist and assertive China, which was keen to establish itself as a separate partner of Southeast Asian countries. China and Japan as the two great powers of East Asia soon began to compete for influence in the region. But it was a competition that was qualified by a degree of partnership. Their economies were both caught up in chains of production and distribution involving all the other East Asian countries where they occupied different but interdependent positions. Japan with its highly advanced technology and service industries was at the top of the value added chain, with China as the intermediary involving the Southeast Asian countries. At the same time the bilateral relationship of China and Japan included mutual engagement as well as rivalry. Neither could allow degrees of antipathy and distrust to overwhelm other dimensions of their relationship. Like its strategic ally, the United States, Japan had a complex relationship with China combining both engagement and deterrence or hedging. China too had to temper its rivalry with Japan with cooperation in order to sustain its "good neighbor" policy, to promote a peaceable international environment and to continue to enhance economic growth at home, on which continued CCP rule ultimately depended.

It is important to recognize that China's dealings with ASEAN continued to be shaped by its larger foreign policy considerations. Thus the Chinese government agreement for the first time in 1995 that the question of the South China Sea could be discussed collectively with ASEAN arose from its relative diplomatic weakness due to its military actions against Taiwan and its secret occupation of Mischief Reef in the Spratlys. Although both before and subsequently Beijing has claimed that the sovereignty disputes over the islands in the South China Sea have to be addressed on a bilateral basis, it conceded that the modalities of conduct in the South China Sea could be subject to multilateral agreements. The concession, which has since served Chinese interests well, was made at the time to avoid diplomatic isolation.[9] The following year China became a formal dialogue partner of ASEAN, like the other major powers. As seen from the ASEAN countries, their role was to try and balance relations between the great powers in their region. That also suited the great powers, as they could not reconcile their conflicting interests sufficiently so as to allow any one of them to assume a leadership role in regional activities or associations. That is why ASEAN tended to take the lead despite its relative weakness and divisions between its members.

However, the 1997 Asian financial crisis (AFC) was a turning point in the relations between the ASEAN countries and China and Japan. China's role was much praised for not devaluing its currency (which was not in its interest anyway) as this was said to have helped stabilize the situation. China also contributed $1 billion to the regional rescue package of $11 billion to Thailand. It was highly praised perhaps because that was the first instance of a Chinese deliberate contribution to safeguarding regional order and security. By contrast Japan was seen to have suffered a setback because its offer to establish an Asian Monetary Fund to be capitalized by $100 billion was rejected by its ally the US (incidentally supported in its opposition by China). Japan's contribution of $4 billion to the Thai rescue package, followed by a total contribution to crisis affected Asian countries of $42 billion received far less attention than China's relatively tiny amount. Attention was also drawn to Japan's relative economic stagnation.[10] At issue was the fact that the ASEAN countries had become indebted to Japan in the late 1980s after the revaluation of the Japanese currency in 1985 and much of the Japanese new contribution of capital was to facilitate repayment of that debt. The deeper problem was that the Japanese economy had not recovered from the collapse of the asset bubble of 1991 and could not act as a market or a new supplier to the ASEAN economies. In stark contrast to Japan, China was emerging as a major source for economic exchanges with the ASEAN countries, aided and abetted by their economically powerful ethnic Chinese communities. They were not only effective makers of deals, especially with places in southern China, from which their families had migrated many years earlier, but they were also major investors in China, and this paved the way for growing trade.[11]

The AFC was also marked by East Asian disenchantment with Washington both because the US did not offer financial assistance and because the IMF impositions seemed to favor the reckless overseas lenders at the expense of the Asian peoples. It marked the beginning of the disenchantment with the so-called "Washington consensus." Perhaps not surprisingly, the AFC also occasioned the coming together of the East Asian countries of ASEAN Plus Three (China, Japan and South Korea) at the ASEAN heads of government meeting in December 1997. An earlier proposal in 1989 by Malaysia to set up an East Asia Group (subsequently modified to East Asia Caucus) in APEC had been rejected by the United States and Japan because it was seen as a political device to marginalize the Pacific countries and in particular the US. But under the new conditions the East Asians clearly felt that a greater degree of self-reliance was needed and that they could do without the participation of the United States.

Beginning as an informal meeting of the foreign ministers of the thirteen countries on the sidelines of the ASEAN Ministerial Meetings, the ASEAN Plus Three (APT) provided the first forum for Southeast and Northeast Asian policy-makers to meet. The APT started with financial cooperation; in particular it explored further the earlier Japanese proposal to establish an Asian Monetary Fund. The Chinese were persuaded to agree in May 1998 to the establishment in principle of an East Asian Fund, as a currency swap arrangement. After consultation among the Prime Ministers of China, Japan and South Korea on the sidelines of the APT in December 1999 it was agreed to set up the currency swap which in 2000 came to be called the Chiang Mai Initiative. The three Northeast Asian countries were the major foreign currency holders and it made sense for them to meet independently, and indeed this set the precedent for institutionalizing the process, which, as we shall see, did not bear fruit until several years later in the form of specific trilateral agreements. Meanwhile it had been shown that China and Japan could cooperate in the larger regional interest despite the competitive dimension of their relationship.

As seen from the perspective of ASEAN countries, access to the Chinese market compensated for what was seen as the divergence of FDI from Southeast Asian countries to China and competition with China for the advanced markets of America, Japan and Europe.[12] Nevertheless the economic relationship with Japan was still important, as its remaining investments in the region were still considerable even though its share of total FDI had dropped from about 28 percent in 1991 to 18.4 percent in 2001. Japanese FDI had contributed to the building of infrastructure and to technology transfers, which all helped to establish a trilateral basis for economic exchanges between ASEAN, China and Japan. Nevertheless China was gradually outpacing Japan in trade with ASEAN.[13]

It was only in the 1990s that China began to forge close relations with the countries of Southeast Asia and with ASEAN. It did so rapidly and, in economic terms, it soon began to catch up and eventually surpass Japan and the United States even though they had been engaged with ASEAN and with the region much longer. The Chinese displayed diplomatic skill in overcoming the distrust still held by many of the ASEAN countries.[14] In particular they embraced the ASEAN style of multilateralism, even to the extent of discussing the modalities of behavior in the South China Sea, despite continuing to insist that specific disputes over sovereignty could be dealt with only on a bilateral basis. They proposed a new consultative security concept in 1997 that was designed to assuage fears of a rising China, but that did not entirely remove suspicions that Beijing sought to supplant Washington and Tokyo, as the proposal was first initiated as an alternative to East Asia's "outdated Cold War alliances." Once, however, this was pointed out to them in Singapore, China's leaders dropped such references to the American alliances in promoting its new concept.[15] But the suspicion remained that China was seeking to reduce and perhaps remove the American strategic presence and leave the resident Southeast

Asian states defenseless against mighty China. Due to its alliance with the United States, Japanese influence in the region came to be seen in an even more positive light.

Partnership and rivalry 2001–08: Southeast Asia

The continuing rapid economic rise of China led to it becoming the economic hub of East Asia. But given the economic interdependence between China and Japan, China's new pivotal economic role did not lead to a widening of the gap between the major countries in either their bilateral or multilateral economic relations in East Asia. To the contrary this led to an intensification of intra-Asian economic relations relative to those relations with the United States. The dynamics of intra-East Asia trade and investment surpassed those of their relations with America. For example, in 1990 only 8 percent of Japanese exports were sent to China and South Korea as compared with 32 percent to the US; in the year 2006 the balance of exports to the two destinations were about the same; but in 2008 the value of Japanese exports to its two Northeast Asian neighbors reached $184 billion as compared to only $139 billion to the US.[16] A similar pattern can be observed in ASEAN's trade relationship with China, Japan and the United States. According to ASEAN statistics its trade in 2009 with China and Japan was valued at $176 billion and $161 billion respectively, as compared with $150 billion with the United States.[17]

The emergence of East Asian and, in some respects, Asian economic regionalism has been widely noted.[18] As the two greatest regional powers and the second and third largest economies in the world, China and Japan have been at the heart of this new Asian regionalism. But that should not be allowed to disguise the fact that the two remained rivals despite their interconnectedness and their respective efforts to promote regionalism. Indeed it has been argued that Sino-Japanese rivalry itself, as expressed in terms of "competitive leadership," has been an important driver of regional economic integration.[19]

The rivalry between China and Japan is not openly declared, but it is nonetheless real. They have competed in establishing FTAs with ASEAN as a whole, with its member states and with others in the broader Asia-Pacific. China tended to take the initiative in first proposing free trade agreements, with Japan playing catch-up. Japan also sought to reduce Chinese influence in continental Southeast Asia, where China has the advantage of contiguity. As previously noted, China and Japan openly promoted alternative visions for the composition of an East Asian grouping. Japan has also countered Chinese attempts to establish exclusive rights in the South China Sea and finally, Japan has sought to consolidate security relations with others in response to China's rise as a military power.

As part of its policy of cultivating neighboring countries and Southeast Asia in particular, China proposed in December 2000 to establish an FTA with ASEAN as a whole (the first country to do so), which was soon known as ASEAN + 1, and an agreement was reached in 2002 for the FTA to be implemented in 2010. Among the goals of China's leaders was to expunge Southeast Asian fears of the so-called "China threat." They also were concerned to demonstrate that China's entry into the WTO in 2001 would provide opportunities rather than challenges to their economies. The Chinese focused on economic exchanges that would benefit the Southeast Asian countries with the political aim of building trust. Japan attempted to follow suit by proposing its own FTA with ASEAN in January 2002. Negotiations began in 2005 and were completed two and a half years later. Called a "Comprehensive Economic Partnership Agreement," it covered not only trade, but also services and investment. Japan's FTA diplomacy suffered to a certain extent in comparison with China's because the domestic political strength of Japan's rural sector led to the exclusion of most agricultural goods. China also benefited from the fact that its economic ties with the ASEAN countries were increasing at a much faster rate than those of Japan. For example, in the period 2000–06 the trade volume between China and ASEAN rose annually by 12.4 percent as compared with only 3 percent by Japan.[20]

Many FTAs of a bilateral character in the Asia-Pacific accompanied these multilateral agreements. These were so diverse (often characterized as a "spaghetti bowl") as to militate against the development of a collective regional approach in accordance with the norms of the World Trade Organization.[21] These FTAs worked against regional multilateralism as they not only had different definitions of the terms of trade, such as the sources of origin of goods and resources, but they also formalized the different comparative advantages between states on a bilateral rather than a multilateral basis. China and Japan have competed with each other in reaching FTAs in Southeast Asia, with China focusing primarily on tariff reductions with the effect of enhancing the attraction of access to its markets and of easing access to Southeast Asian markets for its manufacturers. Japan has tended to focus more on playing to its strengths of services, investment with trade being more problematic.

However, China contributed greatly to a sense of emerging regional order by signing in 2002 the Declaration on the Code of Conduct of Parties in the South China Sea. Although the Code was not binding, by signing the formal declaration the Chinese officially conceded that the behavior of the contestants for sovereignty in the South China Sea was a matter of multilateral concern even if it held onto its view that negotiations over sovereignty could only be addressed on a bilateral basis. In 2002 China and ASEAN also agreed a Joint Declaration on Cooperation in the Field of Non-Traditional Security. China improved its regional image still further in 2003 by being the first outsider to sign ASEAN's Treaty of Amity and Cooperation (TAC), which involved a commitment to settle disputes peacefully. For its part, Japan had been active in convening ASEAN countries to counter piracy in the South China Sea, but both Chinese and Japanese proposals to contribute to providing security in the Straits of Malacca were rejected by the resident states as infringements on their sovereignty, but nevertheless Japanese technical assistance was welcomed by all three of the relevant states (Indonesia, Malaysia and Singapore). Japan signed up to TAC a year after China.

The Chinese side had a head start in the competition for influence over continental Southeast Asia. Its adjoining provinces of Yunnan and Guangxi sought resources from the Indo-Chinese countries and Burma (Myanmar), which also involved building infrastructure projects to improve access and to solidify cross-border lines of communication on a north–south axis, with the goal of eventually reaching Singapore. Much of the Chinese effort has focused on cultivating the countries along the Mekong River. Rising in Tibet, more than half of the river is located in Yunnan before it flows through Myanmar, Laos, Thailand, Cambodia and Vietnam. The Chinese began building dams in the upper reaches of the river in 1986 and their approach received a major impetus when the Asian Development Bank (ADB) advocated the establishment of the Greater Mekong Subregion grouping in 1992. Annual ministerial meetings have been held since then including occasional summit meetings. Many agreements have been reached covering cooperation in transportation, trade investment, environmental protection, human resource development and so on. According to a Chinese source, $100 billion had been spent by the end of 2007 on 180 cooperative projects (of which $76 billion had been granted by the ADB).[22]

Japan was a relative latecomer as a competitor to China in the Mekong Subregion, although it had long been a major investor and trading partner of all the countries of the subregion. Beginning in 1995 Japan organized conferences and workshops including at the ministerial level. From 2001 onwards Japan together with the ADB began to develop an "East–West Economic Corridor," which ten years later was "well on the way to completion as a physical infrastructure." It also announced the development of a trunk road from Ho Chi Minh City to Bangkok via Phnom Penh as the "Second East West Corridor." Like their Chinese counterparts, Japan, together with the ADB, has invested considerable sums on a wide range of projects in pursuit of its east–west projects (in contrast to China's north–south initiatives).[23]

None of the countries of the Mekong River Subregion are content to be dominated by China, especially in view of what is seen as Chinese high-handed unilateralism in building dams in the higher reaches of the river without due regard to the adverse repercussions to the countries downstream.[24] From that perspective Japan's activities in the subregion are welcome by the resident states, as are those by others such as India. Japan's endeavors in the subregion have been officially presented as its contribution to narrowing the gap between the less developed and more developed countries of ASEAN, but they clearly serve the purpose of limiting these countries' dependence on China.

Northeast Asia

The Northeast Asian subregion was an entirely different arena for Sino-Japanese cooperation and competition as it involved the intersection of the strategic interests of all the great powers in the region and the "hot spots" of Taiwan and the two Koreas. In addition the magnitude of the interdependence of the three great economies of East Asia (China, Japan and South Korea), which became clear in the twenty-first century brought the three closer together despite their political and strategic differences. In terms of purchasing power parity (PPP) the three (plus Hong Kong and Taiwan) in 2009 accounted for 21 percent of the world's GDP and 18.3 percent of world trade.[25] It is not surprising, therefore, that the three should have found means of working together on a regular basis in order to address shared functional interests. Moreover in their different ways each of the three had profound domestic political interests invested in their inter-related economies. Continued economic growth was deemed essential to the maintenance of Communist Party rule in China, while both the Korean and Japanese governments recognized that their political fortunes were linked to economic performance.

The strategic issues of Sino-Japanese relations will be addressed more fully in the next chapter. But it is important to recognize that many aspects of the economic relationships had strategic overtones, which necessarily impacted adversely on their capacity to institutionalize their modes of cooperation. For example, relations between Japan and Taiwan remained suspect from Beijing's point of view even if they were confined to the non-official dimensions of economic, cultural and people-to-people exchanges. Since the 1980s the Chinese Ministry of Foreign Affairs has consistently listed Taiwan as one of the problems in relations with Japan, in part because of possible remaining attachments from when Taiwan was a colony of Japan (1895–1945) and in part because of suspicion that Japan (in association with the United States) seeks to keep the island separate from the PRC.

Less overtly, China and Japan have been inherent competitors for influence over the future of the Korean peninsular, at least to the extent of seeking to deny a controlling influence to the other. Historically Korea has been the gateway to attacks on each other, whether as far back as the Yuan Dynasty's failed attacks on Japan in the thirteenth century or the more recent Japanese attacks on China 700 hundred years later in the twentieth century. Ironically, in their different ways both China and Japan have contrived to antagonize South Koreans because of their separate narratives about nationhood. China brought to an end the South Korean "China fever" of the turn of the century by claiming in 2003 the ancient kingdom of Koguryo (or Goguryeo) as Chinese, thereby enraging both North and South Koreans who had long regarded it as one of the precursors of Korea itself.[26] Japan, meanwhile, had antagonized Koreans by claiming ownership of Dokdo/Takeshima (rocky outcrops in the sea between the two countries that were administered by South Korea) on the basis of pre-modern history and in particular on an agreement made with a Korean government in 1905, which was in effect a Japanese protectorate arising from its victory in the 1985 war with China.[27] The Japanese claim had the added insult of reminding Koreans of their brutal annexation by Japan.

As noted earlier, China, Japan and South Korea first began to cooperate together under the auspices of ASEAN in the aftermath of the Asian Financial Crisis in 1997. However, given their collective economic weight, their ministers began to meet outside the ASEAN framework from 1999 onwards as encouraged by their remarkable president and two prime ministers, Kim Dae Jung, Zhu Rongji and Keizo Obuchi, respectively. Annual meetings between their leaders were then held to consult and cooperate on broad economic issues such as trade, finance, energy, telecommunications, labor, social welfare and so on. These were reinforced by China's Bo'ao annual forums (often dubbed as Asia's equivalent to the Davos meetings) first set up in 2001. Indeed it was at Bo'ao 2002 that Japan's Prime Minister Koizumi quelled Japanese concerns about the dangers posed by China's economic rise by declaring that these were overblown and that in fact the Chinese economy should be seen as offering opportunities to Japan. In fact the 2 percent or so of economic growth in Japan in the early years of the twenty-first century owed much to the interchange with China.

At the fifth high-level meeting of the "Plus Three" in 2003 a joint declaration was issued on the Promotion of Tripartite Cooperation among Japan, the People's Republic of China and the Republic of Korea, setting in motion specific plans for cooperation. However, following the sixth summit in 2004 such summits were suspended for two years, because of the deterioration of relations between China and Japan and even between Japan and South Korea. Meetings were resumed after Abe's "ice-breaking" visit to China in 2006. Perhaps the most significant tripartite summit was the ninth, which was held in Fukuoka, Japan on December 23, 2008, as this was the first time that they met separately from ASEAN. A large number of documents was issued committing the three to action plans for cooperation in a wide range of matters including finance, investment, energy, logistics, air and marine pollution, maritime search and rescue, the management of disasters and health. They agreed to institutionalize the relationship by having regular annual summit meetings between the three. They also pledged to promote people-to-people exchanges focusing particularly on youth. Agreements were made to widen the scope of the tripartite institution by holding meetings between cabinet officials and high-level bureaucrats on a regular basis.[28] At the 2011 summit meeting it was agreed to establish a secretariat in Seoul and in May 2012 the three agreed to begin work towards establishing an FTA between them.

The development of Northeast Asian regionalism was driven not only by the logic of the overlapping interests of the three countries but also by the coincidence of changes in the domestic politics of all three countries. In the case of China a new emphasis on development of the country's own northeast (Manchuria) was associated with the leadership changes from the Jiang Zemin administration to that led by Hu Jintao from 2003 onward. South Korea's embrace of regionalism was prompted by the rapidity of the growth of its economic engagement with China beginning in roughly 2002–03 as encouraged by big business and supported by successive presidents from the more leftist Roh Tae Woo from 2003 and the more conservative Lee Myung-bak from 2008.[29] Although Japan remained ambivalent about the orientation towards Asia and weakened by its dysfunctional political system, it was the breakthrough in relations with China carried out surprisingly by the more right-wing leaders of the LDP in 2006–08 that paved the way.

The tripartite institution must be seen primarily as a vehicle for managing functional economic and social relations between the three major Northeast Asian countries. It is not a venue for addressing defense and security issues. It may be suggested that there is an inevitable spill over between deepening economic ties and promoting greater security in the sense that increasing economic interdependency can only be possible on the basis of the maintenance of a degree of order in the region. But it should be noted that the period from late 2008 through 2012 has been marked in the region by an increase in military and strategic tension in the region, centering on what has been regarded as enhanced Chinese military assertiveness and the reaction against it by South Korea and Japan who have drawn closer to the United States as a hedge against Chinese activism. Perhaps the more important point is that the new tripartite framework of cooperation not only survived the challenges of both the international financial crisis and the increased Chinese military and diplomatic assertiveness of 2009 and 2010, but that it also prospered and deepened.

Despite the heightened strategic tensions with China and the deepening of relations between the allies of Northeast Asia, China, Japan and South Korea were still able to press ahead with their wide ranging action plans of tripartite cooperation as set out in the Fukuoka agreements of December 2008. In less than three months after the shelling by the North and of the Senkaku/Diaoyu incident, which had so antagonized South Korea and Japan, they signed an agreement with China to establish a "three way cooperation secretariat" in Seoul the following year.[30] The terrible triple disaster of an earthquake, a tsunami and the radiation leaks at the Fukushima Daiichi nuclear plant that took place on March 11, 2011 provided opportunities for both China and South Korea to provide assistance. However, notwithstanding their closer collaboration over the disaster, the Northeast Asian states continued to register dissatisfaction with each other over long-standing complaints. Thus Japan protested the buzzing of one of its destroyers by a Chinese State Administration helicopter near disputed waters; and South Korea "strongly protested" newly approved Japanese school textbooks for claiming sovereignty of the Dokdo/Takeshima. Indeed it was South Korean objections to Japanese claims to the rocky islands that stopped the two sides from signing a much needed agreement on sharing intelligence about North Korea.[31]

Conclusion

Within the context of China's rise and Japan's relative decline the two major powers of East Asia both competed and cooperated in the various regional organizations and groupings in Southeast and Northeast Asia. The rivalry between the two was mitigated in part by the depth of their economic interdependency and in part by the geopolitics of East

Asia in which China had to balance against the perceived hegemony of the United States. Furthermore China had to contain its nationalistic passions if it were to ensure that its neighborhood would continue to be sufficiently tranquil to enable its economy to grow so as to provide sufficient domestic stability to undergird continued rule by the Communist Party. Japan too found that despite its deepening distrust of China's growing power it had to engage China for economic reasons and to prevent the enmity between them reaching unmanageable proportions.

Both China and Japan faced degrees of distrust in the region. Although China's leaders and historians tend to think of their imperial history as benign that is not the view of their neighbors in either Northeast or Southeast Asia, who can recount many past invasions and attempts to impose Chinese superiority by force. In the modern era, China supported insurgencies in Southeast Asia during the Maoist era and the Chinese and South Korean armies had fought in the Korean War in the 1950s. China attacked Vietnam in 1979 and it also forcibly evicted Vietnamese from islands in the South China Sea, where its territorial and maritime claims clash with others in the region. Japan may not be an immediate threat to its neighbors, but its aggression in the first half of the twentieth century has left scars which have yet to heal, especially in Northeast Asia. It is that combined with Japan's relative isolation derived from its dependence on the alliance with the United States, which caused Japan to be so active in promoting regional groupings in which it was able to use its economic pre-eminence to advantage. China's interest in regionalism was driven primarily by its interest in gaining acceptance as a benevolent regional power. In turn regional groupings were keen to accept China in the hope that it would become more attentive to regional concerns and that it might be socialized into adopting regional norms of behavior.

At first it seemed as if China was being integrated into regional norms of cooperative behavior. In 1995 it met with ASEAN as a whole to discuss the South China Sea, thus dropping its insistence that these issues could only be addressed bilaterally with each of the Southeast Asian maritime and territorial claimants. In 2002 it was a party to the Declaration on the Code of Conduct in the South China Sea. The Chinese also sought to charm the Southeast Asians thereafter. But the prospect of Chinese dominance returned to trouble the region, especially after its assertive behavior following the international financial crisis of 2008. Since then the Southeast Asians have sought to counter China by leaning more to the United States. In Northeast Asia too China flattered only to deceive the South Koreans especially. In the early years of the twenty-first century South Korean ties with China grew at such a pace as to engender what has been called a "China fever" in the South. But the favorable view of China paled after China claimed the ancient state of Kogyero as its own. Moreover the South Koreans began to see China as a rival for economic influence in North Korea. China's stewardship of the Six Party Talks, which the Chinese initiated in 2003, also began to trouble the South especially from 2008 onwards when China's leaders appeared to embrace the North in defiance of UN sanctions, culminating in supporting it over the sinking of a Korean naval vessel and the shelling of an island, causing civilian deaths. That, combined with Chinese assertive behavior in the East China Sea, led to a closer alignment between South Korea and Japan and also the United States. But relations between South Korea and Japan were also damaged by their competing nationalistic claims to sovereignty over the Dokdo/Takeshima Islands.

However, both ASEAN on the one side and Japan and South Korea on the other, have continued to cultivate Chinese membership of their regional groupings. The institutionalization of the tripartite grouping involving China, Japan and South Korea has continued even as troublesome incidents with China continue to take place. Similarly, the attempts on the side both of China and of its East Asian neighbors to build on previous forms of institutional cooperation, continue without interruption.

The apparent discrepancy between the trends of political economy and of national security involving China and the countries of East Asia should be understood in a wider context. First, the economies of China and its Asian neighbors are caught up in world-wide chains of production of which their regional interdependencies are a part. Their economic linkages are a necessary component of the performance of their domestic economies, which undergird the political standing of the leaders and in some cases of the political systems too. Second, China is in the middle of a highly complex series of domestic changes, whose outcome for its political and economic systems is uncertain. Domestic and external affairs are interlinked in ways that are not amenable to control. The outside world and especially China's neighbors, have an interest in avoiding a destabilizing change in China. Third, both China and its neighbors are adjusting to huge transitions in the global and regional order arising in East Asia from the rapid rise of China and the relative decline of Japan as combined with the shift of the center of the world's economic center of gravity towards the Asia-Pacific. Fourth, the United States has so far been the provider of the public goods for the East Asian region, including China, in the sense that it has been the guarantor of strategic stability and of maritime order, without which trade would be adversely affected. For much of the post-Cold War period the openness of the American market has been crucial for the success of the East Asian economies.

The international financial crisis of 2008 has brought to the fore a dilemma that arguably was already beginning to emerge. The value of trade and other economic exchanges between China and each of America's East Asian allies and partners (including Australia and New Zealand) has exceeded that which they have with the United States and the gap appears to be widening. Yet the stability and security of the region in the eyes of most of its members is dependent on maintaining the security links with the United States as a balance or a hedge against Chinese dominance. The security aspects of these changes will be addressed in the next chapter. But from the perspective of the development of Sino-Japanese relations the importance of cooperation in regional institutions cannot be over-stressed.

Cooperation in regional institutions provides opportunities to establish rules and norms to guide not only economic, but also educational, social and many other exchanges. Regular meetings of officials and leaders provide opportunities for building much needed personal linkages and trust. That is particularly important, as generational and political changes have brought to the fore leaders in the elites of both countries who have had fewer means of developing close personal relations as compared to their predecessors. Rivalry between these two very different countries with their very different political systems will doubtless continue and may even deepen, but the growing institutionalization of their relations, including within regional groupings and meetings, could provide mechanisms for reducing tensions and perhaps even addressing potential conflicts.

Notes

1 Sueo Sudo, *The Fukuda Doctrine and ASEAN: New Dimensions in Japanese Foreign Policy* (Singapore: Institute of South East Asian Studies, 1992).

2 See Jusuf Wanandi, "ASEAN–Japan Relations: The Underpinning of East Asian Peace and Stability," in Tadashi Yamamoto, Charles Morrison et al. (eds.), *ASEAN–Japan Cooperation: A Foundation for East Asian Community* (Tokyo: Japan Center for International Exchange, 2003), pp.3–17.
3 For an account of the establishment and processes of these early regional organizations see, Lawrence T. Woods, *Asia-Pacific Diplomacy: Nongovernmental Organizations and International Relations* (Canada: University of British Columbia Press, 1993).
4 For detailed analysis see, John Ravenhill, *APEC and the Construction of Pacific Rim Regionalism* (Cambridge: Cambridge University Press, 2001).
5 For the best account of its establishment see, Michael Leifer, *The ASEAN Regional Forum. Extending ASEAN's Model of Regional Security* (Adelphi Paper 302, IISS, Oxford University Press, July 1996).
6 For accounts of China's relations with Southeast Asian countries in this period see, Steven Levine, "China in Asia: The PRC as a regional Power," in Harry Harding (ed.), *China's Foreign Policy in the 1980s* (New Haven, CT: Yale University Press, 1984); and relevant chapters in Saw Swee-Hock et al. (eds.), *ASEAN China Relations: Realities and Prospects* (Singapore: ISEAS Publications, 2005) and Ho Kai Leong and Samuel C.T. Ku (eds.), *China and Southeast Asia* (Singapore: ISEAS, 2005).
7 It did not apparently object as strongly to the establishment of "places" (not bases), which could be available for temporary use by American forces, such as port facilities in Singapore, or pre-positioned supply depots elsewhere.
8 Linda Jakobson and Dean Knox, *New Foreign Policy Actors in China* (SIPRI Policy Paper No. 26, 2010).
9 Michael Leifer, "China, in Southeast Asia: Interdependence and Accommodation," in David S. G. Goodman and Gerald Segal (eds.), *China Rising: Nationalism and Interdependence* (London and New York: Routledge, 1997), pp.156–71.
10 François Godement, *The Downsizing of Asia* (London: Routledge, 1999), p.180.
11 Lim Hua Sing, *China & Japan in East Asian Integration* (Singapore: ISEAS, 5th edition, 2008), Chapters 12, 13 and 14, pp.271–304.
12 Anne Booth, "China and Southeast Asia: An Economic Perspective," in David Shambaugh (ed.), *Charting China's Future: Domestic and International Challenges* (London: Routledge, 2011), pp.117–24.
13 See Zhang Yunling, "The ASEAN Partnership with China and Japan," in Yamamoto, Morrison et al. (eds.), *ASEAN–Japan Cooperation*, pp.226–27.
14 See Evan Medeiros and Taylor Travel, "China's New Diplomacy," *Foreign Affairs*, November–December 2003. http://www.ou.edu/uschina/texts/FravelMedeiros2003NewDiplomacy.pdf. Accessed March 27, 2013.
15 Michael Yahuda, "The Evolving Asian Order," in David S. Shambaugh (ed.), *Power Shift: China and Asia's New Dynamics* (Berkeley: University of California Press, 2005), p.156.
16 Kent Calder and Min Ye, *The Making of Northeast Asia* (Palo Alto, CA: Stanford University Press, 2010), p.209.
17 Available via www.aseansec.org/. Accessed October 27, 2011.
18 For example, Calder and Ye, *The Making of Northeast Asia*; Naoko Munakata, *Transforming East Asia: The Evolution of Regional Economic Integration* (Washington, DC: Brookings Institution Press, 2006); T.J. Pempel, "Introduction: Emerging Webs of Regional Connectedness," in his (ed.), *Remapping East Asia: The Construction of a Region* (Ithaca, NY: Cornell University Press, 2005), pp.1–28; Kishore Mahbubani, *The New Asian Hemisphere: The Irresistible Shift of Global Power to the East* (New York: Public Affairs, 2008); and Saadia M. Pekkanen, "Asianism Rising," in Gerald Curtis, Ryosei Kokubun and Wang Jisi (eds.), *Getting the Triangle Straight: Managing China–Japan–US Relations* (Tokyo: Japan Center for International Exchange, 2010), pp.191–215.
19 Hidetaka Yoshimatsu, "Political Leadership, Informality, and Regional Integration in East Asia: The Evolution of ASEAN Plus Three," *European Journal of East Asian Studies* Vol. 4, No. 2, 2005, pp.205–32.
20 Lai Foon Wong, "China–ASEAN and Japan–ASEANB Relations during the Post-Cold War Era," *The Chinese Journal of International Politics* Vol. 1, No. 3, 2007, pp.373–404.

21 Razeen Sally, "Free trade agreements and the prospects for regional integration in East Asia," *Asian Economic Policy Review* Vol. 1, No. 2, 2006, pp.306–21.
22 *Xinhua*, "Country Report on China's Participation in Greater Mekong Subregion Cooperation," issued by the Chinese government and published by the *People's Daily*, March 28, 2008.
23 For details see the following drawn from the website of the Ministry of Foreign Affairs of Japan: "Japan's Cooperation for the Mekong Subregion Development" (2001), www.mofa.go.jp/region/asia-paci/asean/relation/subregion.html; and "Chair's Statement Mekong-Japan Foreign Ministers' Meeting" (2008), www.mofa.go.jp/rergion/asia-paci/Mekong/meet08021.html. Both accessed April 9, 2013.
24 Michael Richardson, "Dams in China Turn the Mekong Into a River of Discord," *Yale Global*, July 16, 2009; and Philip Hirsch, "China and the Cascading Geopolitics of Lower Mekong Dams," *Japan Focus*, May 16, 2011.
25 Calder and Min Ye, *The Making of Northeast Asia*, p.3, Table 1.1.
26 Scott Snyder, *China's Rise and the Two Koreas: Politics, Economics, Security* (Boulder, CO: Lynne Rienner, 2009), pp.94–97.
27 The basis of the Korean claim may be seen at "Pride of Korea – Dokdo," www.Dokdocorera.com; and for that of Japan see, Ministry of Foreign Affairs Japan, "Outline of Takeshima Issue." www.mofa.go.jp/region/asia-paci/takeshima/position.html. Accessed March 27, 2013.
28 Ryosei Kokubun, "The China–Japan Relationship. East Asia Community, and the Dynamics of Trilateral Relations," in Curtis et al. (eds.), *Getting the Triangle Straight*, pp.62–63.
29 Calder and Min Ye, *The Making of Northeast Asia*, Chapters 7 and 8, pp.163–83.
30 "Trilateral Cooperation," *Global Times* (Beijing), December 17, 2010.
31 Chico Harlan, "With China's Rise Japan Shifts to the Right," *Washington Post*, September 21, 2012.

Chapter 6

Strategic rivalry

The strategic rivalry between China and Japan, which was largely latent during the Cold War period, began to emerge in the 1990s and has gathered pace in the twenty-first century. China's growing economic and military power has given a sharper edge to its relations with a Japan perceived to be in relative decline. Long-standing disputes about maritime territorial claims have emerged as points of potential crisis. Japan's alliance with the United States has also come under greater pressure as Washington seeks to engage China as a fellow global power, while at the same time reassuring Japan and persuading Beijing that its alliance with Tokyo is not aimed at China. At the same time Washington's reaction to greater Chinese assertiveness in Northeast and Southeast Asia may be seen as reassuring neither. Beijing is fearful of Washington combining with Tokyo to limit its rise even as Washington seeks its cooperation; and at the same time Tokyo fears that Washington will reverse on its commitment to help defend the islands so as to maintain workable relations with Beijing. Should military incidents take place between Chinese and Japanese naval vessels, American pledges to come to the aid of its ally could be put to the test. The United States could be expected to seek to avoid military clashes with China, especially over uninhabited rocky islands of little strategic importance to the US. Washington has used its influence to urge both sides to step back from open hostilities. In the process, however, it is entirely possible that the value of the alliance may be questioned in Japan. Such issues were less of a problem during the Cold War when American and Japanese strategic interests in confronting the Soviet Union were congruent. In the current era the strategic interests of the two allies are not as closely aligned and the broader strategic situation in Northeast Asia is more fluid.

The demise of the Soviet Union had freed both China and Japan from lingering fears of an attack from the north and the end of the Cold War presaged a new re-positioning of the great powers and the unfettered expansion of the sweep of the forces of globalization. It was under these circumstances that, as we have seen in chapter 2, each of the countries began to forge new identities both at home and abroad. If China focused on developing the economy and becoming a great power, Japan was still circumscribed by the legacy of the "Yoshida Doctrine" in having to balance adherence to the Peace Constitution with being an effective ally of the United States, but in a new, uncertain and more fluid strategic situation. The new nationalism in China accentuated the growing divide with Japan, arousing negative responses from Japan. Japanese aspirations to becoming a permanent member of the UN Security Council and their attempt to be a more useful military ally to the United States, combined with the reluctance of many Japanese leaders to come to terms with the country's history of aggression towards China in particular, evoked suspicion and opposition in China.

China also began to develop as a maritime power. For nearly all its history, ancient and modern, China has been predominantly a continental power. Through the centuries China's leaders have understood the strategic dynamics of the balance between land, power, space and time. Mao's writings on strategy and warfare focus entirely on land matters. The current expansion of the Chinese navy from a coastal to a near coastal and now to a blue water navy is unprecedented. Unlike maritime powers, contemporary China has no experience of naval warfare. China has considerable experience of settling disputed borders and territories on land, but little of the maritime variety. The former have been agreed on a bilateral basis, where the underlying principles and rules may vary according to the strategic and tactical considerations of both sides. At sea, however, territorial and maritime claims have to be settled according to universal laws and norms. If Chinese claims did not always seem to be based on current International Law that was because the Chinese Foreign Ministry supported by Chinese legal scholars argued that International Law was set by the Western powers to serve their interests and they used that to seize Chinese maritime territory during the "hundred years of humiliation." Therefore the Chinese side argues that China is entitled to base its claims on historical evidence pre-dating the advent of the West.[1] The expansion of China's maritime interests has brought a new dimension to its strategic rivalry with Japan. The Chinese regard their forays into the Western Pacific Ocean as the initial steps to fulfill their strategic need to protect their sea routes and to control islands in the East and South China Seas over which they claim sovereignty. The Japanese in turn see the Chinese projection of force through straits between their islands as potentially threatening an encirclement of the Japanese archipelago. In the absence of formal or informal strategic understandings between these two great regional powers their relations appear embedded in strategic dilemmas of a structural kind, by which what is seen as a defensive measure by one side is seen as offensive by the other, requiring a response in kind.

China's naval ambitions of deploying in the Pacific Ocean are currently constrained because its navy could only gain access to the Western Pacific by going through international straits that bisect the Japanese archipelago. In so doing China's naval vessels are monitored closely by the Japanese side leading to the possibility that they might be subject to interdiction by Japan, especially in the event of increased tension, let alone armed conflict, involving the two. The Chinese therefore face the prospect of being confined to their coastal waters. Clearly that would be unacceptable to them, less because of the relationship with Japan, than because of the adverse strategic situation in which they would be placed in dealing with the United States especially over Taiwan. China's leaders regard the eventual unification with Taiwan as one of China's core interests and to this end they seek to prevent a possible military intervention by the United States through a strategy of what the Americans call "Anti Access and Area Denial" (A2/AD). Although some military specialists in both the US and China claim that advances in missile and other technology have superseded the strategic significance of these islands, both navies continue to regard them as vital.[2] From a Japanese perspective, the Chinese strategy could threaten the trade routes on which they depend and potentially it could even threaten to encircle the country, especially if it were to succeed in imposing unification upon Taiwan.

As far as the United States is concerned, its ability to deploy its forces in the Western Pacific and in East Asia is dependent on the maintenance of its alliance with Japan and the bases located there. The alliance with South Korea is not an adequate substitute, both because South Korea is located too far to the north in East Asia and because South

Korean interests are more narrowly focused on relations with the North and on maintaining a complex relationship with China. Consequently the US would not have the degree of latitude in East Asia provided by the location of its bases in Japan. The American strategic need to maintain bases in Japan means that it needs to pay heed to Japanese fundamental strategic interests, which in turn affect the Taiwan issue. Taiwan may not be a strategic asset for the United States, as it cannot provide bases for the American military and it is an obstacle to forging better relations with China. But Taiwan is of great strategic importance for Japan. One way in which the Chinese could enjoy unfettered access to the Pacific Ocean would be through the acquisition of Taiwan. From a Chinese perspective, that would free them from the constraints imposed by Japan, but at the same time the Japanese would once again face the danger of encirclement or the possible interdiction of the sea traffic on which the island country depends.

Notwithstanding the economic and political problems of the United States, which are likely to restrict the expansion of its military forces in the Asia-Pacific, American military power is likely to retain its predominance in the region for the foreseeable future, especially with cooperation of its allies and partners.[3] Consequently, the risk of war breaking out between contending regional powers is very low. The low risk of warfare involving China and Japan in particular is enhanced by their economic interdependence and the recognition by China's leaders that the potential disruption of the economy that would follow open warfare with Japan could well undermine Communist Party rule.

One consequence of these huge constraints against warfare between the significant powers in Northeast Asia is the possibility of low-key military incidents fired by nationalism, and driven by local politics in which leaders cannot afford to appear weak in handling disputes with neighbors. These political uncertainties have been aggravated by problems of governance in both China and Japan. In the former, domestic and external policy-making has become bedeviled by the difficulty of coordination between competing interests of powerful regional and economic bodies. In Japan a divided Diet, dysfunctional political parties and the continual rapid change of prime ministers (six since 2006 serving only about a year each and a seventh elected in December 2012) have combined to prevent coherent and consistent foreign and strategic policies. Condoleezza Rice, the US former National Security Adviser and Secretary of State (2001–08) complained in her memoirs of Japan "emerging as a weakening link" in America's "chain" of alliances and that after the end of Koizumi's term in office Japan no longer seemed to be the "confident" partner America "needed."[4]

Disputes over the sovereignty of islands (often little more than rocks) and about jurisdiction of maritime zones have proved fertile grounds for the outbreak of incidents that could potentially lead to military conflict. These relatively minor points of conflict could overwhelm the capacities of leaders in managing the deeper strategic issues between China and Japan that are crucial for maintaining relative regional stability. In fact it was precisely with these concerns in mind that the US secretary of defense warned each side in the course of his visits in September 2012 against the dangers of miscalculation.[5]

The impact of the end of the Cold War

These strategic issues only came to the fore after the demise of the Soviet Union and the end of the Cold War. Following shortly after the end of the Pacific War in 1945, the Cold War saw China and Japan in opposing camps, but the potential rivalry and enmity between them was overshadowed by Cold War rivalry between America and the Soviet Union. It was only after the disintegration of the Soviet Union in 1991 that China and Japan became strategic adversaries. The two emerged as great powers simultaneously for the first time in their long history. Without either necessarily targeting the other, the two became strategic rivals. The rivalry has grown slowly and incrementally in response to China's growing economic and military power and to Japan's determination to resist what it perceived as a growing threat to its security. Underlying the rivalry is a deep distrust between the two sides, which has its roots in their history and divergent identities. But after 1991 it extended to the strategic dimension of their relationship. The last twenty years have also witnessed the balance of power between the two countries change as China's rise has seemingly eclipsed a declining Japan. That may not be true in strict military terms, especially because of Japan's alliance with the United States, but the perception in much of Asia is that Japan has yielded much of the leadership in the region to China. That view, however, is both a product of Japan's relative economic decline in the region and a consequence of its dysfunctional political system, which has prevented Japan from articulating a coherent strategy towards the region.

After their rapprochement in 1972 Japan and China continued to share a common adversary in the shape of the Soviet Union until the end of the Cold War some twenty years later. During that time both sides saw Japan's economic prowess as an asset from which China could benefit. China had no navy to speak of and it regarded the American alliance with Japan in a favorable light, as it served to strengthen opposition to Soviet power and to guarantee strategic stability in East Asia, while also keeping Japan from developing into an independent military power commensurate with its economic strength. In 1978, when the fears of Soviet encirclement by China's leaders was at their height, an anxious China signed a Treaty of Peace and Friendship with Japan and Deng Xiaoping was moved to state in public that his country was no longer concerned about the revival of Japanese militarism and that it approved of the Japanese Self Defense Force.[6] It is true that there were complaints in the 1980s in China from time to time about the possibilities of the militarization of Japan and about aspects of Japan's economic influence in China.[7] But it should be noted that these took place only after China's leaders considered that the threat from the Soviet Union had abated. They were also related to the new significance China's leaders attached to the victory over Japan in the war that ended in 1945. Meanwhile the Chinese side recognized that Japan's massive economic power (which was projected at the time to surpass that of the United States) served China's immediate interests of modernizing the economy by its significant ODA and technology transfers. Moreover after the Tiananmen disaster Japan was instrumental in helping China gain acceptance back into the international community from which it was initially ostracized.

The demise of the Soviet Union in 1991 ended the sense of China's leaders that Japan was strategically useful in dealing with a potential threat from the north. China's leaders then for the first time since the establishment of the PRC turned southward and seaward, initially to develop the economy and then to modernize its armed forces, including especially its naval and related armed services. The independent foreign policy, which the Chinese had proclaimed in 1982, had truly become a reality as they began to forge a new set of policies towards the outside world. The end of the Cold War and Deng's new policies of opening to the world, coupled with the consequences of the Tiananmen massacre, brought to an end the effectiveness of any remaining appeals to socialist ideology as a means of galvanizing the support of the Chinese people. As noted in earlier chapters, the propaganda organs of the Communist Party then turned in the early 1990s to emphasizing a particular form of nationalism, which depicted China as a victim of modern history from which it was saved by the leadership of the Communist Party in defeating the last and most cruel invaders – the Japanese. The nationalist propaganda also sought to demonstrate that Western hostility to China abetted by an unrepentant Japan had never ceased.

Even though the Japanese economy began to stagnate after 1991, Japan too became more independent and assertive internationally as the end of the Cold War brought to an end its fear of the Soviet Union, which had undergirded the rationale for the alliance with the United States. But the alliance, along with the peace constitution, continued to provide the framework within which Japanese foreign and strategic policy was made. Under American pressure, Japan began for the first time to send contingents of its armed forces to participate in international military conflicts (albeit in non-combat capacities).

Japan first began to change its regional strategy in response to North Korea rather than China. Japan's failure to provide military assistance to the US-led coalition in the first Gulf War of 1991 coupled with its inability to cooperate with the United States in managing the 1994 crisis with North Korea led to a fundamental strategic review that contributed to the issuing of new guidelines in 1997. These committed Japan to work more closely with the United States in dealing with regional and international security issues. A North Korean missile that crossed mainland Japan in August 1998 shocked Japan and ensured all round domestic support for carrying out joint research into the development of ballistic missile defense systems. The Diet promptly passed the necessary legislation in 1999. However, China's leaders took the view that the new guidelines were aimed at China, as their announcement came only a year after China's attempt to intimidate Taiwan with the launching of missiles in its vicinity. The Chinese also took exception to the Japanese agreement to work jointly with the United States to develop ballistic missile defense systems. The Chinese protested that such systems would degrade their nuclear deterrent forces and undermine their capability to prevent Taiwan from seeking formal separation from China.

Yet Chinese protests were not wide of the mark. Notwithstanding the importance of the immediate challenges North Korea posed to Japan, in the medium and longer term, it clearly was the strategic relationship with China that would shape the future of Japan and the stability of the East Asian region. Although the political character of Sino-Japanese relations has fluctuated in the two decades since the end of the Cold War the incipient strategic rivalry has continued unabated.

The strategic rivalry has been intensified as a result of the disparity in the growth of their military spending. China's officially announced defense spending between 1989 and 2011 increased by an average of 12.9 percent a year, whereas that of Japan grew between 1 and 2 percent, as it kept the military budget to just below the 1 percent ceiling of its GNP, which, in contrast to the overblown 1980s, grew by only 1–2 percent since 1991. According to the Japanese Defense White Paper of 2012, China's declared military budget had increased thirty-fold over the past twenty-four years (admittedly from a low base), but more pertinently it had doubled in size in the five years since 2007. By contrast Japan's military budget had not increased in the previous seven years and in 2012 the Defense Ministry requested an increase of only 0.6 percent. The official Chinese military budget for 2012 was Yuan 650.3 billion and that of Japan was Yen 46.9 trillion. At current rates of exchange they came to $102 billion and $61 billion respectively. But the Yen was thought to be overvalued in 2012 and the Yuan undervalued. Moreover, if calculated according to purchasing power parity (PPP) the Chinese military spending is over $400 billion. A further difficulty in calculating China's military spending is that various items including procurement and research and development are excluded from the official budget. The US Department of Defense claimed that if these and other excluded items were factored in, China's military budget for 2012 would come to over $160 billion at the official exchange rate.[8]

This does not mean necessarily that the balance of military power has shifted in China's favor. Within the limits of its spending on defense Japan has been able to replace weapons systems with more modern or appropriate ones to meet new contingencies. In addition Japan has been able to develop a formidable Coast Guard, which is not subject to the spending constraints of the Self Defense Forces. Nevertheless the disparity in defense spending and the continual upgrading of China's weapons systems (which now includes the prototypes for the latest stealth fighter planes and aircraft carriers) suggests a continual build-up of military pressure on Japan.[9]

Japan's and China's geographical propinquity and the inexorable modernization and growth of the Chinese navy have resulted in deepening the strategic distrust between the two sides. From a Chinese perspective the development of its naval capabilities is necessary first, to deny Taiwan the ability to separate permanently from China; second, and relatedly, to deny the United States the unfettered capability to come to Taiwan's aid (as in 1966); third, to uphold China's jurisdictional and sovereign claims in the East and South China Seas; and fourth, to meet the growing need to safeguard the maritime routes on which its economy has come to depend. Moreover since the turn of the century maritime power has been seen within China as a prerequisite for its emergence as a truly great power in the contemporary world.

The modernization of China's military forces and especially its development of a blue water navy has brought to the fore a structural basis for the strategic rivalry between the region's two great powers. As already noted, China fears that under certain circumstances Japan could block its access to the Pacific Ocean, leaving the country bottled up within the East and probably the South China Seas; and similarly Japan fears that China could gain command of the maritime trade routes in the sea near Japan. Such calculations mean that Japanese and Chinese security interests are affected adversely by the possible future of Taiwan. Japanese interests are best served by a continuation of the present de facto independence of Taiwan, which keeps at bay possible threats to its sea routes in adjacent waters. However, from a Chinese perspective, an indefinite continuation of the status quo is unacceptable in principle as the unification with Taiwan is seen as the completion of national agenda of finally uniting all those territories seized from China by unequal treaties in the "hundred years of shame and humiliation." Japan's concern, however, is that Chinese unification with Taiwan would result in unfettered Chinese access to the Pacific and Chinese control of the trade routes on which Japan depends.

The disputes over ownership of the Senkaku/Diaoyu Islands and over conflicting claims to their respective Exclusive Economic Zones in the East China Sea, which separates the two countries, both highlight their strategic rivalry and give it a sharp nationalistic dimension. The disputes first surfaced after a report was issued in 1969 by a UN agency, which indicated the probability of oil and gas deposits in the seabed in the East China Sea. However, matters only came to a head with the growth of Chinese maritime power from the 1990s onwards, when Chinese ships first began to survey the region and then to extract oil amid Japanese protests that they were infringing on Japanese claimed rights.

This chapter will first consider the significance of Japan's alliance with the United States before looking in greater detail at the development of the strategic rivalry between China and Japan and concluding with an analysis of its implications.

The alliance between Japan and the United States

The United States figures prominently in the strategic relations between China and Japan. As the ally of Japan, it is not only the guarantor of the country's national security, but the alliance relationship is more generally regarded as the lynchpin of the American strategic presence in the Western Pacific, which has been central to the provision of regional peace. As such it has contributed an indispensable role in providing the public goods on which the rapid growth of the Asian economies (including China's) has depended. However, beginning in the 1990s the alliance has raised problems and ambiguities for China and Japan and hence for the United States as well.

As seen from China, Japan's alliance with the United States has a contradictory character. On the one hand, the alliance still serves to constrain Japan from becoming an independent military power in its own right. As an American admiral once put it, the alliance "keeps the cork (of the Japanese military) in the bottle." On the other hand, the alliance also serves as a constraint on China's rise and it stokes Chinese fears of being contained by the United States and its Japanese ally.[10]

Seen from the American perspective, Japan should contribute more actively to regional and international security. The Cold War arrangement by which Japan granted and largely paid for the stationing of American bases on its territory in return for the security provided by the alliance was no longer satisfactory in the new era in which the United States required more active contributions from allies and partners. There was no longer a common enemy in the shape of the Soviet Union against whom Japan had to be defended. Accordingly, the United States demanded of Japan that it contribute militarily to regional and international security, particularly because Japan was deemed to have a vital stake in energy and regional security so that it was no longer acceptable that Japan's contribution would be limited to money, while others put their soldiers at risk.

As we have seen, Japan came in for criticism in the early 1990s for providing only financial assistance to the conduct of the first Gulf War in 1990/91 and then for failing to provide active assistance in the course of American management of the first nuclear crisis in Korea, which at one point in 1994 threatened to lead to outright military conflict. The alliance was revitalized in 1996/97 as Japan pledged to provide logistical assistance in the "areas surrounding Japan." After 9/11/2001 the Koizumi government rapidly passed laws that enabled the Japanese to make symbolic but important contributions by its SDF to the American led wars in Iraq and Afghanistan. Since then, however, the United States has been frustrated by the exigencies of domestic Japanese politics. These first caused Japan to inject its concerns about North Korean abductions of its citizens into the Six Party Talks thereby threatening to weaken the main purpose of the talks, which was to bring about the nuclear disarmament of the North.[11]

Second, and perhaps more importantly, the apparent paralysis of Japanese domestic politics has frustrated American attempts to readjust military aspects of the alliance to conform to changing American strategic and tactical requirements. For example, the complexities of Tokyo's factional politics and the inability of successive Japanese governments to persuade, or to bring sufficient pressure to bear on, the people of Okinawa to agree to a redeployment of a major American base from an intense urban environment has delayed or prevented the implementation of an agreement that was originally reached in 1996.[12] Sixteen fretful years later in 2012 it appears that a possible compromise has been reached by which the United States has agreed to withdraw up to 10,000 troops from Okinawa as part of its restructuring of its deployments in the Pacific. That would still leave some 10,000 troops in the island chain and it would leave unresolved the question of relocating American troops from the facility in the urban space of Ginowan city to a less populated place. The then DPJ Japanese Foreign Minister, Koichiro Genba, described the new agreement as a "forward-looking and concrete one that prioritizes reducing the burden on Okinawa including the return of land."[13] Nevertheless, the move was still obstructed by popular opposition in Okinawa. The incoming LDP government headed by Shinzo Abe in December 2012 was committed to strengthening the alliance with the US, which indicated the intention to settle the Okinawa problem quickly. But it remained unclear how Abe could overcome or override opposition by people in Okinawa.[14]

China's rise and the relative decline of Japan have modified American strategic relations with both countries in ways that perhaps unintentionally have increased the distrust between the two. The engagement with China has resulted in close economic interdependence and in the encouragement of China to join the United States as a "responsible" great power in tackling global and regional problems. This has led Japan to be concerned about being "by-passed" or of being regarded as a partner of declining importance, even though it has been continually stated to be crucial to the American presence in the Asia-Pacific. At the same time the Chinese side has come to regard the American commitment to Japan, as instanced by their joint development of ballistic defense systems, as evidence of their attempts to contain China. American statements that the treaty with Japan also extended to the defense of disputed islands in the East China Sea also served to deepen Chinese distrust.[15]

Despite American dissatisfaction with the domestic political constraints that hold Japan back from playing a more active military role, there is one strategic area where US–Japanese cooperation has worked best and it is one about which the Chinese complain most. This is the successful collaboration between Japan and the United States in developing ballistic defense systems to meet the proclaimed nuclear and missile threats from North Korea that Chinese regard as a threat to the efficacy of their nuclear deterrent.

As seen from China, the common development of ballistic defense by Japan and the US suggests that, contrary to American disclaimers, the alliance is aimed at China and is a key component of what many Chinese analysts regard as the containment of China. Nevertheless Chinese continually have had to balance the concern about the dangers of the Japanese alliance with the US being directed against them with the benefit to them of the alliance, which serves to prevent Japan from becoming a military power in its own right. From that perspective the American extension to Japan of its nuclear deterrence against North Korea also serves Chinese strategic interests by precluding Japan from developing its own nuclear deterrent. As a threshold nuclear power possessed of large supplies of plutonium and of the necessary technology, Japan has the capacity to become a military nuclear power in a short space of time should a major crisis cause Japanese public and elite opinion to overcome the aversion to nuclear weapons. Despite Japan's continued resolve against becoming a military power the country disposes of significant naval power in its own right. The Chinese also appreciate that the naval power of the United States cannot be ignored as they tussle with Japan in the East China

Sea and as they seek to gain unfettered access to the Pacific Ocean. At the same time Chinese strategists are also concerned about the role that Japan may play in any military conflict involving the United States and China over Taiwan.

From a broader Chinese perspective there is a tension between trying to separate Japan from the United States and the concern that a more strategically independent Japan might prove to be a greater threat to China's rise than the current Japanese–American alliance, which at least has provided the stability and public goods which facilitated China's rise in the first place. Nevertheless as economic interdependency has deepened between China and America's two allies in Northeast Asia, Japan and South Korea, China has sought to establish exclusive institutional relations between the three. As noted in the previous chapter, regular high-level meetings have been taking place between the three since 2008 and the three have reached various agreements to facilitate their economic interactions. Although these meetings and agreements are ostensibly about economics, they also have political and perhaps strategic implications. They constitute a new regional grouping for the key countries of Northeast Asia, from which the United States is excluded and in which the role of China is central.

Although the participants have not publicly explored the broader implications of the new grouping, the format provides in embryo a means for developing a more purposeful institutional basis for deepening cooperation by high-level officials. So far the agenda of the grouping has been focused on economics, but the annual meetings provide a format in which senior officials can become more familiar with the concerns and domestic processes of their partners and hopefully develop greater trust between them. As will be discussed more extensively below there have been times when Chinese and Japanese governments have explored the possibilities of cultivating closer relations that would have the effect of loosening Japan's ties with the United States. But these ended in 2009–10 with a reaffirmation of Japan's alliance with the United States, even though it was not without its problems.

While developing institutional relations with its Northeast Asian neighbors China's leaders have also been careful to cultivate relations with the United States, claiming that the two have global and other interests in common on which they could cooperate. But the Chinese continue to be wary of the United States and what they see as the new Obama policy of "pivoting" to Asia.[16]

In the Japanese perspective, the strategic dependence on the United States leads to continual concerns about being abandoned or downgraded by the United States because from time to time it appears to embrace China to the neglect of Japan. At the same time Japanese have also evinced concern about being embroiled in American conflicts in which their interests may differ and on which the Japanese were not consulted. If Japanese are worried about "Japan-passing" (as happened when President Clinton visited China in 1998 without stopping over in Japan) they are still concerned about being entangled in American military conflicts that do not directly involve them.

As already noted, one issue close to home in which Japanese and American interests may be said to differ concerns Taiwan. The future of Taiwan is of greater strategic significance for Japan as it commands the southern maritime approaches to the Japanese mainland. The principal American commitment to Taiwan is that the outcome of Taiwan's relations with Beijing should be settled in a peaceful manner. In and of itself Taiwan does not play an important role in enabling American forces to continue to dominate the Pacific Ocean. Japan has little influence on American policy-making towards Taiwan, yet its security interests could be adversely affected by either a military conflict over the island or by a peaceable settlement that could place the island within China's sphere of control and threaten Japan with maritime encirclement. However, the differences between the US and Japan are unlikely to surface as long as the status quo of Taiwan continues. Despite a sense of continual tension, that status quo has endured since the Taiwan Relations Act of 1979.[17]

Meanwhile the obstacles presented by Japan's political system to working better with the United States on strategic matters threaten to weaken Japan's role as a bastion of American power in the region. That tends to reinforce the American tendency to develop policies towards China without full consultation with its key ally in the region. Ironically, like its American ally, Japan too seeks to deepen its engagement with China, even as it hedges against its rising military power, and it does so largely independently of the United States, especially in the economic sphere, where, as already noted, it pursues bilateral and trilateral (including South Korea) forms of interdependency with China. At issue is how far the two allies can work together towards this ostensibly common objective.

Last, but not least, the strategic rivalry between China and Japan is taking place in the context of the development by North Korea of nuclear weapons and ballistic missiles, which threaten Northeast Asia as a whole. Chinese and Japanese interests both converge and diverge on the issue. As the convener of the Six Party Talks (6PT) China has played a key diplomatic role in addressing the North Korean problem, but it would appear that its primary interest is maintaining a degree of stability on the Korean peninsula by preventing the collapse of the regime in the North and promoting the cause of economic reforms there along Chinese lines. But the Chinese recognize that the regime fears for its future if it were to follow the Chinese example, especially as its people would be exposed to the South, which enjoys a standard of living infinitely superior to the North. A collapse of the regime would raise the specter of chaos on the peninsular that could damage the Chinese economy and destabilize its northeastern provinces. Longer term, if Korea were to be reunited the Chinese would hope to ensure that its security in the northeast would not be damaged and that Korea as a whole would come under its influence.[18] The question of denuclearization is also a Chinese interest, if only to prevent Japan and others from going nuclear too. But it is clear that in the shorter term China's emphasis is on the survival of the Northern regime in the interest of stability on the peninsula.

Japan by contrast is more concerned with the denuclearization of the North, notwithstanding its diplomatic emphasis on settling the question of abductions. Being in range of its missiles, Japan fears the belligerency of the North and it has worked more closely and strategically with the United States and South Korea since the aggressive acts carried out by the North against the South in 2010, especially as these were seemingly supported by China. Longer term, however, Japan is a potential competitor with China for influence in a united Korea.[19] In fact a potential reconciliation between Japan and North Korea cannot be ruled out, as was illustrated by Koizumi's two visits to Pyongyang in 2004 and 2006 by the previous DPJ administration. The possibility of another unilateral move by Japan towards North Korea was raised again in 2012, and in May 2013 by an emissary of Prime Minister Abe when delegations from Japan visited gravesites in the North amid suggestions that higher-level officials might visit later.[20] If the abduction issue were to be addressed in a way acceptable to both sides, Japan has much to offer to help the development of the economy of the North and it could ease the North's current dependence on China.

As with Taiwan, American and Japanese interests are not identical with regard to North Korea. The United States, as a global power, is primarily concerned with the problems of nuclear proliferation and its main priority is the denuclearization of the North. In the future North Korea may be able to develop nuclear missiles capable of reaching the American mainland at which point it might claim to have a viable deterrence against US attack. But North Korea is geographically close to Japan and the Korean peninsula has been famously described as a "dagger pointing at the heart of Japan." In the short term Japanese and American interests coincide in opposing North Korean belligerency and in demanding its denuclearization. Longer term their interests may diverge as Japan has a direct security interest in preventing Chinese domination of the Korean peninsula.

One of the problems that plagues Sino-Japanese security relations is their security dilemma arising from the fact that whatever measures the one side takes to strengthen its defenses are regarded as offensive and a threat to the other, to which it must respond thereby setting up a vicious circle. For example, Japanese measures to meet the immediate threat from North Korea are often regarded by China as threatening to itself. Similarly, Chinese military acquisitions and deployments aimed at Taiwan and designed to deter American intervention are regarded with concern by Japan.

Both China and Japan recognize the need to keep their rivalry within bounds. Not only would the costs of major military conflict be horrendous and its adverse consequences incalculable, but the two are also economically interdependent. However, such is the distrust between them that they have not been able to work out how to manage the small-scale incidents that regularly occur in the seas and skies between them, let alone an enduring *modus vivendi*.[21]

Finally, another complication especially from the American perspective is the difficulty its two key allies in Northeast Asia, Japan and South Korea, have found in working together to meet the challenges posed by the rise of China.[22] In South Korea the memories of Japan's harsh colonial rule run deep as they involve questions of Korean identity. In part this is because despite the formal apologies by Japanese leaders, issues from that time are kept alive by the refusal of the Japanese government to accept full responsibility for the "comfort women" or "sex slaves" who served the Japanese army and by Japanese claims to small islands in the sea between the two countries that date largely from a treaty imposed by Japan in 1905. In part the Korean objections to Japan also derive from domestic politics involving the emergence from autocratic rule. Especially during the presidency of Roh Moo Hyun (2003–08) charges of collaboration with the Japanese occupiers (1910–45) were made against former military dictators and their associates. These recriminations gave a new and sharper dimension to the recriminations against Japan.[23] Even earlier South Korean concern about Japan has worked against American objectives. For example, following the reaffirmation of the US–Japan alliance in 1995/96 the then presidents of China and South Korea "found common cause" on the former's visit to Seoul in November 1996 in criticizing Japan for failing to address its historical legacy of imperialism in Northeast Asia.[24] Later, when both allies agreed on the need to respond to what they saw as North Korean provocations in 2010 by joining together with the United States in military exercises in the seas near the North, the Japanese were able to participate only as observers. Two years later an agreement between the leaders of the two countries to share intelligence in monitoring North Korea and China failed at the last moment because of domestic opposition in South Korea.[25] Relations between the two

American allies then rapidly deteriorated as the South Korean president angered the Japanese side by suddenly visiting the Dokdo/Takeshima islands, occupied by South Korea, but claimed by Japan. He compounded the "offense" by calling on the Japanese emperor to apologize for past wrongs if he were to visit Korea. Many in South Korea and Japan regarded Lee's sudden visit as an about face with Japan designed to improve his sagging standing in the eyes of the Korean public.[26] But visits in the Spring of 2013 to the Yasukuni Shrine by members of Abe's cabinet, comments by Abe himself casting doubt on whether Japan's war in Asia can be classified as 'aggression', coupled with comments by other senior politicians casting doubts on the significance of 'comfort women' for the imperial army all served to annoy the Chinese, but more importantly they antagonized the new South Korean administration and Washington at a time when the Americans sought a united response by its two allies against the provocations by North Korea.

The beginnings of strategic rivalry: 1990–2005

The decade began with the balance of power between China and Japan largely favoring the latter. But by the end of the 1990s the balance had begun to shift towards China. Japan played the major role in helping China overcome the diplomatic isolation and sanctions imposed on its government after the Tiananmen disaster. Japanese economic assistance that was briefly interrupted in 1989 was resumed the following year and continued to play a significant role in the development of a modern infrastructure in China in the early 1990s. By its actions and diplomacy Japan persuaded its fellow members of the G-7 to cut back on their sanctions. In 1992 the Japanese emperor visited China, bestowing upon it the highest diplomatic accolade open to Japan. That occasion, however, was to be the high point of Japan's relative significance in the balance of power with China. Up to that point Japan's principal strategic concern about China was not about its military prowess, but rather the prospect of its retreat once again into angry chaotic isolation. It was thought up until then that Japan's economic significance and diplomatic standing would enable it to prevent a Chinese return to such a dangerous isolation. By the mid-1990s, after the bursting of its economic bubble and the success of China's renewed economic growth and integration in the world economy, the Japanese found that their economic weight had lost such effectiveness as it may have had of exerting influence over Chinese foreign and strategic policies.

Thus in 1995 and 1996 Japan was unable to dissuade China from conducting nuclear tests and the Japanese symbolic act of withholding grant aid ($86 million – a relatively small proportion of Japan's total ODA given to China for fiscal 1994 – $1.6 billion) only provoked anger in Beijing, which had regarded Japanese aid as reparations in all but name. Japan was also troubled by China's coercive response to the visit by the Taiwanese president (Lee Teng-hui) to the United States in 1995. In particular Japan was alarmed in March 1996 by China's resort to the use of military force by the firing of missiles close to Taiwan's two main ports (the northern of which was within sixty miles of Japan's territorial waters).[27] These came to a halt only with the appearance of two US carrier-led battle groups near Taiwan.

These developments, which from a Chinese perspective were not aimed at Japan, nevertheless proved to be a turning point in their relationship. China's nuclear tests were timed to take place before the coming into effect of the Comprehensive Test Ban Treaty and they were geared towards improving China's nuclear deterrence.[28] The military maneuvers against Taiwan were a reaction to what was seen as a Taiwanese move towards independence that had American backing. Although Beijing had long expressed misgivings about Japan's links with Taiwan, they were not at issue in this case. Against the background of the campaign to promote patriotic education in which Japan was singled out for its brutal aggression in the 1930s and 1940s, for which it was judged not to have properly atoned, the Chinese rejected Japanese complaints about its actions. In their view Japan had no moral standing to object to China's nuclear testing and, as the former colonial overlord of Taiwan, Japan had no business in complaining about Chinese actions to promote unification.

However, security relations had begun to deteriorate even earlier. As early as 1992 Japan sent out elements of its Self Defense Forces (SDF) to participate in UN Peace Keeping Operations (PKO) activities in Cambodia. The event was noted in China, even though no protests were made, as Japan's actions were under the auspices of the United Nations and hence they were seen as legitimate, particularly as Japan had played a leading role in brokering the settlement of the Cambodian problem.[29] In May 1993 Japan's foreign minister protested alleged attacks on Japanese fishing boats in the East China Sea and a year later in January 1994 his successor questioned China's 15 percent increase in military spending.[30] But in a context in which Japan's economic significance for China had rapidly declined Japanese complaints carried little weight. If the complaints about the changing strategic environment had so far come primarily from the Japanese side China soon found cause to complain about Japan for its recalibration of its alliance with the United States.

If the first Gulf War was a wake-up call to the Japanese requiring a fundamental readjustment in their strategic relations with the United States, it was more of a shock to the Chinese. It suddenly and brutally demonstrated to the Chinese military how far behind the American forces it was technologically. Beginning in 1993 a massive modernization of China's forces unfolded. A wide range of state of the art naval and aerial weapons systems began to be purchased from Russia and a fundamental restructuring of the People's Liberation Army (PLA) was initiated. Within a decade both China's navy and air force had been equipped with a growing number of advanced submarines, destroyers and frigates and with many of the latest Russian fighters and fighter-bombers. The number and quality of the various kinds of ballistic missiles were also increased. Just as importantly, China acquired advanced networks of communications and it was beginning to manufacture its own versions of modern weaponry. The transformation of China's military capabilities did not take place with Japan in mind. Rather it was aimed at deterring or preventing the United States from coming to the aid of Taiwan in the event of military conflict across the Taiwan Strait and more broadly at upholding its maritime claims and at defending China's wider interests now that its economy had come to depend so greatly on maritime trade.[31]

Ironically, the enhancement of the Japan–US alliance was not designed with China in mind. Its original purpose was to address Japanese shortcomings in contributing to the American led first Gulf War of 1990/91 and in assisting the United States in the first nuclear crisis with North Korea in 1994. With these in mind Japan issued a new National Defense Program Outline (NDPO) in November 1995 so as to clarify its support for UN PKO and for US "operations in the areas surrounding Japan." The United States and Japan agreed a new set of defense guidelines in 1996/97 along the lines of the new NDPO, which replaced those of 1978. They also agreed to develop jointly ballistic missile defense systems, but the agreement was triggered by concerns about North Korea rather than China.[32]

The Chinese, however, saw the new guidelines as a response to the Taiwan crisis. Chinese behavior in that crisis certainly helped to approve of the guidelines in the Japanese Diet in 1996. For example, one of the missiles fired by the Chinese to the north of Taiwan came sufficiently close to one of the islands in the Okinawa chain that the Japanese prime minister considered evacuating civilians if the situation were to have worsened.[33] But the new guidelines had been conceived before the Taiwan crisis and they were designed to adjust the terms of the US–Japan alliance to meet the new strategic situation after the Cold War in which the Americans demanded more active commitments from its allies.[34] The specific Chinese complaints centered on the extension of Japan's military role from its earlier confinement to Japanese territory. In particular they charged that the "areas surrounding Japan" included Taiwan. It confirmed Chinese suspicions of Japanese continued interest in the island. Their concern was intensified by a remark of the Chief Cabinet Secretary claiming that the guidelines did indeed cover Taiwan.[35]

The fact that Japan and the US had begun to cooperate in the development of theater missile defense suggested to the Chinese side that Taiwan might be integrated into a broader security structure including Japan as well as the United States. The United States had long been accused of interfering in China's domestic affairs through its defense of Taiwan and although the Chinese had long suspected the Japanese of seeking to prevent unification, this was the first time since the end of the Cold War that Japan appeared to be openly doing so as well. Perhaps that was why Chinese ire was directed more at Japan than the United States.[36]

However, from a Japanese perspective the new guidelines were triggered by the North Korean problem rather than by China. The perception of a North Korean threat was galvanized by the North Korean launch of a missile on August 31, 1998 that traversed the Japanese mainland to land nearby in the Pacific Ocean. It demonstrated a new and startling Japanese vulnerability to an autocratic, opaque and unpredictable neighbor that was known to possess chemical and biological weapons and which was in the process of developing a nuclear capability. It was a neighbor who professed abiding hostility towards Japan because of Japanese aggression and the annexation of Korea in 1910 and which condemned the current LDP Japanese government as an American puppet. The North had long been disparaged in Japan. Over the years Japanese citizens had been abducted by North Korean agents and more recently, North Korean spy ships had entered Japanese waters. But suddenly the North appeared as a present and ready danger. As a consequence the following year Japan began a joint program with the United States to develop ballistic missile defense systems for protection against incoming missiles.

However, just as these events seemed to cement the value to Japan of its alliance with the United States in dealing with Northeast Asia doubts began to creep in about Japan's relative value to the US as compared with China. Following the Taiwan crisis of 1995/96, which ended in the deployment by the US of the largest flotilla of sea and air power to East Asia since the Vietnam War, the United States and China sought to improve relations in order to prevent another possible confrontation. In 1998 President Clinton paid a ten-day visit to China and unlike previous presidential visits to Beijing he did not stop off in Tokyo either on his way there or on his return. For good measure he also sided with China in holding Japan at least partially to blame for the 1997 Asian Financial Crisis and in rejecting the Japanese proposal for an Asian Monetary Fund. He aroused acute Japanese fears of being abandoned and he gave rise to the phrase "Japan passing."

Thus it was not until towards the end of the 1990s that the Chinese and Japanese began to recognize each other as major competitors and strategic rivals. Until then the strengthening of Japanese defenses was triggered by the need to revamp the alliance with the United States and to respond to the new threats posed by North Korea. To be sure there had been incidents at sea between Chinese and Japanese fishing vessels and the two sides had complained about various military and strategic developments of the other party. But from the perspectives of each government these were not primarily targeted at the other. Nevertheless Japan's new arrangements with the United States and China's military build-up and actions that were aimed at Taiwan troubled Beijing and Tokyo respectively. They combined to deepen the distrust that was already evident in their relationship.

During this period Japan too had begun to carry out changes in its defense orientation from a preparedness to resist a potential attack by the Soviet Union in the north to meet the need for a more flexible, mobile force capable of undertaking joint tri-service operations with increased interoperability with American forces. Within the framework of the limits set on the growth of its defense budget of 1 percent of GNP, Japan has succeeded in readjusting its military capabilities, by jettisoning those no longer needed after the demise of the Soviet threat and by upgrading existing weapons systems. Japan has also purchased state of the art naval vessels and aircraft from the United States.[37] Moreover the Japanese Coast Guard, which is attached to the Ministry of Land, Infrastructure, Transport and Tourism, is not subject to the same funding constraints as the Self Defense Forces. It disposes of a significant number of advanced naval vessels, aircraft and helicopters.[38]

Chinese and Japanese attempts to improve their security relations through meetings of officials and senior leaders did little to assuage the fears on either side. Part of the problem was the frequency of incidents in the East China Sea involving what the Japanese regarded as unwarranted challenges to their territorial waters and EEZs by Chinese fishing, coast guard and naval vessels.[39] From a Chinese perspective they were only asserting their rights as mapped out in their territorial law of 1992.[40] It will be recalled that by the late 1990s nationalist sentiment in China had taken on a fierce anti-Japanese tone, symbolized by Jiang Zemin's visit to Japan in November 1998 in which he lectured his hosts, including the emperor, about their failure to apologize appropriately for Japan's past aggressive war.

In view of the increasingly troubled strategic relationship between China and Japan, it became difficult to see the strategic logic in China's treatment of Japan between 1998 and 2005. The strident demands for a fuller apology for Japan's war time aggression and brutality associated particularly with Jiang Zemin provoked only resistance from Japan. Prime Minister Koizumi in particular seemed unfazed by Chinese strident demands that he stop visiting the Yasukuni Shrine. As noted earlier, he had his own domestic political reasons for continuing the visitations. But at the same time he depicted Chinese objections as interference in Japanese internal affairs and, by and large, Japanese opinion polls showed majority support for his resistance to Chinese pressure, even though those same polls registered ambivalence about his prime-ministerial visits.[41] The high mark of Chinese demonstrations was sparked by Japan's announced intention to seek a permanent seat in the UN Security Council, signaling Japan's status as a great power. If the purpose of

China's pressure was to bend Japan to its will, it clearly failed. If, on the other hand, the pressure stemmed from the emotional nationalism released by the patriotic education campaigns, or from other domestic political causes, the clamor and pressure demonstrated a dangerous weakness in foreign policy-making. After all, the treatment of Japan did not fit in well with China's more general "good neighbor policy." It raised doubts about the credibility of that policy in Southeast Asia although Southeast Asians were careful to avoid airing the doubts in public.[42]

In fact there were differences in the Chinese leadership about policy towards Japan. It will be recalled that in 2003 two Chinese intellectuals, echoing deeply embedded views in the Ministry of Foreign Affairs, called for "new thinking" in policy towards Japan. Although the angry nationalistic young subjected them to public harassment, their call was heeded, but only after the anti-Japanese hysteria over-reached itself in the riots of April 2005. However, as discussed in chapter 3, the new approach adopted by Hu Jintao was advanced only after the purge of a leader who had been close to the former General Secretary of the Party, Jiang Zemin. In the summer and fall of 2005 it became clear that the Chinese media had been instructed to present news from Japan in a better light.[43]

Beijing, however, had reason to be concerned about the changing scope of Japan's SDF. Following 9/11, the Japanese government passed a number of laws that allowed for the contribution of logistical services by its SDF in the American-led and UN sanctioned war in Afghanistan and in the more controversial war in Iraq, which lacked UN endorsement. The enlargement of the scope of the overseas operations of the SDF was of concern to China, even if these were largely restricted to providing maritime supply services to US ships in the Indian Ocean and to helping in civil construction work in Iraq. The Chinese took greater exception to the Japanese National Defense Program Outline of November 2004, which aimed to strengthen the alliance with the US against a threat from the "West." Beijing took even stronger exception to Japan's Joint Statement with the US in February 2005, which stated for the first time that it had a security interest in the prevalence of peace in the Taiwan Strait.

Despite the growing number of incidents involving Chinese incursions by sea and by air into waters claimed by Japan, each side was careful to avoid allowing the incidents to escalate. For example, there were no reports of actual shooting. Nevertheless tension at sea increased, especially as the Chinese side in 2004 stopped notifying the Japanese in advance about the operations of Chinese research ships in waters claimed by Japan, as had been agreed in 2001. In that same year a Chinese submarine was observed and tracked in Japan's territorial sea in the Okinawa island chain.[44]

The growing pressure from China on Japan since the mid-1990s had adversely affected Japanese attitudes towards China and had reduced Japanese support for pacifistic positions. First, the Japanese public reacted adversely to the stream of anti-Japanese incidents taking place in China. The number of those who felt an affinity towards China declined to less than 30 percent. It may be recalled that in the 1980s the figure was over 80 percent and even after the shock of Tiananmen in 1989 it stood at around 50 percent. Second, and more importantly from a strategic perspective, there was growing support for making Japan a more active military and strategic actor. Public support for revising the Constitution, which had grown to over 50 percent in the 1990s, reached a record 65 percent in 2005.[45]

As discussed in greater detail in the previous chapter, the deepening strategic rivalry was reflected in new regional diplomacy by both sides as they sought to minimize the influence that the other could wield in proposed new regional groupings. In January 2002

Koizumi proposed the establishment of an East Asian community with the ASEAN 10, Japan, China, the Republic of Korea, Australia and New Zealand as core members. As the idea of an East Asian summit took greater hold in 2004, the Chinese indicated that they sought a more limited membership in which they were suspected of wanting a leading role. This was opposed by Singapore, Japan and others, who successfully insisted that Australia, New Zealand and India be included as well in the first East Asian Summit, which met in Kuala Lumpur in December 2005.

The Japanese government had begun to express concern about China's military build-up, especially about the lack of information accompanying it. In December 2005 Foreign Minister Taro Aso described China as a "considerable threat." However, at that point the former head of the Japanese Defense Agency gave a more sober assessment by arguing that the Chinese military did not pose a serious threat to Japan. The relatively low quality and effectiveness of its equipment and the superiority of the Japanese air force and navy ensured that China, for example, would be unable to invade and occupy islands such as the Senkaku/Diaoyu.[46] Nevertheless there was concern about the trend of events and the possibilities of a crisis spinning out of control.

Behind the scenes powerful players on the Chinese side and significant institutions in Japan, including the office of Prime Minister Koizumi, recognized that Sino-Japanese relations had to be put on a sounder footing. The conclusion of Koizumi's Premiership was due in the fall of 2006 and that was seen as an opportunity to make a new beginning. In February 2006 the Chinese and Japanese vice foreign ministers, Dai Bingguo and Shotaro Yachi, began a series of talks that paved the way for the eventual mending of relations in October.[47]

2006–09: political improvement, but strategic distrust remains

These years saw a positive transformation in political relations between the two sides, but an intensification of military rivalry and strategic distrust. The breakthrough in political relations between the two countries took place when the newly installed Prime Minister Shinzo Abe visited Beijing in October 2006. As discussed in greater detail in chapter 3, a Joint Statement was issued, which sought to remove the most important bones of contention that had bedeviled the relationship in the last twenty years. For the first time, the Chinese officially acknowledged Japan's consistent adherence to the "path of a peaceful country for the 60 years since the end of the Second World War." That in effect put to rest Chinese charges of the supposed revival of militarism in Japan. The "history issue" was largely depoliticized by leaving it to be determined by the "joint research" of Japanese and Chinese scholars. The Chinese side reaffirmed its adherence to the path of "peaceful development" and assured the Japanese of the beneficial economic opportunities that would accrue to them as a result. At the suggestion of Abe the two sides pledged to develop a "mutually beneficial relationship based on common strategic interests." In China it was noted that this was the first time that a Japanese leader had used the word "strategic" in defining Sino-Japanese relations.[48] These "strategic interests" were not identified by the two sets of leaders then or subsequently, but the phrase was repeated as a mantra whenever the leaders were to meet in the future.

It was striking, however, that the Joint Statement made no reference to Pyongyang's first test of a nuclear weapon that took place on October 9, a day after Abe's arrival in

Beijing. The absence of such a reference despite the great impact that the test had on the strategic situation for both Beijing and Tokyo suggested that having worked hard to negotiate the terms of their major meeting they were not willing, or perhaps they were unable, to agree on how best to make a common response. Although the nuclear test may be said to have come as a shock, the North Koreans had given China prior notice just six days earlier.[49] Any Chinese fears that Japan might respond by developing its nuclear force (and there were indications that some LDP leaders wanted to open discussions on the subject) were quieted by the speed with which President Bush and his Secretary of State, Condoleezza Rice reaffirmed "the full range" of the American deterrence for Japan and South Korea. By that time Prime Minister Abe had stopped further comment in the LDP, by stating that the discussion was "already finished."[50] The significance of the avoidance of mention of the nuclear issue by China and Japan, and of the very public reaffirmation of extended nuclear deterrence by the US, was that China and Japan did not then and have not since engaged in a serious bilateral dialogue about nuclear strategy. To be sure they discussed the denuclearization of North Korea in the context of the Six Party Talks and Chinese objections to Japan's cooperation with the US on ballistic missile defense, but there is no evidence of their having discussed in depth broader nuclear questions such as Japan's vulnerability to Chinese nuclear missiles. Neither was there evidence then, or subsequently, to suggest that the two sides had discussed their respective strategic concerns about military developments of the other side.

This is not to undervalue the importance of the political breakthrough of October 2006, which was dubbed "ice-breaking" by the Chinese side. It changed the dynamics of the relationship and set the path for more frequent meetings between the top leaders and a range of institutionalized meetings between lower level officials on a wide range of topics. Abe's first visit was followed by an "ice-melting" visit to Japan by Premier Wen Jiabao in April 2007 and by a "spring-warming" visit by President Hu Jintao in May 2008. Many agreements were signed to enhance cooperation in many fields including energy, environmental protection, finance, information and communication technology and so on. Agreements were also reached to promote exchanges and consultation at all levels in the public and private sectors to encompass education, culture, tourism and so on.

But improvements in the vital strategic sector were minimal despite agreements to "enhance mutual trust" through dialogue and exchanges between defense personnel. Prime Ministers Abe and Aso, who had taken hawkish positions on China during the Koizumi administration, openly favored a new alignment involving the US, Japan, Australia and India to be based on "shared values," which clearly excluded China and was seen in China as a call for containment. During the latter part of Koizumi's premiership, Japan, Australia and the US established in May 2005 an annual trilateral security dialogue, which "Abe appeared to see as an important means of mobilizing the three key democracies in the region in order to counter China's rise." During Abe's term Japan deepened the formal defensive link with Australia in March 2007 with the signing of a Joint Declaration on Security. In September that year Japan extended the new multilateral dimension of its defense operations by participating in joint naval exercises in the Bay of Bengal with the US, Australia, India and Singapore.[51] But owing to Japan's constitutional restrictions and the legal limits set to the operations of its SDF, these developments are best understood as soft balancing rather than the kind of hard balancing associated with formal alliances.

Prime Minister Fukuda, who held office in between the Abe and Aso administrations, belonged to the more Asianist wing of the LDP and he did not build on these multilateral defense initiatives. If Japanese policies towards China can be understood as a mixture of engagement and counter-balancing, Abe tended to emphasize the latter and Fukuda the former. Not surprisingly, the Chinese were more forthcoming with Fukuda, who hosted the visit by Hu Jintao in May 2008. Not only did the visit result in more extensive agreements including a "mechanism for high-level regular visits between leaders of the two nations," but also for the first time progress was registered on the divisive and strategically important question of exploration and development of oil and gas in the East China Sea. The two agreed in principle that Japan could contribute to the development of the Chunxiao/Shirakaba oil and gas field, close to the median line. This was seen as a possible tacit endorsement by China of the median line as the dividing line of their respective EEZs rather than the extension of the continental shelf, which the Chinese formally claimed. But the agreement about cooperative development has not been followed by further undertakings about how to implement the agreement and in addition the two disagreed as to how to relate the agreement to other oil and gas fields in the vicinity. However, the fact that the agreement was not developed further probably reflects Chinese unwillingness to consider accommodating Japanese interests with Taro Aso, a prime minister whom they regarded as not favorably disposed towards them.

As outlined in chapter 4, the growing economic interdependence between China and Japan found institutional expression not only in bilateral ties but also in a tripartite new grouping involving South Korea as well. The first trilateral summit between them was held in December 2008. Although that was after Fukuda's resignation in September, it was clear that much of the preparatory work had been completed under his premiership. However important the establishment of regular trilateral summit meetings was for the political economic relations between the three parties, these meetings were not matched on the strategic side. Although some exchanges took place between Chinese and Japanese defense officials and naval ships from both sides visited each other's ports, nothing of substance emerged. A leading Japanese specialist in military studies observed, "frankly, Japan–China 'defense exchanges' had remained high-level ones easily affected by political relations, and had not always achieved the goal to promote building of reliable and cooperative relations between China and Japan."[52] Nevertheless, as the Chinese side tends to see economic and political relationships to be closely connected, it must have seen the tripartite group as politically important in bringing America's two key allies together with China in an arrangement that excluded the Americans.

The advent of the DPJ government in August 2009 provided a new opportunity for Japan to develop closer relations with China and to "rebalance" the relationship with the United States. As discussed in greater detail in chapter 3, important elements in the DPJ had developed new thinking along such lines while in opposition.[53] After its electoral victory the new government produced what a leading American official called "a number of disturbing developments" of which Prime Minister Hatoyama's proposal for a new Asian community that would exclude the United States was said to be "perhaps the most troubling."[54] After all, Japan was the lynchpin of America's strategic deployments in East Asia. Not surprisingly, the proposal was welcomed by China's leader, Hu Jintao, who said that it was "in line with the vision of 'harmonious Asia' and 'harmonious world' advocated by China."[55] But little came of this as Hatoyama resigned in May 2010, in part because of the general incoherence of his government and because of his mishandling of the attempt to renegotiate the location of Futenma, the US marine base in Okinawa.

The political improvement in the relationship was the product of careful management by both the Chinese and Japanese leaderships. But this was not sufficient to overcome their strategic distrust, which had been intensified both by Japanese concern about the rise of Chinese military power and the opaqueness associated with it and by Chinese concern about the perceived attempt by the United States together with its Japanese ally to limit China's rise.

Domestic politics

As noted in previous chapters, the international financial crisis, which began in the US in 2008, was seen by many in China as a turning point in changing the international balance of power, especially in East Asia. By this stage China had changed the pattern of the previous five or six decades by surpassing the value of trade between America and its Asian allies often by considerable and growing margins. In the case of Japan by 2011 its trade with China of almost $340 billion greatly exceeded that with the US of $200 billion. Moreover the modernization and growth of China's military power had reached a point where it could seriously challenge America's ability to come to the aid of its allies and partners in the region.[56] It was in this context that many of China's maritime disputes over sovereignty and rights of jurisdiction gained greater saliency. Although the disputes were not necessarily initiated by China, the Chinese response was often heavy-handed, reflecting its military superiority over its maritime neighbors especially in the South China Sea.[57] Contributing apparent support for North Korea over the sinking of the South Korean corvette the *Cheonan* and the passage of a Chinese flotilla of ten advanced naval vessels through a strait in the Okinawan chain had the effect of reminding the Japanese of their vulnerability and of their need for the protection afforded to them by the alliance with the United States. Arguably, the Chinese implicit accommodation of North Korean aggressiveness was due to anxiety about the stability of the Northern regime and hence the Chinese response may have been defensive rather than aggressive in character. However, from a Japanese perspective China's actions suggested that the immediate developments on the Korean peninsula and the significance of demonstrating the capacity of its navy to access the Pacific were of greater importance to it than the prospect of developing new relations with a Japanese government that in all probability would be unable to deliver on its first prime minister's promise to shift diplomacy more towards Asia. In any event, the next Japanese Prime Minister, Naoto Kan, shifted back to the standard Japanese view on the centrality of the Alliance with Japan. The US now had "living proof that both major political parties in Japan, on the right and on the left could be relied upon to maintain and support the alliance."[58]

A new Chinese assertiveness became evident in 2009–10, which had profound strategic implications even though China's leaders began to draw in their horns somewhat at the end of 2010. The assertiveness took the form of a more confrontationist approach towards China's neighbors over long-standing competing claims to sovereignty and the exercise of jurisdiction in the maritime domains of the South and East China Seas. China also took a tougher stance against the US. This began with a tightly staged management of President Obama's visit to China in November 2009 in which his proposals for closer collaboration to meet global problems were largely disregarded and which was followed by a display of discourtesy when he was berated by a relatively junior official in the course of the UN climate conference in Copenhagen a month later. The Chinese rejected customary international law in their objection to American naval exercises in the Yellow Sea (which were a response to North Korean belligerence). The American exercises were conducted on the high seas and not in Chinese waters.[59] The Chinese authorities had earlier sought to obstruct American surveillance ships from operating in China's Exclusive Economic Zone on legal grounds, which are not accepted by the international community.[60]

However, what drew most attention was China's use of its growing naval power to try to intimidate Southeast Asian fellow claimants in the South China Sea. Much of Chinese activism was in response to what it regarded as provocations by others and there is evidence that Vietnam and the Philippines often took the initiative, but the Chinese were often perceived to over-react. As we have seen, the International Crisis Group called the Chinese approach "reactive assertiveness" designed to change the status quo in China's favor. The diplomatic high point in the exchanges occurred at a meeting of the ASEAN Regional Forum in Hanoi in July 2010, when for the first time as many as ten member states openly complained about Chinese behavior. The American Secretary of State, Hillary Clinton, for the first time intervened in an ASEAN disagreement with China to assert that freedom of navigation in the South China Sea was in the national interest of the US and for good measure added that the US favored a collaborative diplomatic process for resolving territorial disputes. She further stated that claimants should pursue their rights and claims "solely from legitimate claims to land features" in accordance with international law. Her position was in direct opposition to China's long-standing insistence that territorial disputes should be solved only on a bilateral basis and she also by implication rejected any Chinese claims derived from its famous nine dashed lines encompassing much of the South China Sea, which the Chinese had submitted to a UN Committee.[61] The Chinese foreign minister, who was taken by surprise, consulted Beijing, before holding the United States responsible for instigating the Southeast Asian states to behave in this challenging way and in a moment of anger berated them by telling the Singaporean foreign minister, "China is a big country and other countries are small countries and that is just a fact!"[62]

The first major turning point in Chinese assertiveness towards Japan took place in September 2010, and arose from an incident near the Senkaku/Diaoyu Islands claimed by both countries. The incident started with the ramming of two Japanese Coast Guard vessels by a Chinese fishing vessel, whose apparently drunken captain was arrested and was to be put on trial. From a Chinese perspective, that contravened earlier practice by which the Japanese Coast Guard quickly sent back to China Chinese fishermen and others whom they had detained for encroaching on claimed Japanese sovereignty. By threatening to place the captain on trial the Chinese side argued that Japan's legal claims to the islands were being raised to a new level. However, the Chinese reaction was seen to be excessive. Amid shrill nationalist rhetoric, four Japanese were detained in China, political exchanges were suspended, a visit by a student group to the Shanghai World Expo was canceled and the export of rare earths (on which China had a near monopoly) vital for Japanese electronic and other high-tech production was effectively stopped or significantly delayed. Even when the Japanese side released the captain the Chinese did not immediately stop their retaliatory actions. Despite what was regarded as Japan's "maladroit" handling of the incident, the US demonstrated its solidarity with Japan by stating at a very high level that its Defense Treaty covered all the territories administered by Japan, including the Senkakus, even though the US did not officially take a position on whether China or Japan had sovereignty over them.[63]

Chinese assertiveness appears to have been sanctioned, if not actually instigated by the top leaders. Premier Wen Jiabao publicly admonished the Japanese to correct their behavior. China's more confrontational approach seems to have been the result of the concurrence of developments that led to what Henry Kissinger has called Chinese "triumphalism." This stems primarily from the perception of many scholars and officials that China's weathering of the financial crisis of 2008 in a much better way than the US and its allies, the EU and Japan, indicated the beginning of China's eclipse of the US. The main debate in Beijing appeared to be whether the American decline was temporary or permanent. That viewpoint, stimulated by a virulent nationalism (which had been instigated by Beijing especially through its education in defense studies, which permeated the education system at all levels) and enhanced by the rise of China's naval power, was enough to lead to an assertiveness at the expense of its neighbors.[64] This was made more feasible by the multiplicity of maritime enforcers of China's more belligerent approach. In addition to China's three official naval fleets, there were four armed fishery protection fleets belonging to four separate ministries and several others belonging to coastal provincial and municipal authorities.[65] However, as we shall see, when Beijing decided that this new approach was counterproductive it was able to exert sufficient authority to call a halt to its more egregious manifestations.

As a consequence of China's assertiveness the Chinese had aroused the concerns of all its maritime neighbors, driving them to turn more closely towards the United States, which in any event, had decided to focus more closely on Asia. Chinese actions damaged much of its diplomatic success in reaching across to its neighbors in the previous ten years. In the case of Japan, strategic relations with the US were deepened, but perhaps more importantly so were relations between Japan and South Korea. Overcoming its previous historical antipathy towards Japan, South Korea joined with Japan and the United States in coordinating policies and in conducting greater consultations. Japan also participated in more joint naval exercises with the United States and its partners.[66] Japan also drew closer to the Philippines and Vietnam, who were China's principal protagonists in the South China Sea.[67]

However, as China began to withdraw from its exposed and isolated position, as signified first by an article in the *People's Daily* by China's leading diplomat and confirmed by Hu Jintao's fence-mending visit to Washington in January 2011, the friction between China and Japan also appeared to ease.[68] The two sets of leaders agreed to seek to improve relations at an unscheduled meeting at the APEC summit in Yokohama on November 14, 2010. By January of the following year the Chinese side confirmed its desire to resume high level exchanges and in early February the Japanese Prime Minister Naoto Kan declared his desire to rebuild political as well as economic relations.

This return to "normalcy" indicated that despite the fundamental strategic distrust that underlay Sino-Japanese relations, both sides recognized the need to keep their potential conflicts within limits as neither could afford open military conflict. The consequences of that would be ruinous to each side. Japan could not afford the economic and potential social disruption of a break with its most important economic partner and the ramifications for China could be even more disastrous as Communist Party rule could be put at risk by a downturn of economic growth.

But it was clear that mutual suspicion had reached new depths. The Chinese side regarded with concern Japan's enhanced relations with America and some of its allies and partners such as Australia, India and the Philippines. Japan was seen as part of a new strategic American offensive against China, associated with Obama's declared "pivot" to Asia. Japan for its part continued to be concerned by China's naval activism in the waters around Japan and by its continual infringements of maritime domains regarded as within Japanese sovereignty and jurisdiction. In an act of bad timing, when the two sets of leaders had determined to improve relations, the Japanese Ministry of Defense published on December 17, 2010 its new National Defense Program Guidelines (NDPG), which stated that China's military development and its lack of transparency were matters of "concern" to the "region and the international community." The previous NDPG of 2005 merely said that they were worthy of "attention." The new NDPG declared that Japan would adapt a more dynamic defense orientation to the southern islands and increase the number of submarines from sixteen to twenty-two.

Conscious of the problems of possible conflict as their boats and naval vessels encountered each other, especially in the disputed waters of the East China Sea, the two sides agreed in December 2011 to "create a mechanism to discuss maritime security issues."[69] This led to a series of meetings at different levels of authority that included one which brought together the different parties and ministries of both sides with an active interest in the Sea. They agreed to have further meetings to thrash out practical ways of addressing maritime issues from sea rescue to managing fisheries and encounters at sea.[70]

However, such rationality was soon put at risk by yet another fracas over the Senkaku/Diaoyu. The Chinese side reacted strongly in early September to the Japanese government's purchase of three of the islands even though Prime Minister Noda had explained to President Hu that the purchase was to forestall a similar move by the right-wing governor of Tokyo, Shintaro Ishihara, who was determined to enhance Japan's claims at China's expense by building several facilities on the islands. Although Noda had explained to Hu that his purchase was designed to preserve the status quo and to minimize the risk of destabilizing incidents, Hu had his official news agency publish a severe warning by him to Noda opposing the purchase. Noda was seen by Hu as having raised Japan's claims to the islands to a new level. Yet from a strictly legal point of view the purchase did not change the basis of the Japanese claims to sovereignty over the islands. However, in Beijing the purchase was seen as an affront to China's sovereignty. China's Premier Wen Jiabao was then quoted as saying that his government would not retreat "half an inch" from its sovereign territory. A media campaign was then unleashed against Japan, which beginning on September 13 resulted in demonstrations, riots and violence against Japanese and Japanese property in up to eighty-five cities throughout China. Within two days some Chinese leaders and the official media began to urge restraint. Other media outlets, including the nationalistic *Global Times* and the armed forces' *Liberation Daily* continued the anti-Japanese rhetoric, adding for good measure that China could defeat a declining Japan and that America would not come to its aid.[71]

The episode provided yet another example of Chinese distrust of Japan. However, the deliberate incitement of anti-Japanese demonstrations and riots and evidence of official guidance of demonstrators suggested that domestic Chinese politics may have been involved. Commentary by some Chinese academics and others in China claimed that by encouraging the public to focus on opposition to Japan attention would be diverted from domestic political difficulties on the eve of a Communist Party Congress in which power would be transferred to the next generation. Some also claimed that the jockeying for positions of power in the forthcoming ten-year change of top leaders was reflected in the differences in the media between calls for restraint and further demonization of Japan.[72]

Interestingly, unlike previous occasions of official encouragement of anti-Japanese demonstrations, there were no clear demands for the Japanese to desist from particular actions (e.g., refrain from visiting the Yasukuni Shrine, or return a ship captain without a trial). The message apparently was that Japan should simply cease claiming indisputable sovereignty over the islands and recognize that China too had a valid claim. China's Vice President Xi Jinping, who was expected to take over the top leadership within weeks, declared that Japan's purchase of the islands was a "farce" and that Japan should "rein in its behavior" and stop undermining Chinese sovereignty.[73] China's leaders must have known that the Japanese government would not contemplate such an abject surrender, especially after having been condemned at home for conceding to China in the last Senkaku/ Diaoyu incident two years earlier. On the other hand they may have thought, in line with some Chinese media, that a declining Japan could not resist Chinese pressure. Indeed some even thought that the crisis could be used to separate Japan from the United States.[74]

One of the problems for China's leaders as a result of their inciting (or allowing) virulent nationalist demonstrations as a means of bringing pressure to bear on a foreign adversary has long been seen by those foreigners who have to deal with Chinese diplomats. The former US Secretary of State Condoleezza Rice noted: "Time and again we would see this. China would stir up nationalistic sentiment in the population through the state controlled media, diminishing room for maneuver as it reacted to the very passions it had created."[75] What made matters worse in the September 2012 case was that the whipping up of nationalist demonstrations and riots occurred as the leaders were still jockeying for position in the lead-up to a change of Party leadership. No senior official could appear to be weak on Japan and yet there was no sign that Japan was willing to make significant concessions. To the contrary, the Japanese attitude towards China appeared to be hardening.[76]

The US Secretary of Defense, Leon Panetta, happened to visit both Japan and China as some of the events of the crisis unfolded. But far from distancing the US from Japan, he signed an agreement in Tokyo to establish a second advanced radar station in Japan. Not surprisingly, this was criticized by the Chinese, some of whose analysts saw it as having the effect of strengthening Japan's determination to stand firm on the islands dispute with China.[77] Although Panetta pressed both sides to tone down the conflict lest it escalate, the United States continued to declare that the security treaty with Japan covered the islands, even as it reiterated its long-standing position that it took no side on the dispute over sovereignty.[78] Nevertheless sections of the Chinese media and as prominent a leader as Xi Jinping tried to cast doubt on the American–Japanese alliance. The Japanese were warned that the United States would probably not come to its assistance in the event of military conflict, while Xi Jinping sought to persuade the United States that the Japanese government had got very close to the Japanese right-wingers and that Japan had become a threat to regional and international order.[79]

It is difficult to evaluate the significance of the positions taken by China's leaders on the eve of a leadership succession. None of them could afford to be seen as "soft" on Japan at this juncture. Nevertheless, Xi's argument to Panetta about Japan as constituting a danger to regional order does fit in with a Chinese strategic objective of weakening or splitting Japan's alliance with the United States. As pointed out at the beginning of this chapter, the straits between Japanese islands constitute the only gateways to the Pacific open to the Chinese navy. The islands in dispute have a bearing on this issue, even though they do not command any straits. If the Chinese were able to persuade the Japanese that they could not rely upon the US to come to their aid over what one unnamed American senior official called a "few barren rocks" they would succeed in weakening Japanese confidence in the American deterrent. If the Chinese were also able to persuade the Americans that Japan and its "tilt to the right" was the problem and the Americans should exert pressure on their ally not to "provoke" China, China's leaders would have gone far in achieving their larger aim. Beginning in September Chinese Coast Guard vessels began to patrol the coastal waters of the islands and in December occasional flights by Chinese surveillance propeller aircraft took place near the islands' airspace. These developments were part of a mission to demonstrate Chinese sovereignty and to undermine Japanese claims to administer the islands. However, the advent of the new Abe government provided an opportunity for both sides to reduce tensions.[80]

In conclusion it is clear that the strategic rivalry between China and Japan, bolstered by popular animosity and distrust, is deep and enduring. Notwithstanding China's inexorable rise as an economic and military power and the relative decline of Japan, there is no question of Japan yielding to Chinese pressure. Japanese defiance is based on its long-standing historic unwillingness to defer to Chinese superiority and by its reliance on its alliance with the United States, which is likely to remain the superior military power in East Asia for the immediate future. However, much will depend on how Washington balances its engagement of China with its hedging against Chinese assertiveness. The Chinese side will also have to take into account that Japan's military and technological capabilities provide a solid basis for it to remain a naval military power of great regional significance should it choose the path of strategic independence. Moreover, as a threshold nuclear power Japan could rapidly acquire an independent nuclear deterrent, which of course is one of the unstated factors that cause the Chinese to treat Japan with care.

As Richard Bush has argued, this strategic logic could well be undermined by the lack of effective crisis management organizational tools on both sides of the East China Sea. Neither China nor Japan have an administrative unit that brings together all the different relevant agencies (intelligence, the military, the diplomatic, etc.) under one central command under the leadership of the head of government. In a context in which there is no agreement about how to deal with incidents at sea, the possibility of unwanted escalation from minor incidents remains a serious threat to the maintenance of order and clarity of understandings between the two sides.[81]

Yet even if the two great powers of East Asia are condemned to be strategic rivals their mutual economic dependence and the enormity of the stakes of open warfare ensure that the two are also driven to cooperate. Finally, the role of the United States as the offshore balancer, which is also allied to Japan is perhaps the key to determining the character of Sino-Japanese strategic relations as being neither too hot nor too cold. In other words it is not in American interests for Sino-Japanese relations to be put on a warlike footing, nor for them to become too cordial in an Asian partnership that would exclude the United States. The complex adversarial and cooperative relationship between these two great power neighbors coupled with American overwhelming military power are sufficient to ensure that the American interest is by and large upheld. Nevertheless, the different weaknesses in the respective governmental systems of each of the three parties provides for uncertainty in the capacity of their respective leaders to provide always the necessary prudence and control to ensure that Sino-Japanese animosities do not explode. To rephrase a well-known saying, the price of Sino-Japanese peace is eternal vigilance.

Notes

1 See for example, the White Paper issued by the PRC's State Council, "Diaoyu Dao, an inherent territory of China," September 25, 2012. http://news.xinhuanet.com/english/china/2012-09/25/c_131872152.htm. The historical basis for the Chinese claim is not currently recognized in International Law, a fact that the Japanese government has pointed out. See www.mofa.go.jp/region/asia-paci/senkaku. Both websites accessed April 9, 2013.
2 AP, "Disputed Asian islands part of 'first island chain' that could restrict China's navy," *Washington Post*, December 24, 2012.
3 Cheryl Pellerin, "Panetta: Rebalance to Asia-Pacific Region Shows Early Progress," *American Forces Press Service*, November 12, 2012. www.defense.gov/news/newsarticle.aspx?id=118518. Accessed March 27, 2013.
4 Condoleezza Rice, *No Higher Honor: A Memoir of My Years in Washington* (New York: Broadway Paperbacks, 2011), pp.648–49.
5 *BBC News Asia*, "US Defense chief Panetta warns on Asia territory rows," September 16, 2012. See also comment by Kurt Campbell, Assistant Secretary of State for East Asian and Pacific Affairs, "in the current environment, we want cooler heads to prevail," *South China Morning Post*, September 13, 2012.
6 Cited by Liao Chengzhi in his report to the Standing Committee of the National People's Congress on Deng Xiaoping's visit to Japan (November 4, 1978).
7 See, for example, Allen S. Whiting, *China Eyes Japan* (Berkeley: University of California Press, 1989), pp.138–41.
8 Jane Perlez, "Continuing Military Build up, China Boosts Military Spending more than 11 Percent," *New York Times*, March 4, 2012.
9 The figures are drawn from Defense of Japan 2012-E-White Paper, www.mod.go.jp/e/publ/w_paper/2012.html. Accessed April 9, 2013. Regarding Japan's spending on defense, see Sisi Tang and Tan Ee Lyn, "Japan Defense Ministry: No Rise in Budget Request," *Reuters*, September 30, 2011, in *Aviation Week*, September 9, 2011. See also the accounts in Christopher W. Hughes, *Japan's Remilitarization* (Oxford: Oxford University Press, Adelphi Paper Vol. 48, issue 403, 2008); Richard C. Bush, *The Perils of Proximity: China–Japan Security Relations* (Washington, DC: Brookings Institution Press, 2010), Chapter 5, "Navies, Air Forces, Coast Guards and Cyber Warriors," pp.41–62; and Richard J. Samuels, *Securing Japan: Tokyo's Grand Strategy and the Future of East Asia* (Ithaca, NY: Cornell University Press, 2007), Chapter 6, "The New Threat Environment," pp.135–57.
10 Banning Garrett and Bonnie Glaser, "China and the US–Japan Alliance at a Time of Strategic Change and Shifts in the Balance of Power," *Asia Pacific Research Center*, Stanford University, October 1997.
11 Maaike Okano Heijmans, "Japan as a Spoiler in Six Party Talks: Single Issue Politics and Economic Diplomacy Towards North Korea," *The Asia Pacific Journal: Japan Focus*, October 28, 2008. www.japanfocus.org/-maaike-okano_Heijmans/2929. Accessed March 27, 2013.
12 William L. Brooks, "The Politics of the Futenma Base Issue in Okinawa: Relocations Negotiations in 1995–97, 2005–6," *Asia Pacific Policy Papers* Series No. 9, 2010 (Washington, DC: Reischauer Center for East Asian Studies, SAIS, Johns Hopkins University).
13 Thom Shankeri, "US agrees to Reduce Size of force on Okinawa," *New York Times*, April 26, 2010.
14 "Abe named prime minister, vows to strengthen national security," *Asahi Shimbun*, December 26, 2012.
15 Jing-Dong Yuan, "Chinese Responses to US Missile Defenses: Implications for Arms Control & Disarmament," *The Nonproliferation Review*, Spring 2003, pp.75–96.

16 This discussion of China's strategic views has benefited greatly from a reading of Gilbert Roznan, *Chinese Strategic Thought Toward Asia* (New York: Palgrave Macmillan, 2010), which provides a cogent analysis of writings by Chinese analysts.
17 For an account of why this has endured see, Alan Romberg, *Rein in at the Brink of the Precipice: American Policy Towards Taiwan and US–PRC Relations* (Washington, DC: Stimson Center, 2003).
18 A senior Chinese diplomat openly told me that in Seoul, December 23, 1996.
19 See, Scott Snyder, *China's Rise and the Two Koreas: Politics, Economics, Security* (Boulder, CO: Lynne Rienner, 2009), Chapter 8, "The Korean Peninsula and Sino-Japanese Rivalry," pp.183–98.
20 Kyodo, "Japanese visit North Korean gravesites," *Japan Times*, October 3, 2012.
21 Interview with a senior official in the Ministry of Foreign Affairs Tokyo, August 29, 2012.
22 See Victor Cha, *Alignment Despite Antagonism: the US–Korea–Japan Security Triangle* (Palo Alto, CA: Stanford University Press, 1999); and Alexis Dudden, *Troubled Apologies Among Japan, Korea and the United States* (New York: Columbia University Press, 2008).
23 "Korea: Ex-Leader Park on list of 3000 Japan Collaborators," *Korea Herald/AsiaMedia-UCLA*, August 30, 2005.
24 Snyder, *China's Rise and the Two Koreas*, p.88.
25 Choe Sang-Hun, "South Korea Postpones Military Pact with Japan," *New York Times*, June 29, 2012; and Choe Sang-Hun, "South Korea Fires Top Presidential Aide Over Pact with Japan," *New York Times*, July 5, 2012.
26 J. Berkshire Miller, "Lee's Dokdo Visit Sinks Hopes for South Korea–Japan Détente," *World Politics Review*, August 14, 2012. www.worldpoliticsreview.com/articles/12258/lees-dokdo-visit-sinks-hopes-for-south-korea-japan-d-te. Accessed September 4, 2012.
27 Yoichi Funabashi, *Alliance Adrift* (New York: Council on Foreign Relations, 1999), p.352.
28 Ming Wan, *Sino-Japanese Relations* (Palo Alto, CA: Stanford University Press, 2005), p.281.
29 For an account of Japan's successful initiatives in solving the Cambodian crisis at that time see, Michael Jonathan Green, *Japan's Reluctant Realism* (N.Y.: Palgrave 2001) pp.172–76.
30 Ming Wan, *Sino-Japanese Relations: Interaction, Logic and Transformation* (Washington, DC: Woodrow Wilson Center Press / Palo Alto, CA: Stanford University Press, 2006), p.36.
31 For details consult the *Military Balance*, published annually by the International Institute for Strategic Studies (IISS), London. See also Bush, *Perils of Proximity*, Chapter 5, "Navies, Air Forces, Coast Guards, and Cyber Warriors," pp.41–62.
32 Green, *Japan's Reluctant Realism*, p.90.
33 Bush, *Perils of Proximity*, p.34.
34 See the discussion in Green, *Japan's Reluctant Realism*, pp.88–93.
35 Ming Wan, *Sino-Japanese Relations*, p.37.
36 Christopher W. Hughes, "Sino-Japanese Relations and Ballistic Missile Defense (BMD)," in Marie Soderberg (ed.), *Sino-Japanese Relations in the Twenty-First Century* (London and New York: Routledge, 2002), pp.69–87.
37 For details and analysis see, Hughes, *Japan's Remilitarization*.
38 For details see, IISS, *The Military Balance* (London: Routledge, 2012).
39 Ming Wan, *Sino-Japanese Relations*, pp.37–38.
40 Promulgated by the Chinese People's National Congress (NPC) in February 1992. Inter alia it set out Chinese claims in the East and South China Seas, which were disputed by others. Japanese scholars maintain that the Senkaku/Diaoyu islands were included only after the leaders of Guangdong insisted when the draft law had been circulated within China before being presented to the NPC. This was reported on September 19, 2011 by Dr. Akio Takahara in the course of the verbal presentation of his paper, "Japan–China Relations and the Implications for the United States and Okinawa," to a conference, "The Okinawa Question," held at the Sigur Center for Asian Studies, George Washington University, Washington DC.
41 Mong Cheung, "Political survival and the Yasukuni controversy in Sino-Japanese relations," *The Pacific Review* Vol. 23, No. 4, September 2010, pp.527–48, p.537.
42 Personal interviews with scholars and officials in Tokyo and Singapore, 2005 and 2006.
43 Personal interviews in Beijing and Tokyo, October 2006.
44 For a description of these and other similar incidents see, Ming Wan, *Sino-Japanese Relations*, pp.38–43.
45 Ibid., p.161.

46 See, Samuels, *Securing Japan*, note 73, p.241.
47 Ryosei Kokubun, "The China–Japan Relationship," in Gerald Curtis, Ryosei Kokubun, and Wang Jisi (eds.), *Getting the Triangle Straight: Managing China–Japan–US Relations* (Tokyo: Japan Center for International Exchange, 2010), p.58.
48 Jin Xide, "Hu Jintao's Visit to Japan and New Trends in Sino-Japanese Ties," *International Review*, December 2008.
49 UPI, "North Korea to conduct 'safe' nuclear test," October 3, 2006.
50 See, Hans Kristensen, "Reaffirming the Nuclear Umbrella: Nuclear Policy on Autopilot," FAS (Federation of Atomic Scientists) Strategic Security Blog, October 20, 2006. http://blogs.fas.org/security/2006/10/reaffirming_the_nuclear_umbrel/. Accessed April 9, 2013.
51 Hughes, *Japan's Remilitarization*, p.90.
52 Masayuki Masuda, "Tokyo and Beijing in Search of 'Strategic Relations': A Roadmap for Japan–China Military Diplomacy," in Gerrit Gong and Victor Teo (eds.), *Reconceptualising the Divide: Identity, Memory, and Nationalism in Sino-Japanese Relations* (Newcastle Upon Tyne: Cambridge Scholars Publishing, 2010), p.194.
53 D. Sneider, "The New Asianism: Japan's foreign policy under the Democratic Party of Japan (DPJ)." www.nbr.org/publications/element/aspx?id=504. Accessed March 27, 2013. Also in *Asia Policy 12* (July, 2011).
54 Jeffrey A. Bader, *Obama and China's Rise: An Insider's Account of America's Asia Strategy* (Washington, DC: Brookings Institution, 2012), p.43.
55 Ministry of Foreign Affairs of Japan, "Overview of Japan–China Summit Meeting (Outline)," April 13, 2010. http://www.mofa.go.jp/region/asia-paci/china/summit_meet1004.html. Accessed March 18, 2012.
56 Interview with a Japanese scholar in July 2009, that is, before President Obama had announced the pivot to Asia.
57 Michael Yahuda, "China's Recent Relations with Maritime Neighbors," *The International Spectator* Vol. 47, No. 2, June 2012, pp.30–44.
58 Bader, *Obama and China's Rise*, p.47.
59 Elizabeth Bumiller and Edward Wong, "China Warily Eyes U.S.–Korea Drills," *New York Times*, July 20, 2010.
60 Christopher Twomey, "The Military Security Relationship," in David Shambaugh (ed.), *Tangled Titans: The United States and China* (Lanham, MD: Rowman and Littlefield, 2012), pp.238–39.
61 See the discussion in Michael D. Swaine and M. Taylor Travel, "China's Assertive Behavior – Part Two: The Maritime Periphery," *China Leadership Monitor* No. 35, September 21, 2011, pp.1–29.
62 "China's military rise: The dragon's teeth," *The Economist*, April 7, 2012.
63 Bader, *Obama and China's Rise*, p.107. For an account of the September incident and its immediate aftermath see, Akio Takahara, "Japan–China Relations and the Implications for the United States and Okinawa," paper presented to the conference, "The Okinawa Question: Regional Security, The US–Japan Alliance and Futenma" held at the Sigur Center for Asian Studies, The Elliott School, George Washington University, September 19, 2011.
64 For an account of the militaristic education see, Christopher Hughes, "Nationalism and Foreign Policy: The Problem of Chinese Militarism," paper presented to conference on "China's Strategic Intentions," Lingnan University, Hong Kong, February 24, 2012.
65 Linda Jakobson and Dean Knox, *New Foreign Policy Actors in China* (SIPRI Policy Paper No. 26, 2010).
66 Bumiller and Wong, "China Warily Eyes U.S.–Korea Drills." See also, Mure Dickie, Song Jung-a and Kathrin Hille, "US, Japan begin naval drills near China," *The Financial Times*, June 21, 2012.
67 Richard Colapinto, "Vietnam Key to Japan's Southeast Asia Policy," *Atlantic Sentinel*, May 2, 2012; Jerry E. Esplanada, "Philippines to get 12 new patrol boats from Japan," *Philippine Daily Inquirer*, July 30, 2012; and Yoree Koh, "Tokyo and Manila Strengthen Defense Ties With an Eye Toward China," *Wall Street Journal*, September 28, 2011.
68 For an account of the Hu Jintao visit to Washington see, Bader, *Obama and China's Rise*, pp.126–29.
69 James J. Przystup, "Japan–China Relations: Another New Start," in *Comparative Connections*, January 2012. www.csis.org/files/publication/1103qjapan_china.pdf. Accessed March 27, 2013.

70 Interview with a senior official in the Ministry of Foreign Affairs Tokyo, August 29, 2012.
71 There are many accounts of the demonstrations and the rioting as they unfolded. For a useful account of the build-up to the crisis see, Przystup, "Japan-China Relations: Happy 40th Anniversary ... ? Part 2," in *Comparative Connections* (Hawaii, CSIS) Vol. 14, No. 1, September 2012. For an analysis see, Ian Johnson and Thom Shanter, "Beijing Mixes Messages Over Anti-Japan Protests," *New York Times*, September 17, 2012.
72 William Wan, "Chinese government both encourages and reins in anti-Japan protests, analysts say," *New York Times*, September 17, 2012.
73 *BBC News*, September 19, 2012.
74 See for example, Li Xiaokun, Wang Chenyan and Wu Jiao, "Tokyo 'must realize this is serious'," *China Daily*, September 10, 2012; and Raymond Li, "Papers go ballistic over Diaoyu dispute with Japan," *South China Morning Post*, September 20, 2012.
75 Condoleezza Rice, *No Higher Honor*, pp.46–47.
76 Chico Harlan, "With China's Rise Japan Shifts to the Right," *Washington Post*, September 21, 2012.
77 Thom Shanker and Ian Johnson, "US Accord with Japan over Missile Defense Draws Criticism in China," *New York Times*, September 17, 2012.
78 "Treaty with Japan covers islets in China conflict: U.S. Official [Kurt Campbell, Assistant Secretary of State Department]," *Reuters*, September 20, 2012. US Secretary of Defense, Leon Panetta, when asked in Tokyo about the islands dispute between China and Japan called for restraint and added, "we stand by our treaty obligations." www.defense.gov/news/newsarticle.aspx?id=117891. Accessed March 27, 2013.
79 See for example, "Diaoyu Islands 'Purchase' reflects weakened Japan: experts," *Xinhua*, September 15, 2012; and "Discard the illusion of friendly times with Japan" and "US costly option for cornered Japan," *The Global Times*, September 5, and 12, 2012, respectively. Xi Jinping's comment was told to me by a knowledgeable American official.
80 AFP, "China urges Japan's Shinzo Abe to meet 'halfway' over East China Sea," *South China Morning Post*, December 27, 2012; and "China trying to assess Abe's approach to future ties," *Asahi Shimbun*, December 24, 2012.
81 This is the principal theme of the most thorough study of the subject, Bush, *The Perils of Proximity*.

Conclusion

Looking ahead

Since the end of the Cold War, relations between China and Japan have taken place in the context of a shifting balance of power in which Japan's ascendancy has been replaced by the rise of China. The dynamics of the change are best illustrated by the phenomenal growth of China's GNP, which ranked tenth in 1991 and replaced that of Japan in 2010 to take over second place. The change is also reflected in terms of China's military challenge to Japan. At the end of the Cold War China's military capabilities were relatively backward and there was no navy to speak of. By the second decade of the twenty-first century China's military spending had greatly surpassed that of Japan and a modernized Chinese navy and coast guard was challenging Japan's maritime claims in ways that worried Japan's defense planners.

The dynamic of China's rise and Japan's decline have brought to the fore fundamental contradictions between their strategic interests, between their economic interdependency and the mutual antipathy of their people and also between their respective national identities, all of which combine to deepen the distrust between the two countries. None of these can be resolved in the near future, but at the same time it does not follow that open warfare between China and Japan is imminent. For one thing China is likely to be deterred by Japan's alliance with the United States and, by the same token, that alliance serves as a constraint upon Japan's re-emergence as a military power capable of significant offensive warfare. Beyond the constraining effects of America's role, both sets of leadership are aware of the enormous economic costs of potential military conflict, which in China could undermine the rule of the Communist Party, which heavily depends upon the country's economic growth to maintain its position of power. Nevertheless given the strength of nationalism in both countries and especially of that in China, when combined with the growing dysfunctional character of governance in each country, military conflict cannot be ruled out even though it would be contrary to the fundamental interests of both countries. I shall look in more detail at how these different contradictory factors may play out and also suggest ways in which potential military conflict may be avoided.

Conflicting strategic interests

The previous chapter showed how China's new naval capabilities and its ambitions to reach out beyond the "near seas" to the "far seas" require its naval vessels to cross through straits between the island chain that constitutes Japan. As seen from China these are part of what its strategists call the "first island chain" that stretches from north of

Japan through the Okinawa islands incorporating Taiwan and on to the Philippines. It is regarded as critical for the defense of China as it is a gateway to the wider world, which if controlled by an adversary would bottle up most of China's fleet in the South and East China Seas (the "near seas"). The ability to pass through the gateway and, if necessary, to stop primarily the United States from penetrating it to reach China's coastal waters is deemed vital for the defense of China's coastal waters and, perhaps even more importantly, to weaken or block the American capacity to come to the aid of Taiwan in the event of conflict. In fact given the range and accuracy of modern weaponry, Chinese strategists deem it important for China to deny the United States dominance of the maritime area between the first and second island chains, which stretches from the northwest of Japan via Guam to south of the Philippines to Indonesia. The United States calls the object of this Chinese strategy A2/AD (Anti Access and Area Denial). In other words, if the Chinese strategists see their strategy as defensive, the Americans see it as offensive, designed to leave Taiwan defenseless and to undermine the American position in the Pacific where it has kept the peace since 1945 and provided the public goods, which have facilitated the economic rise of East Asian countries, including notably China itself.

In the Japanese perspective a Chinese naval ascendancy that would allow it unfettered command over the straits between the East China Sea and the Pacific would be an unmitigated disaster. It would effectively cede control of Japan to China. Not only would the vulnerabilities of Japan's trade lifelines be at Chinese mercy, but the connections between Japan's main islands and even the country's independence would be in jeopardy. It comes as no surprise therefore that Japan has responded to Chinese increased naval activities in the East China Sea by shifting to a more active defense strategy focused on the islands in the southern part of the Okinawan (or Ryukyu) island chain.

For its part, the United States seeks to calibrate its interest in not alienating China by pursuing a policy of part engagement and part hedging or deterrence. In many respects China and the United States share both regional and global interests. But at the same time the alliance with Japan remains the lynchpin of the American ability to retain its hegemony in the Western Pacific and beyond. Thus the United States has to combine reassurance to Japan about its obligations as an ally to come to its aid in the event of attack not only against the Japanese main four islands, but also any territory currently being administered by Japan including the Senkaku/Diaoyu, whose sovereignty is also claimed by China. It is therefore in the strategic interest of the United States that neither China nor Japan should allow their strategic rivalry to reach the point of armed conflict. The problem, however, is that neither China nor Japan trust each other in strategic matters and that neither trusts the United States to abide by its commitments. If the Japanese worry that the United States might not come to their aid in a timely and effective manner were the Chinese to use force to establish what they see as their rights over, say, the Senkaku/Diaoyu Islands, the Chinese do not trust American claims that they support the emergence of a strong and prosperous China. Indeed the Chinese regard the Obama administration's "pivot to Asia" with the "rebalancing" of its forces by 2020 to a ratio of 60:40 in favor of the Pacific over the Atlantic as directed against them, regardless of Washington's statements to the contrary.

It is this widespread strategic distrust which underlies much of the ongoing crisis of claim and counter claim between China and Japan over the Senkaku/Diaoyu Islands. The

Japanese regard the strengthening of their forces deployed in its southerly islands of Okinawa as defensive and the government's purchase of three of the islands as an act designed to uphold the status quo by forestalling the maverick right-wing former governor of Tokyo from buying them and building structures upon them to bind them more closely to Japan at the expense of China. The Chinese, however, regard all these moves by Japan as provocative changes of the status quo and as indications of a rightward shift by the Japanese government. In other words, each side sees its own positions and actions as defensive against the other side's actions as provocative challenges of the status quo. The relationship may be described as the classic security dilemma in which the attempts of one side to strengthen its defenses is immediately seen as a threat by the other and at the same time any perceived sign of weakness by one accentuates the fear that it would be taken advantage of by the other side.

The Chinese government meanwhile has sought to bolster its diplomatic and strategic position by seeking common cause with South Korea against Japan (the two have their own territorial dispute over the Dokdo/Takeshima islets in the sea between them). If the approach had been successful it would also have troubled Washington greatly, as it has been alarmed by the sudden outbreak in August 2012 of discord between its two major allies. In the event the Chinese sounding was rejected. Beijing had also failed in its effort to make common cause with Taiwan over their respective claims in the South China Sea.

Beijing and Taipei separately claim sovereignty over the Senkaku/Diaoyu islands (or Tiau Yu Tai, according to the transliteration in Taiwan), but here too Taipei followed its own path. Taiwan's President, Ma Ying-jeou, has called for "decorous" behavior and for a multilateral approach (presumably including all three parties) instead of the unilateral measures so far followed by Japan. He also called for the reaching of agreements over fisheries and the joint exploitation of such resources as may be located in the adjoining maritime domain. The proposal was received favorably in Tokyo, but the government of Japan has yet to make proposals of its own as to how to end the impasse. However, it so happens that talks about extending a fisheries agreement between Japan and Taiwan that had expired in 1996 were being held when the latest dispute flared up. To the surprise and annoyance of China, an agreement was reached on April 10, 2013, which allowed Taiwanese fishing boats to operate around the disputed islands (although not within Japan's claimed territorial waters). By the agreement the Taiwanese leader not only satisfied an important domestic constituency, but he also demonstrated diplomatic independence from Beijing, which had long sought to incorporate Taiwan within its approach to the islands and hoped to offer protection to Taiwanese fishermen in the name of China. The Japanese side was delighted with a move that had the potential to reduce tensions and that supported its wider goal of enhancing Taiwan's de-facto independence. It also inserted something of a wedge between Taipei and Beijing.[1]

The agreement is unlikely to provide a model for a similar agreement between China and Japan at least until the two can reach an understanding about managing their differences over sovereignty, which would allow them to "shelve" the issue along the lines suggested by Deng Xiaoping back in 1978. For the present the Shinzo Abe government has rejected the "shelving" proposal as it sees that as a retreat from its claim that its sovereignty over the islands is indisputable. Meanwhile the new Chinese leadership under Xi Jinping shows no signs of backing down from its strategy of "reactive assertivenes" designed to change the status quo in its favor.

A related problem is currently being considered and that concerns the establishment of rules or procedures that China and Japanese naval and civilian vessels should follow in both the high seas and in disputed waters when they encounter each other. The prospects for this were increased by the Chinese decision in March 2013 to unify their various coast gaurd commands into one, which would ensure tighter central control. During his first stint as prime minister in 2007, Abe and Chinese premier Wen Jiabao agreed to start talks on creating a maritime hotline. But first talks about the matter involving reprsentatives of each country's relevant shipping and naval bureaucracies were not held until December 2011 and a further round was held in May 2012. They were then suspended in view of the heightened tensions. However, it was agreed in April 2013 to reopen the stalled talks as a senior Japanese Defense Ministry official noted that "an emergency communication framework is all the more necessary because there is no political dialogue." An incident in January when a Chinese frigate aimed weapons-guiding radar at an SDF destroyer in the East china Sea prompted the Japanese side to insist on setting up such a maritime communications mechanism as a matter of urgency.[2]

In a context in which both sides were increasing the patrols of their coast guard vessels in the vicinity of the islands with their naval warships at a further distance the agreement to resume talks on establishing maritime emergency communication may be seen as both a signal or reassurance and of concern. Better communications should help prevent accidental clashes and in particular prevent escalation arising out of incidents should they occur. The concern is that both sides seem to suggest that they are settling in for the long haul, with no imminent accommodation in sight. Indeed both their defense white papers, which were published in the Spring of 2013 broke new ground in identifying each other as a potential threat and in indicating that they would increase the number of their coast guard vessels as well as those of their navies.

Nationalism and problems of governance

Earlier chapters showed how nationalism in China and Japan was closely linked with domestic politics and questions of identity. It is important, however, to distinguish between the forms of nationalism in China and Japan as they have developed since the end of the Cold War. In China nationalism has become one of two pillars on which the legitimacy of Communist Party rule depends (the other is economic performance). It grew out of the patriotic education campaign in the early 1990s, which portrayed China as a peaceable world leader in economics and culture until brought down low in the "century of shame and humiliation" and which is now in the process of rejuvenation despite continuing foreign hostility, especially from the West, headed by the United States. The Communist Party is portrayed as the savior of the Chinese nation through the establishment of a strong state under Mao's leadership and developing the economy as begun under the leadership of Deng Xiaoping. Much emphasis in this officially inspired campaign has been placed on the horrors perpetrated by the Japanese aggressors in the 1930s and early 1940s and on the possible revival of militarism in Japan, especially in the light of its judged failure to atone properly for its past aggression. China throughout is portrayed as the innocent victim. This campaign has continued inexorably through to the present through the school system in textbooks and magnified through all media outlets, from comic books, television, films to museums and so on.[3] It has been thoroughly imbibed by the younger generation and it dominates discussion on the Internet, to the extent that only a few bloggers challenge the nationalist discourse and they do so at their peril.[4] While the leadership, with a domestic security system whose budget exceeded that of the military in 2012, was able to stifle or suppress other kinds of demonstrations, it did little to stop nationalist demonstrations until they seemed to reach a point at which the government's interests may suffer. Indeed, as we have seen, at times it even encouraged them.

Japanese nationalism since the end of the Cold War and indeed since 1945 has been of a different order. Only rarely have there been street demonstrations, the most recent involving only a few hundred people in downtown Tokyo. Indeed the most numerous demonstrations have been in Okinawa against America and Tokyo over American basing policies in the islands. To be sure there has been a small but persistent demand by right-wingers to amend the peace constitution, and transform Japan to an independent military power. But even these are divided between those who favor the alliance with the US and those who seek to remove what they regard as a foreign presence, which demeans Japan culturally as well as depriving it of strategic independence. But despite the shift towards conservatism in Japan after the end of the Cold War, the attachment to the peace constitution has continued to be strong enough to preclude the constitutional revision sought by the right-wingers. If the Japanese public has adopted a more severe approach to China in recent years it is because of what is seen as an increasingly over-bearing China that has accompanied its rise, but not necessarily its growing military pressure. According to an opinion poll taken in late January 2013, 88 percent of Japanese respondents said they trusted China "not much" or "not at all".[5] In this respect the Abe government may be said to be ahead of or separate from general public opinion. Unlike the situation in China the overwhelming bulk of the people in Japan may be insular, but they are not as nationalistic as they were in the 1930s. It is mainly among the elite associated with the more hawkish elements of the LDP that right-wing nationalism is to be found, which finds expression in denial of Japan's recent history of brutal aggression. Ironically as self-proclaimed upholders of their country's dignity and self-respect they damage Japan's standing in Northeast Asia and weaken Japan's reputation as a uniquely peaceable country for the past seven decades.

Problems of domestic governance in both countries have had the effect of increasing the enmity between China and Japan, reducing the scope for each to deal rationally and flexibly with the problems that arise in their difficult relationship. The Japanese governmental system is seen as dysfunctional, especially due to the rapid displacement of prime ministers of which Prime Minister Abe is the seventh in the six years since the resignation of Junichiro Koizumi. The failings of Japan's bureaucracies as well as the political class became plain for all to see in the great shortcomings displayed in the handling of the March 11, 2011 disasters of the earthquake, the tsunami and especially the Fukushima nuclear power failure and its aftermath. It was the resilience of Japanese society in responding to the tsunami in the main affected area calmly with self-reliance and mutual help which was most noticeable. These developments have resulted in the absence of effective leadership able to provide consistent and effective policies for Japan in tackling either the pressing economic and social issues at home or the immediate problems balancing relations with the United States, South Korea and an increasingly assertive China. The disappointment in the DPJ government was reflected in the massive majority vote gained by the LDP in December 2012. Shinzo Abe's second term of government has seen a remarkable turnaround from his ignominious first of 2007/2008. He has provided vigorous leadership that at the time of writing (May 2013) promises to pull Japan out of the doldrums of the past two decades. With what he calls his "three arrows" Abe announced a Yen 10.3 trillion fiscal stimulus, an inflation target of 2 percent (and a new governor of the central bank committed to the necessary financial easing) and finally, a commitment to structural reform through seeking to join the Trans Pacific Partnership (TPP), which would transform many aspects of the economy. Dubbed Abeconomics, his approach has fundamentally transformed the economic outlook in Japan and it has begun to inject the kind of optimism about the future that has been lacking for more than twenty years. No wonder Abe repeatedly declares "Japan is back".

Externally, Abe has made it clear that he will stand up to Chinese military pressure and domestically he has been buoyed by favorable opinion polls of over 70 percent and he is favored to win the July elections to the Upper House, which will give him a majority in both Houses – something that has eluded the governing party since he was last prime minister in 2007.[6] Abe has indicated that he will introduce changes to the constitution that will move Japan towards becoming a "normal country" with a standing armed forces able to play their part in defending allies. But Abe has a broader more nationalistic agenda that goes beyond strengthening Japan to stand up to China. It is one that harks back to the imperial past. Perhaps inspired by the euphoria of his achievements in the last five months Abe has publicly sided with the right wing revisionist historians by openly querying whether the Japanese were aggressors in the wars in Asia. His chief cabinet secretary, Yoshide Suga, hurriedly assured the outside world that Abe still stood by the apologies for the suffering inflicted by the war as issued by previous prime ministers.

But the damage was done. Abe's comments were particularly ill-timed, given the American and South Korean attempts to present a common front against yet another series of provocations by North Korea. At a stroke Abe had unnecessarily antagonized the newly elected President of South Korea and dismayed the Obama administration for undermining relations between its two key Asian allies at a time the strategic situation called for a unified approach. The episode may be seen as an example of how strategic interests can be undermined by domestically focused nationalistic hubris.

The Chinese case is somewhat different. The new Chinese leadership after the 18th Party Congress in November 2012 faces a deep set of problems that call into question the option of continuing with the current model of economic development and the political system that underpins it. In the view repeated several times by the outgoing premier, Wen Jiabao, the Chinese economy is "unstable, unbalanced, uncoordinated, and unsustainable." A lengthy study by the World Bank and the Development Research Center (DRC) of the State Council of February 2012 also called for fundamental reform of the Chinese economy. In the view of a deputy director of the DRC the government needed first, to focus on the provision of services instead of controlling and driving industrial growth; second, to shift the economy from exports to domestic consumption; third, to reduce the power of state enterprises and state banks to allow for more private firms and financial mechanism to create new waves of consumers; and finally to restructure the system in an orderly manner to avoid chaos.[7] The problem is that many leaders in the Party believe that the current economic system is the bedrock for Party rule. The new leader, Xi Jinping indicated that he upheld Party censorship and he invoked the example of the collapse of the Soviet Union in expressing his determination to hold on to maintaining Party command of the armed forces, rather than placing them under the control of the state.[8] Moreover, even if the new Standing Committee of the Political Bureau wanted to carry out fundamental reform the consensus based collective leadership is ill placed to overcome resistance from the powerful vested interests, who would be the main losers in any such reforms, especially as most of China's top leaders together with their families are the primary beneficiaries of the current system.[9] Further, the fragmentation of authority that is already evident in Chinese politics creates many obstacles to fundamental change. Yet in addition to the structural problems of the economy, rural citizens continue to launch "mass incidents" in their tens of thousands against what they see as land grabs by local officials and pollution of their arable lands. Urban citizens too are increasingly active in airing their grievances about corruption, inequalities, worsening pollution, affordable housing, employment and so on, and are demanding a greater voice in the making of policies directly affecting them. China's new leaders are likely to focus their attention on these and related domestic issues rather than on foreign relations and on coming to grips with the views and interests of their neighbors. This would suggest that there will be greater tolerance for demonstrations against Japan and other foreign countries, reflecting a general tendency to distrust foreign countries, especially neighbors allied to the United States, and a greater readiness to allow domestic driven discontent to be expressed in anti-foreign demonstrations.

The significance of economic interdependence

As argued in chapter 4, the vast scale of the economic relationship between China and Japan ensures that it greatly influences the evolution of relations between the two countries. There is little doubt that their mutual dependence has reached a point at which the consequences of it being disrupted would extend beyond the economic sphere to cause social and political problems sufficient to threaten the power held by one or both of their governments. At issue, however, is how far China in particular can use the importance of the economic relationship to bring sufficient pressure to bear on Japan to make it concede to Chinese demands. At the same time the Chinese have to exercise care, lest their economic pressure rebounds on them by making Japanese companies (and possibly others) seek to invest elsewhere.

Both China and Japan have used their economic strengths to gain political advantage notably in Southeast Asia and Africa. Indeed as noted in chapter 5, the rivalry between the two takes mainly an economic form. However, the question here is the extent to which the two sides use their economic strength to penalize others for political purposes. There is evidence of China having done so on several occasions, sometimes directly hitting imports and exports. For example, in the earlier dispute of September 2010 involving the arrested captain, the Chinese delayed and cut back for a while the export of rare earths to Japan, which were crucial ingredients to many of Japan's manufactures. On that occasion Japan acceded to Chinese demands. Another example concerns a dispute with the Philippines of the ownership of Scarborough Shoal in the South China Sea in 2011. The Chinese engineered delays in distributing imported bananas from the Philippines for the purposes of so-called inspection. A significant number of batches of bananas rotted as a result. At other times China has used popular actions, such as consumer boycotts of products, to punish the offending country. For example, attempts to do so with regard to the French major supermarket Carrefour in 2008 in response to French protests about Chinese behavior in Tibet and in 2012 with regard to Japanese products and cars in particular. However, these boycotts can backfire as in the case of Carrefour, where it was soon recognized that the sufferers in the first instance were the numerous Chinese employed by the French company. The Japanese side expects that similar considerations will end Chinese boycotts of their products. They note that Japanese manufacturers in China employ more than 10 million workers. A *People's Daily* editorial of September 28, 2012 summed up the broader issue well:

> In recent years, whenever China's relations with another country took a turn for the worse, calls for a boycott of that country's products would ring out. So it has been with the Diaoyu Islands dispute.
>
> Any major disruption to bilateral trade would hurt both countries. Yet some scholars argue otherwise. They say Japan is more reliant on the Chinese economy than vice versa. Hence if China were to pull the "economic trigger", it would cripple the Japanese economy.
>
> This is more guesswork than fact-based analysis. Let's not even consider what a sluggish Japanese economy will do to the world economy.
>
> Japan is at the high end of the global industrial chain, while China is at its low-end manufacturing base. Every year, China imports parts and components or the assembly of products that are then exported worldwide. These Japanese made components include hi-tech and high-value-added products that are not easily replaced. Just recall how the tsunami and nuclear accident in Japan last year set back the electronics and auto industries in the US, Europe and China.

It should be noted that the editorial indicated a division of opinion in Beijing about using China's economic power against Japan, but it seems as if moderate voices have prevailed. Nevertheless the genuine popular anger against Japan is reflected in the significant scaling down of tourism to Japan and in a popular boycott of Japanese goods. But these are not expected to endure. However, some Japanese businesses have been sufficiently discomforted to ask the government to soften its stance against Chinese demands that it recognize that the sovereignty over the islands in dispute – an act that would go a long way to undermine Japan's legal case for exercising sovereignty over the islands. Not surprisingly the Japanese government has refused.[10] The Chinese side clearly hopes to exploit the differences that have been exposed in Japan. But the argument has shifted from talk of using China's economic strength as a weapon. Instead the Chinese claim has moved on to suggesting that Japan and the United States have not paid sufficient attention to the recent shift in the balance of power in China's favor that has taken place in recent years.[11]

China's leaders have tried to build diplomatic pressure on Japan by canceling official meetings, including the celebrations for the fortieth anniversary of the establishment of diplomatic relations, refusing to send ministerial-level representatives to an IMF meeting held in Japan. But as already noted they failed in attempts to take advantage of the divide that occurred between South Korea and Japan over the islands in dispute between them. Instead South Korean and Japanese finance ministers have pledged to cooperate closely. A further indication of the separation of economics from the political tensions was evident from the continuation of talks over a trilateral free-trade agreement between the three Northeast Asian powerhouses. The leaders of the three states met in November in Cambodia (at an ASEAN meeting) to kick off higher level negotiations.[12]

In sum the Chinese side has inflicted some economic costs on Japanese manufacturers, especially auto-makers based in China; and on airlines and hotels in Japan (especially in Okinawa) which had expected to profit from Chinese tourists during the week long national day holiday in the first week of October. But these are expected to be temporary losses. Longer term it is unclear how the costs and benefits will be distributed between China and Japan, especially if Japanese companies were to become more cautious about basing so much of their manufacturing capacity in China, given that other safer opportunities exist elsewhere in Asia. It would seem therefore that the scale of Sino-Japanese economic interdependence is indeed a constraint on the escalation of conflict – at least as far as these rocky islands are concerned.

Future prospects

The underlying causes for conflict between China and Japan are unlikely to change – at least in the near future. In fact they are likely to get worse. The continual rise of China's economy and its growing military power will probably accentuate the drive of the Chinese navy to reach the blue waters of the Pacific and escape the confinement of China's "near seas." That will entail increasing use of the international straits traversing the Japanese archipelago thereby deepening Japanese fears of encirclement and Chinese concerns about the straits being closed to their navy in the event of hostilities.

Japanese popular fears of the pressure exerted by China's rise as accompanied by concern of Japan's relative decline will likely continue to harden attitudes towards China. If Abe were to succeed in turning around the Japanese economy and put it on the path to long term growth he would likely preside over a more assertive Japan, which would insist on countering their giant neighbor. The current rightward trend of Japan's political parties is unlikely to be reversed anytime soon, which will make it less likely that Japanese history textbooks will encourage students to reflect on and come to terms with their country's past history of aggression in Asia, and hence make it less likely for a sense of community to develop in East Asia. Similarly, there is no sign in Beijing of a readiness to review the teaching of history in China, which for the last two decades or more has encouraged a view that, as in the period that ended more than sixty years ago, China is a victim surrounded by hostile countries, notably Japan and the United States. The continual vilification of Japan in school curricula, the mass media and so on, continues to ensure that hatred of Japan will be at the forefront of Chinese nationalism.

These two structural dimensions of the conflicts inherent in the relations between the two major powers of East Asia, however, are countered by two structural constraints. These are to be found in the security and socio-economic dimensions of the relationship. As already pointed out, Japan's alliance with the United States is the cornerstone of America's strategic presence in East Asia and the Western Pacific. Its geopolitical position is vital as it is at the center of the means of limiting China's capacity to challenge successfully American power in the region and it is also conveniently located as the link between Northeast and Southeast Asia. The alliance also serves as the guarantor of Japan's security and militates against Japan's emergence as an independent strategic and military actor. Such a development would be seen in Beijing as highly threatening to its core strategic interests.

The other structural constraint is the depth of the economic interdependence between the two countries. As noted above, that has already persuaded Beijing to avoid taking significant economic measures designed to hurt the Japanese economy. It has also had the effect of causing Japanese business leaders to press their government to lower tensions with China over the island disputes. At issue is not just economics, important as it may be in its own right. The political consequences for Japan at a time in which it had still not recovered from the March 2011 triple calamity of the earthquake, the tsunami and the nuclear disaster could be devastating. China's leaders have even more deep-seated reasons to fear an economic downturn as it could unleash precisely the kind of social instability that could undermine Communist Party rule.

Given the many aspects of this complex relationship that could lead to an outbreak of military hostilities, which all sides recognize would be highly damaging to their respective interests, there is a need for better and more effective management of the interactions between China and Japan. The immediate problems are whether Abe's newly established government in Japan will suceed in reversing the country's decline and how soon the new leadership in Beijing can consolidate its power in order to carry out its difficult but needed economic reforms. Lacking a dominant leader it will probably have to operate by consensus. Not only will the new leaders have to deal with a system in which authority is fragmented with powerful vested interests opposed to change, but also much time will have to be spent in the lead-up to the next CCP Congress in five years' time in maneuvers to place favored candidates to replace five of the current seven on the all important Standing Committee of the Political Bureau who have to retire. Consequently it will be difficult for the new leadership to initiate fundamentally new policies in foreign affairs, especially with regard to Japan.

Nevertheless there are some positive developments that are currently taking place on which significant improvements in managing relations can be built. In the economic sphere the trilateral arrangement of regular meetings between Chinese, Japanese and South Korean leaders, which began in 2008, has not been greatly affected by the disputes over islands involving all three parties even though the projected meeting in May 2013 was postponed at the insistence of Beijing. The leaders met at the ASEAN meeting in Cambodia in November 2012 and are due to conduct a tripartite meeting in 2013. The three have already reached a raft of agreements designed to ease their economic transactions and they have even agreed to work together on some non-traditional security issues. A secretariat has been set up in Seoul. Beyond the annual summit meetings, representatives of a variety of ministries involved in economic issues meet more frequently on a regular basis. The significance of this trilateral institution transcends the immediate functional issues it addresses. It helps the different levels of government to gain a better understanding of their viewpoints, their key interests and their methods of operation. It helps consolidate their mutual dependence and strengthen the position of those in their respective governments who are committed to upholding cooperation between these three major states.

In the security realm a start has been made between the main Chinese and Japanese parties engaged in maritime activities in the seas between them to try and reach agreements about what might be called rules of conduct when they encounter each other either on the high seas or in waters closer to their respective coast lines. These are still early days and as yet no firm agreements have been reached. A real breakthrough could be achieved if a code of conduct could be agreed as to how their fishing fleets, coast guard vessels and naval vessels should behave relative to each other and how to communicate with each other in timely fashion in the event of emergencies. Such an outcome could not be reached quickly given the depth of distrust between the two sides and the institutional limitations apparent in both Japan and China in handling such matters.[10] Meanwhile the dangers of incidents at sea are increasing as Chinese coast guard vessels patrol the waters adjacent to the Senkaku/Diaoyu Islands so as to undermine the Japanese claim to administer the islands.

In looking ahead, it is apparent that the Sino-Japanese relationship encompasses not only fundamental distrust and the potential for conflict, but also elements of cooperation. The American presence both as an ally of Japan and as the provider of public goods in the Western Pacific has been the unacknowledged guarantor of peace between these two very different countries. In the more than twenty years that have passed since the end of the Cold War these two major powers of East Asia have emerged with new identities, which have yet to be settled. The balance of power between them has shifted from a Japanese ascendancy to one that is increasingly favorable to China. During this time the relationship has experienced ups and downs, but it has continuously been marked by both rivalry and cooperation. Both countries have a stake in the continuing viability of the other as a relatively stable economic partner. It would seem, therefore, that the interests of both China and Japan lie in continuing to coexist with each other. In that sense the two tigers have no alternative but to share the same mountain.

Notes

1 For an account of the agreement see, "Editorial: Japan-Taiwan fishing deal exemplifies diplomatic ingenuity", *Asahi Shimbun*, April 11, 2013 (www.asahi.com/english).
2 "Japan, China to reopen talks on maritime hotline" *Asahi*, April 24, 2013.
3 For a detailed account of the campaign and its significance in Chinese politics and foreign relations see, Zheng Wang, *Never Forget National Humiliation* (New York: Columbia University Press, 2012).
4 Peter Hays Gries, *China's New Nationalism* (Berkeley: University of California Press, 2004)
5 "50% consider ties with the US to be positive/Survey: 85% have dim view of China", *Yomiuri Shimbun*, February 16, 2013.
6 "Briefing, Japan and Abenomics: Once more with feeling", *The Economist*, May 18th–24th, pp. 24–26.
7 James McGregor, "Heroically Transcending the Existing International system", *No Ancient Wisdom, No followers: the Challenges of Chinese Authoritarian Capitalism* (Westport CT: Prospecta Press, 2012), pp. 103–113.
8 "Leaked Speech Shows Xi jinping's Opposition to Reform." http://chinadigitaltimes.net/2013/_01/leaked-speech-shows-xi-jinpings-opposition-to-reform/ Accessed March 27, 2013.
9 Linda Jakobson and Dean Knox, *New Foreign Policy Actors in China* (SIPRI, Policy Paper No. 26, 2010); and James McGregor, *No Ancient Wisdom…*, op.cit., p.2.
10 "Keidanren chief blasts handling of Senkaku issue, *Asahi*, September 29, 2012.
11 "Japan must make a strategic choice", *People's Daily*, October 6, 2012.
12 *Asahi* April 18, 2013; Martin Fackler, "Japan and South Korea Seek to Strengthen Economic Ties", *New York Times*, October 11, 2012; and Alastair Gale and Rosalind Mathieson, "China-Japan Tensions Concern South Korea", *Wall Street Journal*, October 11, 2012.
13 This is one of the themes covered in depth in Richard Bush, *The Perils of Proximity* (Washington DC: The Brookings Institution Press, 2010).

Select bibliography

Bader, Jeffrey A., *Obama and China's Rise: An Insider's Account of America's Asia Strategy* (Washington, DC: Brookings Institution, 2012)

Berger, Thomas U., Mochizuki, Mike and Tsuchiyama, Jitsuo (eds.), *Japan in International Politics: The Foreign Policy of an Adaptive State* (Boulder, CO: Lynne Rienner, 2007)

Bush, Richard C., *The Perils of Proximity: China–Japan Security Relations* (Washington, DC: Brookings Institution Press, 2010)

Calder, Kent and Min Ye, *The Making of Northeast Asia* (Palo Alto, CA: Stanford University Press, 2010)

Callaghan, William, *China, the Pessoptimist Nation* (Oxford: Oxford University Press, 2010)

Cha, Victor, *Alignment Despite Antagonism: the US–Korea–Japan Security Triangle* (Palo Alto, CA: Stanford University Press, 1999)

Curtis, Gerald, Kokubun, Ryosei and Wang Jisi (eds.), *Getting the Triangle Straight: Managing China–Japan–US Relations* (Tokyo: Japan Center for International Exchange, 2010)

Dower, John W., *Embracing Defeat: Japan in the Wake of World War II* (New York: W.W. Norton, 1999)

——, *Ways of Forgetting, Ways of Remembering: Japan in the Modern World* (New York: The New Press, 2012)

Drifte, Reinhard, *Japan's Quest for a Permanent Security Council Seat: A Matter of Pride or Justice?* (New York: St. Martin's Press, 2000)

Dudden, Alexis, *Troubled Apologies Among Japan, Korea and the United States* (New York: Columbia University Press, 2008)

Finkelstein, David, *China Reconsiders its National Security: "The Great Peace and Development Debate of 1999"* (Alexandria, VA: CNA Corp., 2000)

Fogel, Joshua A. (ed.), *The Nanjing Massacre in History and Historiography* (Berkeley: University of California Press, 2000)

Funabashi, Yoichi, *Alliance Adrift* (New York: Council on Foreign Relations, 1999)

Goldstein, Avery, *Rising to the Challenge: China's Grand Strategy and International Security* (Palo Alto, CA: Stanford University Press, 2005)

Goodman, David S.G. and Segal, Gerald (eds.), *China Rising: Nationalism and Interdependence* (London and New York: Routledge, 1997)

Green, Michael J., *Japan's Reluctant Realism: Foreign Policy Challenges in an Era of Uncertain Power* (New York: Palgrave, 2001, for the Council on Foreign Relations)

Gries, Peter Hays, *China's New Nationalism: Pride, Politics and Diplomacy* (Berkeley: University of California Press, 2004)

Hughes, Christopher R., *Japan's Re-emergence as a "Normal" Military Power?* (Oxford: Oxford University Press, 2004)

——, *Chinese Nationalism in the Global Era* (London and New York: Routledge, 2006)

Jain, R.K., *China and Japan 1949–1980* (Oxford: Martin Robinson, revised 2nd edition, 1981)

Jakobson, Linda and Knox, Dean, *New Foreign Policy Actors in China* (SIPRI Policy Paper No. 26, 2010)
Jansen, Marius B., *The Making of Modern Japan* (Cambridge, MA: Harvard University Press, 2000)
Johnson, Chalmers, *Japan, Who Governs? The Rise of the Developmental State* (New York: W.W. Norton, 1995)
Kingston, Jeff, *Contemporary Japan: History, Politics and Social Change since the 1980s* (Chichester, West Sussex, UK: John Wiley, 2011)
Lee Chae-Jin, *China and Japan: New Economic Diplomacy* (Palo Alto, CA: Hoover Institution, Stanford University Press, 1984)
Leifer, Michael, *The ASEAN Regional Forum. Extending ASEAN's Model of Regional Security* (Adelphi Paper 302, IISS, Oxford University Press, July 1996)
Mendl, Wolf, *Issues in Japan's China Policy* (London: Macmillan, 1978)
——, *Japan's Asia Policy* (London and New York: Routledge, 1995)
Meyer, Claude, *China or Japan: Which will Lead Asia?* (New York: Columbia University Press, 2011)
Ming Wan, *Sino-Japanese Relations: Interaction, Logic and Transformation* (Washington, DC: Woodrow Wilson Center Press / Palo Alto, CA: Stanford University Press, 2006)
Munakata, Naoko, *Transforming East Asia: The Evolution of Regional Economic Integration* (Washington, DC: Brookings Institution Press, 2006)
Pilsbury, Michael, *China Debates the Future Security Environment* (Honolulu: University Press of the Pacific, 2005)
Pyle, Kenneth B., *Japan Rising: The Resurgence of Japanese Power and Purpose* (New York: Public Affairs, Perseus Books, 2007)
Rose, Caroline, *Interpreting History in Sino-Japanese Relations* (London and New York: Routledge, 1998)
Roznan, Gilbert, *Chinese Strategic Thought Toward Asia* (New York: Palgrave Macmillan, 2010)
Samuels, Richard J., *Securing Japan: Tokyo's Grand Strategy and the Future of East Asia* (Ithaca, NY: Cornell University Press, 2007)
Shambaugh, David S. (ed.),*Tangled Titans: The United States and China* (Lanham, MD: Rowman and Littlefield Publishers, 2012)
Shambaugh, David and Yahuda, Michael (eds.), *International Relations of Asia* (Lanham, MD: Rowman and Littlefield Publishers, 2008)
Snyder, Scott, *China's Rise and the Two Koreas: Politics, Economics, Security* (Boulder, CO: Lynne Rienner, 2009)
Soderberg, Marie (ed.), *Sino-Japanese Relations in the Twenty-First Century* (London and New York: Routledge, 2002)
Vogel, Ezra F., *Deng Xiaoping and the Transformation of Modern China* (Cambridge, MA: Harvard University Press, 2011)
Vogel, Ezra F., Ming Yuan and Akihiko, Tanaka (eds.), *The Golden Age of the U.S.–China–Japan Triangle, 1972–1989* (Cambridge, MA: Harvard University Press, 2002)
Whiting, Allen S., *China Eyes Japan* (Berkeley: University of California Press, 1989)
Yahuda, Michael, *The International Politics of the Asia-Pacific* (London and New York: Routledge, revised 3rd edition, 2011)
Ye Zicheng, *Inside China's Grand Strategy*, edited and translated by Steven L. Levine and Guoli Liu (Lexington: The University Press of Kentucky, 2011)
Yinan He, *Search for Reconciliation* (Cambridge: Cambridge University Press, 2009)
Yoshida, Takashi, *The Making of the "Rape of Nanking": History and Memory in Japan, China and the United States* (Oxford: Oxford University Press, 2006)
Zhao Suisheng, *A Nation-State by Construction: Dynamics of Modern Chinese Nationalism* (Palo Alto, CA: Stanford University Press, 2004)
Zheng Wang, *Never Forget National Humiliation: Historical Memory in Chinese Politics and Foreign Relations* (New York: Columbia University Press, 2012)

Index

Note: Page numbers followed by 'n' refer to notes